Your Book
Starts Here

ALSO BY MARY CARROLL MOORE

Nonfiction

Genre: Cooking

> *Healthy Cooking*
>
> *The New Gourmet*
>
> *The No-Cholesterol, No Kidding! Cookbook* (with Hal Straus)
>
> *Prevention's Low-Fat, Low-Cost series*
>
> *Prevention's Quick and Healthy series*

Genre: Health

> *Cholesterol Cures* (with Richard Trubo)

Genre: Self-Help/Memoir

> *How to Master Change in Your Life: Sixty-seven Ways to Handle Life's Toughest Problems*
>
> *Turning Points*

Fiction

> *Breathing Room* (forthcoming)
>
> *Qualities of Light*

Contributor to:

> *Best of Food & Wine*
>
> *Betty Crocker's New Low-Fat, Low-Cholesterol Cookbook*
>
> *Capturing Radiant Light and Color*
>
> *Dr. Dean Ornish's Program for Reversing Heart Disease*
>
> *Time-Life Great Meals in Minutes series*

PRAISE FOR MARY CARROLL MOORE'S
Your Book Starts Here

"The consummate How-To Guide for everyone who has a book percolating inside them."

—Nancy Slonim Aronie, author of *Writing from the Heart: Tapping the Power of Your Inner Voice*

"Moore packs *Your Book Starts Here* with years of gritty good sense and big-picture perspective. Her techniques for drafting, organizing, and polishing a book are practical and time-tested. Here is a first-time book-writer's best companion."

—Elizabeth Jarrett Andrew, author of *Writing the Sacred Journey: The Art and Practice of Spiritual Memoir*

"At the Loft Literary Center, I can always tell which students in my classes have taken Mary Carroll Moore's class on book-writing. They talk about writing their book in 'islands' and using storyboards to figure out how those sections relate to each other. When another student confesses to feeling overwhelmed by the material her memoir might include, they readily advise, 'You should try Mary Carroll Moore's method.' I second that."

—Cheri Register, author of *Packinghouse Daughter,* American Book Award winner

"If you believe you have a book inside you just waiting to come out, here is a guide that will ensure your book's arrival in the world."

—Rebecca McClanahan, author of *Word Painting*

"With specific advice, focused writing exercises and generous encouragement, her clear, personal voice guides developing writers through the process, from first steps to final launch. They—and their future readers—will be grateful."

—Catherine Watson, author of *Home on the Road,* 2008 Minnesota Book Award finalist

"I had a contract but not the first clue how to transact a book. Every morning I tried to move walls with my forehead. I wanted answers and I wanted them yesterday. Mary showed me I wasn't yet ready to ask the questions. More importantly, her method provided an invaluable blueprint that, I suspect, will be useful for every book I write."

—Tom Swift, author of *Chief Bender's Burden*

"With storyboards, collages, image-based writing exercises, and charts, Mary Carroll Moore shows writers how to really see their writing in a new way. Her book-structuring method teaches them to zoom out from the detail level of sentences to see the big picture of the entire book. This ability to control focus—from words and sentences, to scenes and chapters, to the wide angle of themes and flow—is crucial. *Your Book Starts Here* is a valuable resource in developing this skill."

—Rosanne Bane, author of *Dancing in the Dragon's Den: Rekindling the Creative Fire in Your Shadow*

"I came to Mary Carroll Moore's workshop, 'How to Plan, Write, and Develop a Book,' filled with ideas, thoughts, and feelings—all inchoate—about the two books I wanted to write, but I had little thought of how to begin. I was all creator and no editor. The practical information I gained in one short day gave me exactly what I needed to get going—ideas on tag lines, storyboards, focus statements, finding a form for my book, organizing the material. I can't imagine anything more useful, for someone who wants to write not just a book but a good book, than Mary's methods. It's like flopping around scared in the ocean and having a lifeguard come, kindly pull you out, and teach you how to swim."

—Sharon Charde, six-time Pushcart Prize nominee and author of *Bad Girl at the Altar Rail*

YOUR BOOK STARTS HERE

Create, Craft, and Sell Your
First Novel, Memoir, or Nonfiction Book

MARY CARROLL MOORE

CREATOR OF THE
"HOW TO PLAN, WRITE, AND DEVELOP A BOOK" WORKSHOP

RIVERBED PRESS

Your Book Starts Here

Copyright © 2011 Mary Carroll Moore

Library of Congress Control Number: 2011900786

Cover design by Carbon Creative
Interior design by RMcB Creative Services

ISBN 9–78061–523–1389
Printed in U.S.A.

Publisher's Cataloging-in-Publication
(Provided by Quality Books, Inc.)

Moore, Mary Carroll.
    Your book starts here : create, craft, and sell your first novel, memoir, or nonfiction book / Mary Carroll Moore.
        p. cm.
    Includes bibliographical references and index.
    LCCN 2011900786
    ISBN-13: 9-78061-523-1389
    ISBN-10: 061-523-1381
    1. Authorship. 2. Selling—Books.   I. Title.

PN145.M66 2011   808'.02
                        QBI11-600033

CONTENTS

PART ONE—PLAN: GETTING TO KNOW YOUR BOOK

PART TWO—WRITE: MANIFESTING YOUR BOOK'S INNER AND OUTER STORY

PART THREE—DEVELOP: MAKING YOUR BOOK SHINE

APPENDIX

With gratitude for all the books
that have changed my life and
the writers who keep writing them

Deepest gratitude to Barb Chintz, editor extraordinaire, who skillfully shaped this manuscript so that readers could follow its winding path. I'm also grateful to the Monday morning writing class at the Hudson Valley Writers' Center, who reviewed early drafts of this manuscript, and to Nancy McMillan, my faithful writing partner, who gave helpful feedback every step of the way. Thank you to the writers, instructors, and students at the Loft Literary Center and the Hudson Valley Writers' Center who asked for this book for so many years—their persistence and love for the topic made me finish it. Thanks also to my first online class, who tested Part 1 and shared their feedback. Finally, I'm ever grateful to my students and clients who generously shared their personal experiences on the long and beautiful road to writing and publishing a book.

To protect these writers' privacy, real names and the details of books-in-progress have been changed, except where a writer gave express permission to use name and circumstance.

Sections of this book first appeared in *A View from the Loft*, publication of The Loft Literary Center, Minneapolis, *www.loft.org*, and on my blog *http://HowtoPlanWriteandDevelopaBook.blogspot.com*.

To my family and friends who believe in me, especially Becca.

INTRODUCTION

Writing a book is a wonderful journey like no other. It will ask for your time, love, insights, and determination. In return, you'll make your mark on the world as a published author, touching readers' lives.

With *Your Book Starts Here*, my goal is to help you write the book you dream of writing. I am offering you what I needed back in 1988 when I tackled my very first book. Back then, I couldn't find even one comprehensive field guide to help me plan, write, and develop my book. I crafted my early books by intuition, groping for whatever seemed to work at the time. Basically, winging it.

Unfortunately, this is what a lot of first-time authors do. It's not the only way.

If only I had then, what you are holding now: a practical roadmap for any writer who dreams of finishing a book manuscript—in any genre.

In the chapters that follow are the very best tools I've culled from writing thirteen books in three genres. These tools guided me through each phase of planning, writing, and developing—and selling—my books. For the past ten years, I have been sharing these tools with students in my book-writing classes and workshops. Many have used them to finish their books—and have gone on to successfully publish.

Here's my very favorite experience: often, a year or two after a writer takes my class and puts these methods into practice, they appear at my classroom door with a copy of their published book in hand.

"Here," my former student says, with an intensely satisfied smile. "Because of your class, I finally finished this. And it was just published."

From the tools in *Your Book Starts Here*, these writers gained enough belief and stamina to realize their dream.

You can too.

What You Can Expect

Together we'll be exploring the three stages of the book-writing journey, so *Your Book Starts Here* is divided into three sections, each examining one of these stages.

"Part One: Plan" takes you step by step through the initial stage: exploring your book's topic, meeting your ideal reader, facing your own Inner Critic. You'll strengthen your writing practice, craft a premise statement for your book, then launch into learning about structure via the three acts and storyboarding.

In "Part Two: Write," I'll guide you through completing your first draft, then deeper into refining the trio of dilemma, characters, and container (the environment of your story). You'll come away with a working manuscript, ready for revision.

"Part Three: Develop" helps you revise your book, developing voice and theme, fine-tuning pacing and transitions. Then you'll learn how to work with feedback as you bring your masterpiece to the world of waiting readers.

Each chapter gives you specific writing exercises and tools to practice, so you don't have to wing it like I had to, before I learned this method.

You'll read stories from writers like yourself, working in different genres—fiction and memoir, biography and nonfiction, children's and young adult, even poetry. You'll hear their obstacles and lessons, how they've demystified the book-writing process, how they finished their books and went on to publish. You'll find out why it's easier to write your book in sections, with the aid of visual maps like the storyboard. You'll learn why revision comes last, after you have grown into your creative voice.

About the Writing Exercises

If there's one truth I've learned in ten years of teaching, it's this: Writers learn by writing.

So almost every chapter in *Your Book Starts Here* offers writing exercises to put into practice the skills you're reading about. Some exercises are set up in workbook format, with space for you to answer questions or make checklists. Others ask you to pull out your writer's notebook (see page 9 for more about this essential book-writing tool). Feel free to use the wide margins on each page for notes.

The writing exercises will give you a sense of where you are on the book-writing journey each step of the way. They'll make your skills a practical reality on the page.

Your Book Starts Here also uses a three-part learning model from my book-writing classes, proven to help writers retain more information and build skills. First, you'll get new information about book writing and see how it's been applied by other writers. Immediately, you get to practice this new information with your own manuscript—via the writing exercises in each chapter.

Finally, I ask you to keep notes on what you've learned. This last ingredient—feedback—lets your brain and creative self integrate what you've read and practiced.

Other Ways to Use This Book

I love to skip around in books, landing on what appeals to me in the moment. Don't feel you have to read *Your Book Starts Here* chronologically. Make it a browsing guide, if you prefer.

Already have a manuscript-in-progress, maybe one that hasn't sold yet? Use this book as a good editor. Check your book's structure against the storyboard diagrams in chapter

11. Peruse "Part Three: Develop" to see where you might need to dive deeper in order to interest an agent or publisher.

But if you're just beginning, you'll get the most if you approach *Your Book Starts Here* as if you were attending one of my book-writing workshops: Read it chapter by chapter, trying each exercise, taking notes on what you learn, incorporating the new information directly into your own manuscript. Form a book-writers' support circle for feedback and encouragement.

Book-Writers' Support Circles

We need other writers, especially when we're writing a book. On the next page are ideas on how to form a book-writers' support circle. Using this guide at each meeting will propel you forward and help you avoid discouragement and writer's block. You can cheer each other on as you finish—and publish—your books.

Sound good? Are you ready?

Let's get started.

And, by the way, if I see you someday at one of my classes, standing in the doorway with a satisfied grin and a copy of your published book in hand, I won't be surprised. Be sure to tell me about your journey. There's nothing I love more than a good story.

> "I'm writing a book." I sure wish I had a dime for every time I told someone that. Thanks to Mary's book-writing class, I have something even better: royalties. What I learned in her class—from exploring my book idea with a reader in mind, to structuring it via storyboarding, to revision with heart—helped me complete two books, one of which has been translated into five languages. What's more, Mary gave me the skills to complete many more.
>
> —Beverly Bachel, author of *What Do You Really Want? How to Set a Goal and Go for It*

Suggestions on How to Use This Book: A Loose Guide for Book Writers' Circles

Gather weekly, if you can, spending a month on each chapter from this book. Here's a loose guide that's worked for others:

1. Read the month's chapter before each group meeting. Mark it up with questions and notes to bring to the group.

2. Spend the first meeting on the information in the chapter, going over its points and seeing how they fit each writer's understanding of their book. What applies? What doesn't quite?

3. Spend the second meeting on the chapter's exercise(s). Try at least one exercise in the group or first at home, and bring in results to share.

4. For the third meeting, bring in favorite books you are reading, which connect in some way with the topic of the month. Discuss examples from these authors.

5. Use the last meeting to share your work. Either do a freewrite in the meeting and share raw writing, or using the feedback techniques in chapter 23, bring in written work and ask for specific feedback.

Book writers get their books done most easily when they share the journey with other book writers. We are a special breed of artists, and we need each other. Foster community.

PART ONE

PLAN:
GETTING TO KNOW YOUR BOOK

PLAN: GETTING TO KNOW YOUR BOOK

What is your book about? Why are you writing it? What do you want to include? Planning is a free-form stage, where you'll begin to answer these all-important questions. Your goal in the planning stage is to write your book in open-ended sections. By keeping your book sections random and changeable, by holding back from sequencing them in any flow, you'll keep open to the best structure for your book. This is radically different from the traditional method of outlining and then writing. It takes into account two sides of the creative self: the linear and the free-flowing.

Writers following this method will emerge from this stage with enough material to organize into a book.

1

WHY ARE YOU WRITING THIS BOOK?

Books often start with a simple yearning to explore new territory: a fascinating topic, characters who won't leave you alone, a good story.

No surprise that writing a book can be one of the most far-reaching journeys a person can take.

If holding your finished book in your hands is your ultimate destination, you need to know that your book doesn't always provide road signs. It's easy to get lost along the way. Often you won't know if you are getting anywhere at all. You may have experienced the excitement of starting a book. You may have also experienced the frustration of stalling out midway through a manuscript because you didn't know where to go next.

A book is much more than just producing pages. A book demands your belief, your stamina, and a strong structure that your reader can follow. It's a lot easier if you have two things: a good guide and a good map.

The summer I turned nineteen, I was sleeping on the floor in a bookstore in Paris called Shakespeare & Company when I overheard some Australian students talking about a beautiful ruined temple overlooking the Aegean. Ancient and mystical, the Temple of Poseidon was perched on the edge of Cape Sounion, open to the sky. It sounded amazing. It was August, too hot in Paris, and my college semester didn't start for three weeks. I wanted to see this wonder.

I had just enough money to buy a ticket on an overnight train. In Athens, trying to figure out how to get to Cape Sounion, I was stuck with no place to stay. I didn't know the language or the country. And at the time, Greece was seething with intense anti-Americanism.

A book demands your belief, your stamina, and a strong structure that your reader can follow.

But I had to see that temple.

I struck up a conversation with a young British couple. They wanted to hitchhike along the coast and visit some islands then end up at Cape Sounion. They let me tag along. We figured out the route as we traveled. We got rides in trucks, slept along roadsides, ate baklava for breakfast. My new friends paid our ferry trips to each island. We washed our clothes in the Aegean and dried them on the beach.

After asking directions and getting lost many times, we finally stood at sunset under the ancient white columns of the Temple of Poseidon. I sat on the crumbled steps at the edge of a cliff, staring at the impossibly blue sea, watching sea birds coast the wind currents, thrilled to be there.

Looking back, I realize how lucky I was to have made the trip unscathed. As much fun as it was to travel rough, Greece in the 1970s offered too many close calls for an American girl alone. Luckily I had help, because at nineteen, I didn't know better.

I began my first book without a map too, and as with my trip to Greece, unexpected help arrived to get me through the journey.

An expert in gourmet natural foods, I co-owned a cooking school that was reviewed in *USA Today*. One day, a publisher called: Would I write a book about my methods? Yes! It was a dream come true.

I soon learned that books are impossible to navigate blindly. Fortunately I was assigned an editor who worked closely with me every step of the way. During our collaboration, we created a plan for the book's flow, we researched other books to find the best possible structure, and during revision we took out what didn't serve the reader. He helped me learn to make the book's map.

Without that map, giving up would have been a given. I felt discouraged many times, but my editor called at just the right time, pointed to our mapped-out plan, and I carried on.

This first book, *The New Gourmet*, introduced the home cook to everyday fresh foods prepared elegantly. Because my lack of book-writing skills was balanced by a good editor and good recipes, *The New Gourmet* became a bestseller and won an International Association of Cooking Professionals (IACP) award. Winning that award was just as thrilling as seeing the Temple of Poseidon for the first time.

As I published more books, I learned the value of creating a new map for each book project and, too, securing a helpful guide. Book writing became much more enjoyable. I now knew where to turn when the road disappeared, when my enthusiasm flagged, or when my manuscript overwhelmed me.

Start with a Good Map

How do you get a map for your book? It is something you create as you go. It starts easily enough with a written conversation between you and your book project. Get yourself a new notebook. In it, you will begin "talking" with your book on paper, and from the answers that come, you will create your book's map.

During the book-writing journey, your writer's notebook will become a valuable aide. In it, you can collect ideas for scenes, character sketches, research notes—whatever might deliver both inspiration and signposts when you get lost. But first you'll use it to answer three important map-making questions.

With my first published books, I learned that a good manuscript needs to satisfy in three basic ways:

1. the writer's need to write it
2. the reader's reason to read it
3. how it contributes to the world of literature

So making your map starts with asking yourself the right questions that help you explore these three needs. Your answers will tell you where you are already on solid ground, and also where you need a guide to help you develop certain book-writing skills.

Get yourself a new notebook. In it, you will begin "talking" with your book on paper, and from the answers that come, you will create your book's map.

> ## THREE QUESTIONS
> 1. Why am I writing this book?
> 2. Why do I feel a reader will want to read this book?
> 3. What do I think about this book's purpose in the world or the greater mission it could fulfill?

At first glance, these questions seem fairly simple. I thought so too. But most of us never think about all three in depth, and it's a great place to begin your book-writing journey. Because the answers to each question will help you create your book's map.

Question #1: Why Am I Writing This Book?

Quite a few writers know the answer to this question, if they have a book percolating inside. As author Brenda Ueland says, "Everybody is talented, original, and has something important to say." Having something to say is why many of us want to write a book in the first place.

Over the ten years I've taught writers of all skill levels how to plan, write, and develop their books, I've gathered the top reasons—practical, professional, and personal—why we write our books. Is your reason on this list?

> ## TOP REASONS WE WRITE BOOKS
> ✓ To document a life-changing event
> ✓ To help others improve their lives
> ✓ Characters won't leave me alone
> ✓ My friends tell me I have a great story to tell
> ✓ To leave my family a written legacy
> ✓ To make some money, retire rich

✓ It's publish or perish at my job
✓ I need a book to sell at my workshops
✓ To promote my expertise to business clients
✓ My crazy family story would make a great novel
✓ I'm published, but I want to try a new genre
✓ To share what I've learned
✓ I need a creative outlet
✓ To compile my published pieces into a book
✓ To publish my dissertation
✓ I have a story I must tell

Take some time to think about your reason for writing your particular book. Why is it so important to you? Ask yourself what is driving you to take this journey.

Question #2: Why Do I Feel a Reader Will Want to Read This Book?

For many writers, the second question, *Why do I feel a reader will want to read this book?* is harder to answer. This question requires you to look up from your book, face your reader, and consider seriously:

- What you imagine your reader experiencing as he or she reads your book
- How this reader is reacting to your ideas
- What benefit the reader is getting from your story

A publishing industry friend once told me that people read books for a certain pay off. They read to be informed, entertained, or inspired. Ideally, they get all three. Writers who only write for their own reasons produce books that sound as if they're talking only to themselves, and there's little benefit to the reader.

Take some time to think about your reason for writing your particular book. Why is it so important to you?

So how do you answer question #2? Your first step is to get familiar with your book's genre and find out what readers love most about it.

Margo, a published nonfiction author in one of my classes, was writing her first mystery novel. When she couldn't answer question #2, I suggested she skim five of her favorite mysteries and write down what she loved about them, what drew her as a reader. She discovered she loved the entertainment, all that tension and excitement in a highly plotted mystery. We worked together on a brainstorming list in her writer's notebook, exploring how Margo might bring more entertainment—tension and excitement—to her manuscript. Because she asked this important question #2, Margo accumulated twelve plot ideas that fired her enthusiasm after one month. She now knew where her book was going, why it would be read by others. Her new plot ideas created a page-turner.

Sometimes, asking this question about your reader can bring up fears. David, another beginning author, was writing his memoir. But he started getting scared thinking about how his relatives might read it someday. So he began to omit key elements that make books sing, such as the more human side of people he loved.

Readers can spot a writer's hesitation a mile away—they suspect there's a better story hidden somewhere, and if it isn't revealed, they get impatient and stop reading. Seeing David's stall-out, I suggested an experiment. He would write everything that came to him for one week, without censoring, just to see what emerged on the page. As David began allowing the richness of his full story to come through, he found the stories much less risky than imagined. The fuller writing made the story more universal, less personal. His reader became his ally, rather than his enemy.

The process of discovering your real reader is a fascinating journey. As you ask yourself, *Who is my reader? Why would this reader want to read my book?* you'll look at your material in a new way. You'll begin to ask what serves the story best, rather than what just serves you.

Question #3: What's the Book's Larger Purpose?

Our final map-making question asks about the book's uniqueness, its larger purpose in the world. This question most interests publishers. Understandably, publishers and agents want to be sure the manuscript will make its mark, before they invest their time and money.

Linda, a respected clinical psychiatrist, was writing a book about couples in transition, her first attempt at writing more than papers and articles. But her book struggled with its larger purpose. No surprise she was having trouble finding an agent.

We went over questions #1 and #2—these seemed easy answers. Linda knew why she was writing the book—she had a passion for her work and wanted to share the insights she discovered. Her readers were obviously fellow academics. Or so she thought.

When I asked about question #3, Linda fell silent. She knew the book's larger purpose only in theory. Her mission was to help couples communicate from the heart. So why was there no heart in her writing? The chapters felt dry and academic, as if she were lecturing from a distant room. Frustrating to a woman who knew she had more to say than what she was writing.

Heart comes via voice. I knew what was wrong with Linda's book. Her own experiences were largely absent. So I gently asked about this, why her own journey had been omitted. She said because her colleagues would think less of her if they heard about her personal learning curve in relationships, or in sessions with clients. It was a dilemma because these very experiences had led to her most valuable insights about couples communication.

"Let's go back to question #2," I said. "Who are your real readers?"

Linda visited several bookstores, researching other volumes in the body/mind/spirit genre, looking at how similar

Heart comes via voice. I knew what was wrong with Linda's book. Her own experiences were largely absent.

topics were presented. "My reader is primarily the layperson, not the clinician," she discovered, to her surprise. "And almost all the books for those readers are full of the author's personal experiences! Even those written by very respected clinicians." So Linda began to include her own struggles with relationships.

As she revealed her personal vulnerability as a therapist on the page, it brought authenticity to her theories. Readers could now trust this writer's words.

Paul, a business educator, had a similar experience with this important question of his book's purpose—and a similar reason for not yet achieving it in his manuscript.

A skilled speaker with great material, Paul was approached to write a book by his boss who admired Paul's seminars on team-building. To the boss, the book's goal was clear—for use in training seminars. But feedback from the boss on Paul's first draft was discouraging. The manuscript felt slick, as if it were blatantly selling an idea, promoting a prescribed agenda. Paul's boss wanted a book that would inspire, not sound like propaganda.

Paul began to realize that even a business book needs a strong personal voice to convey meaning and purpose to a reader. If his voice was completely missing from the manuscript, he could remedy this by adding a bit of his own story, sharing the steps he'd personally been through with this team-building method. Adding real-life examples from his clients, too.

Although Paul at first couldn't see what good it would do "to make the book all about me," his boss encouraged him to include a few stories about his own process. Each new anecdote made the material much more readable—and ultimately more useful to his company.

Julie, a beginning novelist, easily answered the first question. Pages in her writer's notebook showed why she was driven to write a novel based on her crazy family—the chaos of growing up with a psychotic mother and disappearing brother was such a compelling story, she had to tell it.

Researching questions #2 and #3, Julie looked over recently published books with similar voice, language, and tone. She realized her ideal reader was actually a girl in her late teens, the same age as Julie herself had been when the family craziness accelerated. Her book's purpose? To give young adults inspiration and strength.

This wonderful discovery changed the map for her entire book. A synergy occurred and Julie began to dream about her book, a common occurrence when writers open up the dialogue between themselves and their creative work. The book itself begins to give the writer new directions. Maybe you've overheard writers say, "Those characters are talking to me." Maybe you thought they were crazy. But this ongoing dialogue is magical; it's one reason writers love to write.

During sleep, Julie came up with unexpected ideas: a memory she'd forgotten, a detail about the setting, a plot twist. It was as if the book was talking to her, and in her dreams she could hear what it was trying to say. When Julie only put attention on her own reasons for writing her book, she was unable to see the path ahead. Her book is now moving forward beautifully; the sequence of the three questions created a functional map and her book's inner dialogue became her guide.

Each Author's Voice Is Valuable

Your unique voice as a writer comes through as you contemplate these three questions, answering them as best you can with what you know now about your book. Each author has an authentic way of telling her story. We're sometimes hampered by our preconceptions about the book-writing process, what it takes to get published, or what others feel we should write. These three simple questions help you discover what you alone can offer the world of readers, through your book.

I'm a great believer in short writing exercises to deepen this discovery process. Even twenty minutes of exploring on paper can reveal new directions. As author Adriana Diaz says, "The creative act is a courageous, ancient gesture, a dynamic

The book itself begins to give the writer new directions.

Each author has an authentic way of telling her story. These three simple questions help you discover what you alone can offer the world of readers, through your book.

Writing is a great way to find out what you believe and who you are, to listen to yourself on paper and make sense of what you hear.

exploration of the . . . mystery that is human existence." I couldn't agree more. Writing is a great way to find out what you believe and who you are, to listen to yourself on paper and make sense of what you hear.

Writing exercises help you hear what your creative self is trying to say, get in touch with that mystery. They are also one of the quickest ways to access both the linear (planning) and the nonlinear (random), or outer and inner story. We'll talk more in the next chapter about how these two aspects of your book open doors to new ideas, explore places you haven't yet traveled, and let you adjust course when needed. This last benefit is huge.

As you try the writing exercises in this book, be careful to avoid producing "good" writing. The goal of the exercises is to simply take you outside what you know now, away from your cherished notions about your book, and allow you to explore.

Exercise: Why Am I Writing This Book?
Time needed: 20–30 minutes

---

1. Close your eyes and imagine your book—its topic, its design, its plot and characters. What does it look like? What is it about? Open to an imaginary page. What is going on? Are characters talking? Is there an exciting moment in the plot? Note anything you feel or sense about your book now.

2. Open your eyes and write for ten minutes. Write whatever comes, let it flow, no editing. Read over what you wrote. Is there anything that surprises you?

3. Now ask yourself, *Why do I want to write this book? What is driving me?* Write whatever comes, for a few minutes.

4. Next, ask yourself, *Why would a reader want to read this book?* Is it fun? Fascinating? Moving?

Even life changing? Write whatever comes.

5. Think of a reviewer commenting on your book. What would this reviewer say? What is the larger purpose of your book, its impact on the world? Write for a few minutes about this.

6. Look over your responses. Circle or underline the question that was hardest to answer or had less truth for you. (That tells you something about where you are right now in your book journey.)

7. Jot down a few action steps to explore this question. Maybe "visit a bookstore," "do some journaling," "read books in my genre to see what's published recently."

8. Brainstorm ideas with fellow writers for any area you haven't yet explored or don't understand.

2

INNER AND OUTER STORY: DOORWAYS INTO YOUR BOOK

Every book has an outer story and an inner story. No matter the genre, a book first engages us through an outer event, information, or theory, then takes us to the inner meaning. Think of a thriller—the outer actions create its suspense, and as the writing moves along, we absorb the impact of that event on the inner lives of the book's characters.

I learned about outer and inner story back when I was writing my first nonfiction book. I didn't call them by those names. I called the outer story "information." I worked hard at bringing this information to life for a reader, giving it "meaning," or inner story. As I published more, I learned about the unique ways a book's outer and inner story balance each other in different genres of literature.

Together they make a book much more than entertainment or information. Literature becomes as much about exploring new meaning as savoring a good tale.

First, Build Outer Story's Stucture

Because outer story grounds the reader in your material, whether you are writing about people, politics, or potatoes, it is the foundation of all good books. Outer story creates the basic structure of what you're sharing with the reader, the logical sequence of events or information. It puts this in a believable time and place.

Well-crafted outer story lets your book track for a reader like a train smoothly traveling from one city to another.

So your first job is to find the outer story of your story. How do you do this? By writing specifics.

- *where* the story takes place
- *what* happens

Outer story creates the basic structure of what you're sharing with the reader, the logical sequence of events or information.

- *who* is doing what
- *what* theories and techniques are most important
- *what* obstacles or conflicts are encountered
- *how* is an idea tested or used

Outer Story in the Different Genres

In nonfiction, outer story is your information, facts, opinions, and ideas—what your book is about, what information it will pass along to the reader, what method you are teaching.

In memoir and fiction, outer story is plot: the events or actions that are externally realized. Outer story is not what a person thinks or dreams or writes or emails about an event. It's the event itself. Because true outer story is always external, it must always be outside a narrator's head or emotions. It must be something readers can witness and be part of.

Why? Compare "I think my brother is a loser" to "When my big brother came home crying, I saw he had a ripped shirt, muddy sneakers, and a black eye." Which version lets you into the story faster? Readers believe first what's shown, or demonstrated, before they believe what a narrator is trying to tell them. Externally realized, dramatic events speak louder than words.

So, in essence, outer story is truth revealed in action.

The Undercurrent of Inner Story

Inner story answers the question *Why?*

It contributes discovery to your book because it takes the reader along on a journey of meaning. Good inner story surprises writer as well as reader as it emerges on the page.

Because inner story is also shown more often than told—telling too much defeats its delicate nature—writing effective inner story means not knowing everything when you begin. From a map-making viewpoint, this sounds counterintuitive. How do you plan the meaning of your book if you don't know what it is? By discovering as you go, by being willing to take the reader along with you.

For example, when I began learning to write inner story, the process of discovering it was a huge mystery. Then I read Vivian Gornick's *The Situation and the Story*. A landmark book on writing outer and inner story, Gornick gives examples of how nonfiction writers seamlessly build inner-story meaning directly into outer events. Her examples show how skilled writers use theme, repetition, pacing, and setting—all inner-story tools—to create meaning organically. No longer just reporting facts or opinions, such writing contains an undercurrent that stays with the reader long after the book is finished.

Gornick suggested that to get to this meaning writers must ask deeper questions of themselves and their material, to write not just the situation but also the story behind it.

I first tackled this process in my book *How to Master Change in Your Life*, a memoir/self-help hybrid. In it I wanted to explore why change, for some, is an impossible feat. But I didn't want to stand on a soapbox and deliver profound truths. I wanted to weave them into the outer events I was describing.

I began exploring the main question of my book: Why do some people bloom from life's upsets, happier and healthier than before, and others lose their way? Asking myself this deeper question taught me a lot about the balance of outer and inner story. First, I realized I needed to explore how I personally handled change. This meant disclosing many of my own traumas: divorce, business failure, cancer diagnosis. As dramatic as these changes were, I needed to look deeper at the inner impact of each.

Balancing Outer Structure with Inner Discovery

Two other writing instructors were also encouraging in showing me how to balance outer and inner story. Kenneth Atchity's *A Writer's Time* and Natalie Goldberg's *Writing Down the Bones* both promote a balanced approach of fact

Skilled writers use theme, repetition, pacing, and setting—all inner-story tools—to create meaning organically.

and intuition in writing the two sides of any story.

They suggested writing small dramatic units unbounded to any other section in order to let the meaning, the inner story, emerge organically onto the page. In other words, inner story comes only after you have written enough outer story. An intriguing idea! Keeping the writing unstructured, for now, allows the inner story to show up more fully and faster. A writer can tell this is happening if she is surprised by new directions, if there's more energy in the writing, if it rings with authentic voice.

For me as a nonfiction writer, this approach was illogical and scary at first. I was used to working from an outline and filling in with writing accordingly. Even though outlines bored me, I leaned on their reassurance.

But I really wanted to learn how to write good outer and inner story. So I put my outline aside and began to brainstorm a list of topics that I wanted to include in my book on change. These topics became the subjects of my small dramatic units, or what Atchity calls "islands." I chose one topic at each writing session and wrote my island, not forcing any connection of each day's writing to any other island, keeping the dramatic units without beginning, middle, or end for now. Slowly I noticed my writing changing.

Certain topics led to predictable places with specific outer information—a trip across the U.S. in my Volkswagen, business change and its effect on people. But other topics opened up a completely different kind of writing, such as how my life shifted the day my grandmother died. It was new to me, full of unexpected images and memories, revealing surprising insights on lessons learned, the meaning of what I'd gained from my life-changing events. The inner story was emerging on the page.

Because inner story is born of the discovery process, because it can surprise the writer as it emerges, it is often dismissed by our linear minds.

But this is its beauty. The point of inner story is to discover and demonstrate the less obvious. Inner stories are essentially what we take away from the books we read: the point of the story, the meaning, transformation, or discovery that takes place.

And inner story can change people's lives—both writer and reader. As a reader wrote me after *How to Master Change* was published, "Your book gave me hope that I can learn to navigate my life." That is one big reason why we write our books, isn't it?

If you are willing to follow the unexpected in your writing journey, you'll get to the inner story. It finds its way to your page via nonlinear and non-sequential "freewrites," a type of islands writing that Natalie Goldberg introduces in her book *Writing Down the Bones* (see page 155 for more on freewriting). These unconnected sections allow you time and space to explore unlooked-at possibilities, to dive into subtler ideas.

Whenever I need more inner story in my manuscript, I try exploring what I don't know yet about my book. Yes, it seems illogical. But my creative self knows more than my logical mind. My book's inner story appears in unexpected places, if I follow it.

My creative self knows more than my logical mind. My book's inner story appears in unexpected places, if I follow it.

Exercise: Following the Unexpected
TIME NEEDED: 30 MINUTES

1. Make a list of ten words that interest you. They can be favorite foods, colors, a city with a strange name that intrigues you.

2. Spend a few minutes quickly jotting down what comes to mind for each word.

3. Do any connect with your book in some unexpected way? Choose one and follow it in a twenty-minute freewriting (no editing) session.

4. Finish with a list of questions about your book. What don't you know, at this stage?

This exercise is about looking for sidetracks that surprise you, that might reveal the inner story.

Best Ratio of Outer Story to Inner Story

Over the years since I began using this method of developing both outer and inner story, I've coached hundreds of writers how to manifest both in their books. I've found that outer and inner story exists in all good writing, no matter the genre.

Bert, a nonfiction writer in one of my classes, who was at first skeptical about whether his fact-based book on geology would need inner story, took on an assignment. He compared two single-subject nonfiction books: one on potatoes, the other on corn, neither riveting subjects. Both authors included history, facts, and interesting information. But the potatoes book had zero inner story, or as Bert said, "No personality. It was as if the writer had very little passion for his subject. I couldn't read past the fifth chapter."

The other book, Betty Fussell's *The Story of Corn*, later won an award for food writing. Full of anecdotes and memories of the author's growing-up years, this personal, lyrical material engaged readers easily. Bert, convinced, went on to model its approach. He used many personal stories and fascinating research tidbits in his book. Writing dramatic moments independent of structure, then organizing them after the inner story emerged, made use of Bert's linear and nonlinear creativity. The result was quite enjoyable—even to our class of writers who knew nothing about geology.

RATIOS OF OUTER AND INNER STORY BY GENRE

Nonfiction: Nonfiction writers use a lot of facts (outer story), but their anecdotes (inner story) bring the potentially dry material alive, showing how a theory or a method can be applied in real life.

Nonfiction writing engages a reader via inner story.

Most nonfiction requires a 70/30 ratio; about 70 percent of the manuscript is facts, information, theory, or method (outer story), and 30 percent is illustrative anecdotes (inner story).

Entertainment fiction: Plot-driven novels, such as mysteries or romance, called genre fiction or entertainment literature, also depend on a 70/30 balance of outer story (plot) and inner story (meaning).

Creative nonfiction: Creative nonfiction, such as memoir, needs illustrative events but also more reflection on the meaning of those events (inner story), about a 60/40 ratio. That makes sense—creative nonfiction includes slightly more human stories than regular nonfiction. Writers must balance events with personal reflection to humanize the facts with emotional truth. More is shown than told.

Literary fiction: In some literary fiction, the inner story comprises 60 percent, or much of the book. This level of meaning is hard to manage but when done well it creates characters with vast inner landscapes, people who stay with us for weeks after we finish reading their stories. This delicate balance is only effective if the inner story is woven seamlessly into every outer action, if we naturally derive meaning from each event.

Exercise: Finding the Outer and Inner Story in Published Writing
TIME NEEDED: 15 MINUTES

1. Get two highlighting markers, one yellow, one blue.

2. Choose a chapter of a published book you've read in your genre. Read through it again, looking for outer and inner story. Photocopy three pages to work with.

3. Highlight any outer story on these three pages in yellow.

4. Highlight any inner story in blue.

5. Are you able to notice both? Is one color dominant?

To learn how to balance outer and inner story, we next study how the author's dramatic moments are organized. Does outer story precede inner story? How does the inner story emerge organically through the chapter (shown, not told)?

Below are synopses of three books analyzed by my book-writing classes for outer and inner story—books enjoyed by their readers because the balance was appropriate to the genre.

Seven Habits of Highly Effective People
by Stephen R. Covey

(nonfiction)

What it's about: Seven ways to change your life and live with more fairness, happiness, and kindness.

Outer story (information): A paradigm shift is required to change our perspective on how the world works; Covey presents step-by-step theories, methods, and research.

Inner story (anecdotes): Family and business stories show people who struggled then thrived as they began to live according to these seven habits.

Bel Canto
by Ann Patchett

(novel)

What it's about: Unlikely alliances form when guests gathering at a birthday celebration find it is invaded by a terrorist organization which holds the guests hostage.

Outer story (plot): A birthday party is invaded by terrorists and guests are held hostage.

Inner story (shown meaning): Loyalties are tested when unexpected love develops between two hostages: a Japanese businessman and an opera singer.

The Duke of Deception:
Memories of My Father
by Geoffrey Wolff

(memoir)

What it's about: Growing up with the Great Pretender, a son learns that the guilt of betrayal lives in the soul of the betrayer.

Outer story (plot): Twenty-five years of living on the run with a shifty father, who outwits creditors and invents credentials for jobs.

Inner story (reflection): Psychological changes inside a boy's heart and mind illustrate his love-hate relationship with his father.

Which Door Do You Choose?

Learning to achieve outer-and-inner-story balance appropriate to your genre is a wonderful part of your book journey. You may lean toward one more naturally than the other, at first. Linear, left-brain writers often prefer outer story more—since they enjoy plot, organization, and structure. Right-brain-dominant writers, who like the nonlinear, often find inner story comes naturally, because their brains easily embrace images and randomness.

There is no down side to which one comes first. You just need to eventually welcome both—especially the door you are not yet opening wide enough. If you're primarily an outer story writer, if your writing is event or fact based, you must learn to add meaning via image-rich moments which humanize your material. If you're an inner story writer, you need to begin to ground your imagery in the specific details of time, location, and outer event.

Try the exercise that follows, as a starting place. It will test your natural writing strengths, reveal how you most

Learning to achieve outer-and-inner-story balance appropriate to your genre is a wonderful part of your book journey. You may lean toward one more naturally than the other, at first.

readily engage a reader. It'll also show you what balance of outer and inner story you use now, and what goal you can look forward to as you continue with your book.

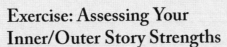

Exercise: Assessing Your Inner/Outer Story Strengths

TIME NEEDED: TWO 30-MINUTE SESSIONS WITH 1 HOUR BREAK BETWEEN

1. Write about an event you experienced this week, something that actually happened. Write until you have three or four pages. Try not to edit. Let yourself go wherever you want in the writing.

2. Set the writing aside for an hour, then go back to it. Read it through.

3. With a yellow highlighter, underline anything that seems to be outer story: the plot, events, or specific action.

4. With a blue highlighter, do the same with any images, thoughts, feelings, interpretations, or meaning about what happened—the inner story.

5. Look at the balance. Which was more plentiful in your writing, outer or inner story? Which doorway do you choose naturally?

6. Finally, answer the questions on the next page, as best you can with what you know now about your book.

What is my book about?

What is my book's outer story?

What is my book's inner story?

You may not be able to answer these questions yet. Don't worry. It will come. A lot of writers are so close to their writing, it's hard to get distance. Do your best and know that your outer and inner story will become more and more apparent, as you move forward on your book-writing journey.

3

DEVELOPING A WRITING PRACTICE

Few books arrive fully formed. Rather they grow from regular, unflinching practice of our art and craft. Writing a book takes the same everyday hard work that tennis players put in practicing their volleys, violinists their scales.

Practice leads to developed skills.

I've found that approaching writing as practice, taking small steps rather than big leaps toward your goal, is a great soul-soother. It fosters the belief that your book will arrive if you practice enough, just as you will eventually play the violin if you focus on your fingering.

So . . . how is your writing practice going?

How much of your time and attention do you devote to your book?

If you experienced some blips, as we all have, how can you renew your purpose?

A Professional Writer's Schedule

In his wonderful book *On Writing*, Stephen King describes how he writes every day. He once told a reporter he skipped his birthday, Christmas, and Fourth of July, because he thought it would sound more reasonable. But actually he writes every single day, including vacations, Sundays, birthdays, and holidays. Writing every day makes him happy.

Practice brings him joy, and "if you can do it for joy, you can do it forever," he says. So how do you find the joy that is the key to successful writing practice?

First, you need to let go of expectations. This isn't about creating prize-winning material each time you sit down. It's about making yourself sit down and write every day because

How do you find the joy that is the key to successful writing practice? First, you need to let go of expectations.

you enjoy the benefits of practicing your art.

In *Thunder and Lightning*, Natalie Goldberg wrote of a time when she and a friend were in the dumps. They first tried a long hike to cure it. That didn't work. They sat *zazen* (meditating), but both women still felt bad. Finally, Natalie suggested writing practice. "We wrote for half an hour, read to each other, wrote another half hour, read aloud," she said. "By the end we were both beaming. Writing practice had done it again—digested our sorrows, dissolved and integrated our inner rigidity, and let us move on."

Goldberg adds, "Writing practice lets out all your wild horses. Everything you never dared to utter—didn't even know you thought—comes galloping and whinnying across the page. This is good. You become connected with a much larger force field, one where you're not in control."

It is just this simple. It has worked for me more times than I can count. Although writing regularly has produced many books, stories, and articles, that wasn't the point of my practice.

The practice itself was the point.

Finding Your Ideal Practice

I always give my book-writing classes this exercise: Experiment for a week writing at different times and in different places. Try midnight then noon then first thing in the morning. Write in libraries, restaurants, doctor's offices, bus depots. Figure out when and where, for you, the writing rolls out easiest.

First you may find times and places that don't work: two or three in the afternoon when blood sugar dips can shut down any writer, as will a train commute to NYC when strangers read over your shoulder. For some, a too-quiet empty house stops them cold.

I ask my students to experiment until they find the right time, where they can give attention to their writing every day. Repeating the length of time and the setting is often vital—especially when you're just developing a writing rhythm.

One writer discovered she loves to write late into the night. She says she is less bothered by people's thoughts, her day's responsibilities are over, and she can focus on her own images. Another is sleepy by 9:30 p.m., so pre-dawn is best. A third writes first thing each day, right from the dream state, especially when he's working on the first draft of a new book. Ideas come through as small snippets and scenes and are often clearest when he emerges from dreaming.

Some writers learned they work best in intense bursts, between predictable fallow periods. One published author of many novels will do no writing for three months, then write like a madwoman for four months, working every day for seven or eight hours. Dry spells are all about filling the well again after a book is published.

Others are more methodical; like Stephen King, they write until they have reached a certain number of words or pages for the day, no matter how long it takes. The page count is the practice.

Finding your rhythm and honoring your practice will slowly grow your confidence in your commitment to your craft. You will begin to trust yourself, that you'll deliver on your promise to this book. And, like any practice, you gain stamina.

Stamina equals momentum. When we write for a set time every day, we don't need as long a warm-up time. Early in my writing career, a teacher told me about the three-day limit: if we miss three days, we lose the thread of the writing dream and have to work harder to pull up memories, inspiration, and characters from the inner worlds. The muse gets huffy and goes on vacations if we ignore her too long.

Saboteurs and Their Antidotes

Julia Cameron, in her book *The Artist's Way*, talks about predictable reactions artists get as they begin to request time for their art. "Such time, space, and quiet will strike our family as a withdrawal from them. It is."

Finding your rhythm and honoring your practice will slowly grow your confidence in your commitment to your craft. You will begin to trust yourself, that you'll deliver on your promise to this book.

She explains that if we don't honor our need for the private time and space to create freely, we begin to die a slow death. Often we don't recognize this is happening. Or we may shrug it off—What can a busy person do? Of course, family, job, life responsibilities cannot be ignored. But there's a place for creativity too.

Virginia Woolf wrote an entire book about the basic human need to be creative and have your own space to do so. Reading *A Room of One's Own* spurred me on during my first few books. I learned that not having time and space to write is an excruciating experience, as not only did my book abandon me, but I abandoned myself. Whenever I compromised my need to have privacy and writing time in a busy life, I soon lost the threads of my creative ideas. But worse, I began to feel discouraged, so much so that I doubted I was ever creative at all. Re-establishing a writing practice again slowly helped me regain confidence in myself and joy in my creative life.

Writer David Ogilvy, author of *Confessions of an Advertising Man*, joked that he's developed certain ways of keeping open "the telephone line" to his unconscious, in case that "disorderly repository" has anything to say. Poet and essayist Lewis Hyde speaks of the invocation that's an essential part of any artist's life. "Part of the work cannot be made," he says, "it must be received."

But receiving requires taking a stand against the demands of our lives. And this conflicts with our desire to be good people, contributors to society, supportive of our family, to say nothing of showing up for our job. "We want to be generous, of service to the world," Julia Cameron says. "But what we really want is to be left alone. When we can't get others to leave us alone, we eventually abandon ourselves. To others, we may look like we're there. We may act like we're there. But our true self has gone to ground."

Practicing art is a constant balancing act. How much time and energy you can devote to your book depends on your life responsibilities. Be realistic, but also realize that saboteurs come not only from without. They also come from within ourselves.

One way to keep a balance is to start small and negotiate each stage. If you tell yourself you'll write three hours each morning and know full well that life usually prevents that, it sets you up for failure. There is no benefit with managing two days then giving up.

Build your writing practice gradually. Start with ten minutes a day for two weeks, the same time each day if possible. See if you can maintain this, get used to the new rhythm, grow confidence in your own trustworthiness and your own commitment.

Five Fundamental Practices

It isn't talent that makes an artist succeed. Talented people fail all the time. Success comes from belief in yourself, persistence with your craft, and a good routine—setting aside regular, sacred time to make art. To dedicate time, you must believe in your worth.

As the painter and author Frederick Franck wrote in *The Awakened Eye*, "You shall not wait for inspiration, for it comes not while you wait, but while you work."

You must believe your art is important and deserves your attention. So must your family and friends. I've found five ingredients that make a book writer's practice successful. If all five are in place, they will support and sustain the long journey.

Success comes from belief in yourself, persistence with your craft, and a good routine—setting aside regular, sacred time to make art.

FIVE FUNDAMENTAL PRACTICES
1. Find and honor your best time to write.
2. Keep writing equipment private, secure, and in good working order.
3. Have a dedicated writing space.
4. Have a set time to write.
5. Close the door to the world when you are writing.

When We Sabotage Ourselves

Some writers try a writing practice, have good success for a while, then suddenly give up. Life intervened. But a close examination of what "life intervening" means, comes down to choice. There are always ten minutes to write, but when stress is high, it's easier to face the evening news than face ourselves.

Writing takes us to scary places sometimes. Our interior lives are often more frightening than anything television can offer. We get overwhelmed with our books, the enormity of the project we've taken on. We begin to resent the routine, the demands of the book. We want to rebel, say, "Forget this!"

I watch for three signs of this: increasing self-critique, getting sick, and other people who "suddenly" need me.

Self-critique comes via that small voice that whispers, "Why bother? This is all terrible anyway." It fuels self-doubt—Who are we to think we're writers? Sometimes it also fuels anger, nudges us to prove we're the boss and show it by breaking the writing rhythm.

If derailment doesn't come via doubt or anger, it shows up with getting sick. I've come down with unexplainable headaches or colds in the middle of important writing projects, and I've begun to see this as a sign of self-sabotaging.

A third derailment comes via people who suddenly need rescuing. I believe in my own perverse ability to "manifest" this: I think it's a law of attraction in the universe that when I need to rebel, someone needs me urgently. A dear friend will get sick and I'll just have to stop writing to make chicken soup.

When my practice gets derailed by these kinds of fears and frustrations, I go back to my original vision. I revisit my original motivation for writing this book.

Whenever I mention to my writing classes to be on the look-out for writing-practice sabotage, I am always amazed to hear of their own experiences with it. My classes shared these examples of self-sabotage: They are amusing, but don't be fooled. These are deadly stories.

A sixteen-year-old daughter shares her mother's computer so the writer can't finish a scene in her memoir, fearing her daughter might read it.

The only writing space is the dining room table and research piles have to be put away every night for meals.

Writing time is frequently interrupted by non-emergency calls—spouse is too busy to take care of it so the writer (who isn't "really" working) has to stop writing and take care of the non-emergency.

Nothing but a closet to work in—the only private space in a four-bedroom home.

Growing up in a family where closed doors were considered unfriendly so as an adult the writing space that seems most natural is the highest-traffic corner of the kitchen.

Any of these sound familiar? Then try the exercise below. It is a simple self-assessment. It lets you know where you might be unconsciously self-sabotaging, and where you can improve your chances of successfully establishing a writing practice so you can write and finish your book.

Exercise: Facing Common Saboteurs
TIME NEEDED: 20 MINUTES

Answer the questions below, then take action on one of the solutions.

1. *Do you try to fit writing in between everything else?*

    Solution: Make a daily date for your writing and mark it into your calendar each week.

2. *Do your family, spouse, partner, pets, children, or roommates highjack your writing time?*

Solution: Have a family meeting to discuss why it's important to you to write regularly. Ask for their help.

3. *Do you lack the equipment you need to write well?*

   Solution: Get a laptop or desktop computer and printer. Organize computer files to keep research manageable. If you prefer to write longhand, get a really great pen and stacks of legal pads.

4. *Does someone else commandeer your writing equipment?*

   Solution: Talk with them about the need to keep your writing private. This is basic. If you have to share a computer, get a password to protect your privacy. If it's a desk you must share—then create a portable one. Put pen and paper in a briefcase, lock it, and leave it by your writing chair. You don't want to feel restricted about which topics you can safely explore.

5. *Do you have high-traffic writing areas, no privacy, not enough light, constant interruptions?*

   Solution: Think about your ideal writing space. What would be possible? How can you get it? Can you go to the local public library? Or barter with someone for a quiet hour in a quiet room?

6. *Can you give yourself permission to close the door to the world when you need privacy?*

   Solution: Journal about your need to put everyone else first, your creative life last. List the benefits of creative practice for your life—and how a more fulfilled you can benefit others too.

Benefits of a Writing Practice

Aside from making us happier and more creative, regular writing has also been documented for its healing benefits. James Pennebaker, professor at the University of Texas, Austin, and author of *Writing to Heal*, studied the effects of writing on groups of medical patients. His landmark study showed marked improvements in immune function and general well-being from patients who wrote regularly.

Dr. Louise DeSalvo, in *Writing as a Way of Healing*, narrowed it down. She listed three areas writers must tap into, to benefit the most from writing practice.

THREE AREAS

1. How did the person feel then (during the event)?
2. How does person feel now, by comparison?
3. Which specific, concrete details, especially sensory detail, describe the past event?

Say you are writing about a difficult crisis you, a client, or a character went through. For the writing to be transformative, it must reveal how the person or character felt when it happened, as well as afterward, and the comparison of feelings between the two. It must also use sensory detail to describe the past event.

To test this theory, I scanned favorite nonfiction books, memoirs, and novels from my bookshelf, ones I reread often and feel transformed by. In every one, the authors showed people who felt things in the present moment, remembered past feelings via backstory, and compared the feelings of present and past, demonstrating change. Well-crafted scenes also used specific sensory details to illustrate those feelings.

When I looked at my own books, my best-loved moments also showed these three healing aspects.

Now I try to include these three transformative areas in my writing practice, as questions to ask about my story.

When I can, I find using these healing guidelines increases my joy in my practice of my craft.

When I can, I find using these healing guidelines increases my joy in my practice of my craft.

Writing practice becomes easier as you do more of it. You see how it changes you for the better, how it helps you be happier, how it even keeps you out of trouble. "I create every day," a painter told me, "because it keeps me happy. I'm less likely to cause problems for myself." So it is with writing practice.

In *Women Who Run with the Wolves*, Clarissa Pinkola Estés wrote, "It is the love of something, having so much love for something—whether a person, a word, an image, an idea, the land, or humanity—that all that can be done with the overflow is to create. It is not a matter of wanting to, not a singular act of will; one solely must."

A radical thought: The act of writing can keep you so at peace that you don't search for problems where there aren't any.

Exercise: Starting a Regular Writing Practice
TIME NEEDED: 10 MINUTES A DAY FOR 3 WEEKS

1. Find ten minutes a day that you can devote to your book.

2. Put your writing time on your calendar. Make it the same time every day.

3. Talk with your family, roommates, spouse, or kids. Explain that you'll be spending fifteen, thirty, ninety, or more minutes a day on your writing. Ask their cooperation: when you are in your writing space, you are off duty. You can't be asked questions or talked with.

4. Make a sign that says "Writer at Work" and put it near your writing space or on your door.

5. For the first week, do freewrites for ten minutes each day. Write about something that stuck with you, something that happened recently.

One student wrote about going to a movie that week where the audience was primarily elderly people and how the way they laughed, moved her. Another wrote about taking her son to dinner at a Chinese restaurant where large cylindrical red-and-orange paper lanterns hung along the walls and how the conversation blossomed in this colorful atmosphere.

6. Keep these writings in a file on your computer called "Week One."

7. Start a new file called "Week Two." Day one of the second week, make a list or freewrite for ten minutes on possible topics for your book—anything you can imagine including. The rest of week two, choose one of these topics each day and write for ten minutes on it.

8. The third week, write about a new topic from your list each day but add one observation of something you experienced, saw, felt, or learned that week. See if you can blend the exercises from weeks one and two.

A Word about Stumbling Blocks

The most important part of this exercise is noticing what it was like to have a regular writing rhythm. How did it feel to keep your practice going? What voices or interruptions blocked you?

If you had problems, take a moment and ask yourself what first came up to stumble you—was it a self-defeating thought or was it an external interruption? The next chapter explores our patterns of creative interference and offers ways to think about what might clear them.

How did it feel to keep your practice going? What voices or interruptions blocked you?

4

LISTENING TO THE INNER CRITIC

In each stage of writing your book, chances are you'll meet a most unsavory part of yourself: the Inner Critic. It's a negative self that delivers negative self-talk.

Many writers have different names for their critics. Sue Grafton, the mystery writer, calls hers *ego*. "Ego is the piece of me that's going, How am I doing, champ?" she says. "Is this good? Do you like this? Do you think the critics will like this? Because that has nothing to do with creating." In order to "get in touch," Grafton adds, "I have to block out ego."

For me, the Inner Critic reminds me of a helpful, slightly worried elderly aunt. "Are you sure you want to write about this, dear?" she'll whisper in my mind. "What will people say if they know that about you?"

I always ask my book-writing classes to start a log of negative comments from their Inner Critics. The idea is to write down those moments of discouragement, doubts, or boredom. Why write them down? Because only after reading those comments can my students realize that they aren't actually true.

I sometimes ask them to bring the notes to class after a week of logging. We may laugh over the Inner Critic's sneakiness, but we marvel at how common the problem is.

We learn that, at first, the Inner Critic starts with slightly unhelpful comments and small doubts. These comments grow. They may seem logical, even worth listening to, but gradually they erode confidence. It's self-talk that leads to discouragement or avoidance.

As you read the sampling on the next page, you may find your own Inner Critic's voice.

The Inner Critic is a negative self that delivers negative self-talk.

49

FAVORITE INNER CRITIC COMMENTS

"You need a lot more backstory here."

"This section will take months of research. Stop writing and get started. It'll be a good distraction."

"You need to explain what your character is thinking here. Your writing isn't good enough to just let the action show it."

"For God's sake, use bigger words. Everyone will think you're uneducated."

"Get to the action. How is anyone going to know what's happening if you go on and on about setting?"

"This is pretty boring, you know. Maybe wrap it up faster."

"Your mother will hate this section. Kill it."

"Why don't you run out and get the dry-cleaning now, then write when you get back?"

Let's face it. The Inner Critic is part of any book journey—no matter how many books you've published. That's why your first step is to disable its influence. How? Common wisdom suggests you fight it with any means you can. But that often turns into a neverending battle.

I've discovered another way: Get to know your Critic and make it an ally, not an enemy.

Facing the Inner Critic

The Inner Critic can be both strong and sneaky. As you explore and plan your book, it will first worry that you don't have a good enough idea. It will hint your ideas are seriously lacking and can't be put into a book. Then, as you write your book and form the chapters, it will convince you the draft is definitely good enough to show your best friend—right now, today! This, of course, is a not-so-subtle sabotage attempt, made real when your friend asks about missing parts and you crumble with the realization that you have omitted half your story.

Or as you revise, the Critic will get bored with inner story, theme, or pacing, those essential fine-tuning steps each book writer must implement. It will even tell you to edit out the juicy parts because all your relatives will shun you when they read them.

And as you try to sell your book, the Critic will come into full battle mode. It may suggest you stop now before any rejection letters arrive.

What's a hapless writer to do? Turn and face yourself. Get to know your own Inner Critic and how it delivers its particular sabotaging self-talk.

The Inner Critic as a Gatekeeper

One morning, I was finishing up a chapter in my self-help/memoir that centered on my business bankruptcy back in the 1980s. As I wrote, the Inner Critic began flooding me with feelings of shame about my failure. I began writing more slowly, reluctantly. The voice inside my head got louder, warning me to stop my exploration. "Why bring up this all over again?" it argued. "Totally in the past, not helpful to anyone else. Let it be."

I persisted, angry at its interference. Suddenly I had to run to the bathroom. I was very ill, vomiting and dizzy. As I lay on the bathroom floor, the cold tiles against my face, I wondered if this was the work of the Inner Critic. Had it escalated the sensation of shame so strongly, that it turned into a physical reaction?

After a while, I came back to my desk. I was shaken. How could I keep writing if I was going to make myself sick? But I knew in my heart that the bankruptcy story was important in my book. During the 1980s recession, I met so many people who were devastated by failing businesses and personal loss. I wanted to help them with my own and others' experiences. How could I do this if I couldn't get past my own Inner Critic?

Turn and face yourself. Get to know your own Inner Critic and how it delivers its particular sabotaging self-talk.

So I did what I tell my writing students to do: take a break and do a freewrite—write outside my story.

I located my writing notebook under the manuscript pages. (See page 9 for more about writing notebooks.) I began writing about being literally sick with shame. As I wrote, I got the idea to start a "treaty" letter to this Gatekeeper-as-Inner-Critic, thanking it for its help in keeping me safe all these years. I wrote about how I appreciated its role. I wrote how I understood why it brought caution to my writing life because it had my best interests at heart. With each sentence, I felt a lessening of tension in my gut, a softening in my heart. No longer waged in battle, I was able to see my Inner Critic in a new way.

Then I asked it kindly to step aside, to let me write this chapter. I explained why I needed to write it, reassured the Critic that this story didn't have to end up in the final book. I just needed to get it on paper.

When the letter was finished, I closed my notebook and went back to my dsk. The chapter flowed out better than I could've imagined and the Inner Critic was noticeably calmer the rest of that writing session.

My Inner Critic only wanted to protect me from the shame of fame: people looking at me in a different way because I told about a business failure many years before. By collaborating with this gate-keeping voice, instead of rejecting its help, I was able to proceed.

As Hal and Sidra Stone, authors of *Embracing Your Inner Critic*, write, "To go beneath the criticisms of the Inner Critic and convert your distress to understanding, you must always remember how and why the Critic was born. You must remember the important role it has had to play in protecting that very young, vulnerable, unprotected, and sensitive child that you used to be."

One student of mine was so intrigued by this idea of converting her very severe Inner Critic into an ally that she sought out a Voice Dialogue facilitator to learn how. With the help of facilitator Judith Hendin, author of *The Self behind the Symptom*, my student learned that her Inner Critic came into being when she was a small child for the express purpose of protecting her from the very real consequences of revealing anything personal (be it in writing or even talking with friends) that would expose family secrets.

Once her Inner Critic realized that she was now safe and the threats were no longer valid, the Inner Critic could back off. My student thanked this gatekeeper for a job well done and asked for its support so she could write what she wanted.

Dr. Hendin says the group of inner selves called "gate-keepers" are sincere inner guardians, concerned about our safety. They often prevent us from doing things that might put us at risk as we move into new territory. So the Critic's negativity often hides a real fear and must be addressed.

According to Dr. Hendin, the Gatekeeper might tell us, "Don't go into unknown territory," while the Inner Critic scolds, "You're no good, you can't write." The Inner Critic is "like a sledgehammer that attacks us," Dr. Hendin says, "until we learn to deal with it and develop a creative alliance with it."

When we forge this alliance, miracles happen. My book, *How to Master Change in Your Life*, was finally published, and I got more letters and comments about that bankruptcy chapter than any other.

My intuition was right—people needed to hear about self-forgiveness for big mistakes.

The group of inner selves called "gate-keepers" are sincere inner guardians, concerned about our safety.

Exercise: A Letter to the Inner Critic
TIME NEEDED: 30 MINUTES THEN 5 MINUTES CHECK-IN A WEEK LATER

1. Set aside thirty minutes and begin a letter to your Inner Critic.

2. First, ask it what it's contributing to your life. Listen inside for anything that might come, even small things it does for you.

   ✓ How does it keep you safe?

   ✓ How does it keep you connected to others?

✓ How does it keep you responsible?

✓ How does it make you feel intelligent?

✓ How does it bring you respect of peers?

3. Thank it for its help in these areas. If more comes to mind as you write, add your gratitude about those.

4. Now write a request to the Inner Critic: ask it to step aside for a week. Tell it you'll be exploring a new avenue in your writing and you feel you need freedom. Ask for its help in letting you try it.

5. Mark on your calendar to follow up in a week.

6. After one week, spend five minutes freewriting about any changes you've noticed. Are there fewer blocks in your creative process? Is your writing any different? Do you experience less negative self-talk?

When You Can't Write At All

Sometimes when our Inner Critic has really shut us down and we can't write, it takes time to reacquaint ourselves with the "muscle memory" of our imagination. Writing practice restores muscle memory, but when it's starting to come back it can feel tingly like pins and needles on the brain's numbness. Or very mechanical, artificial, awkward, as if you're making it up. "What I try to do is write," novelist Maya Angelou said in an interview. "I may write for two weeks 'the cat sat on the mat, that is that, not a rat,' you know. And it might be just the most boring and awful stuff. But I try."

Regular writing practice is a huge skill in controlling the Inner Critic. Even ten minutes of writing a day keeps the imagination limber, the mind open, the words and images flowing. So when you get hit with disappointment, it's easier to start again if there's momentum from routine.

As one of my students said, "We'd never expect to pick

up the violin again and play well if we haven't practiced for a long time. Putting things together in a different way to create a book is a new skill. We have to put in practice time. Eventually we'll be able to do it, but we have to give ourselves permission to practice."

What if you miss writing because of illness, travel, or pure terror of the material? Beware a too-sudden, too-enthusiastic return. Fantastic fodder for the Inner Critic who will be all over it. Any false starts will bring its nagging voice, telling you that you've lost it for sure, your words are repetitious, you're wasting your time.

Expect interference and plan a gradual, steady return to your writing practice. Remind yourself that it takes time to get back into the groove of it. Listen respectfully to the Critic's voice in your head and thank it for its effort, but tell it you have some new things to try. And let your creative self out.

Creative Voice or Inner Critic?

If you think all this talk about Inner Critic is just fanciful nonsense, then rename it your "negative thoughts." Rick Carson, in his well-loved book *Taming Your Gremlin*, says the inner voice that nags, belittles, and shames us exists in everyone—we're just not always conscious of it. In fact, if we've believed that voice for years, we may not hear anything different.

It takes time to hear and separate the negative self-talk from our true creative voice. For me, the creative voice always opens doors; it never shuts them. It's responsible and ethical, it doesn't harm others, and it certainly doesn't harm me. It encourages me to explore and grow, realize my potential. It helps me believe in myself.

It reassures me that I can finish my book.

One writer put a sign on his computer: "Who's telling me this? Creative voice or Inner Critic?"

Writing practice tames the negative voice. It's a sure way to begin hearing yourself again.

One writer put a sign on his computer: "Who's telling me this? Creative voice or Inner Critic?"

5

Content versus Product: How to Keep Them in Balance with Brainstorming Lists

A skilled journalist once attended my weekly book-writing class in New York. John was writing his first memoir, about growing up on a farm.

He worked as a professional magazine writer, winning many awards for his interviews and profiles, but he hadn't much opportunity to explore his own story. He enrolled in my class, ecstatic to learn he could use his non-linear, non-logical self in his writing. He felt like a man let out of prison.

With this new-found freedom, John drafted raw scenes (or islands) each week, jetting through a hundred pages—two hundred—with no trouble. "Amazing experience for me," he said at our weekly class. "I usually get writer's block with this much writing."

I've encountered this reaction many times, especially from professional writers used to the constriction of outlining and deadlines. From the gleam in John's eyes, I knew his volume of weekly unedited writing was immensely pleasing to him; after all, he was a professional who measured each word carefully.

John wrote each day for as long as possible. He re-arranged his work schedule, and absented himself from child-care and household duties. He woke early, wrote for many hours. When the energy was high, he wrote until exhausted.

Like a happy accountant, he totaled the number of words he wrote each day. The more he wrote, the more it fed his desire to write.

While word count is obviously essential to your book, there's another part that is equally important: meaningful content. John's excellent journalist skills made him a keen observer, so he was used to watching from the sidelines. But

While word count is obviously essential to your book, there's another part that is equally important: meaningful content.

in his memoir he needed to become a participant in his life and his writing. That was really difficult for him.

John would not let himself become vulnerable on paper. He accumulated piles of pages, but when I read them, they were all flat. Meaning only comes through to a reader when a writer experiences something new about himself or his material and reveals the inner story of his book.

That kind of experience requires being fully present, open, and receptive to the material you are trying to write about. This writer wasn't ready for that yet.

I foresaw a fall. It took six months. It came unexpectedly. It stopped him cold.

One evening, talking with a colleague about his book and bragging about his production of pages, John was completely thrown by his friend's question: how would he fit his son into the memoir?

John hadn't planned on including his son. They were estranged.

He went home from the evening confused. At first he shrugged off his friend's question, but as he thought more about it, the more he realized his memoir would be incomplete without the inclusion of his son. He saw that adding his son would make the memoir deeper, truer.

When he came into class that week, I could tell something had changed. He drew me aside during our break: What about all the pages? he asked. He had written nearly one-third of his manuscript. Should he scrap it, start over? How should he factor in his estranged son into his memoir?

Starting a Brainstorming List of Topics

I suggested John start a list of topics to explore in future writing sessions (his is the first list on page 62). He added to it each week in class. This brainstorming list surprised him as it grew—topics appeared that he'd never imagined including. Just writing them down, in a few words, allowed memories to bubble up in his writing brain. His book was being approached from different angles, considered in new ways. Each time he chose one of the list's topics for that day's writing session, he was pleased by the direction it took him.

Much more settled into his writing life, John returned to his normal life. His paid work wasn't suffering, yet he was still getting his memoir written. Pages still mounted up, 90,000 words in total. After a year, he completed a strong draft of the manuscript and was ready for revision.

On the last day of class, he told me something that's stayed with me. His grandmother was a wonderful cook, and she taught him how to make soup. "What I learned with my book was that what goes in to good writing is a lot like making a good soup," he said. "You can't just chop vegetables, throw them in water, cook for an hour, and expect a great-tasting soup. Flavors have to blend before anything becomes good enough to eat."

In the same way, writers must be active participants in their writing, engaged in it, not passive.

Writers must be active participants in their writing, engaged in it, not passive.

Developing your book takes a balance of two aspects of the book-writing journey. You must produce writing (product) but you must also think carefully about the meaning of this writing to yourself and others (the content). Writers who incorporate both have books that speak to others.

Product: Fresh Writing Every Day

Product is production. You must produce pages of writing, regularly and methodically, to finish a book. But you must be able to do this without exhausting your creative energy. This means being open to explore, via fresh writing, new avenues that your book presents.

Even when I am knee-deep in editing a book, I try to produce fresh writing every day. It keeps my Inner Critic at bay. It keeps me alert, energized, and discovering.

How much is enough? New writers can start out writing two pages, about 500 words, per sitting. This is enough to engage the creative self but not overwhelm it. It's fine to keep the pages unpolished for now or lightly revise as you go. The goal is to build stamina for your writing practice. Once you are producing 500 words regularly, see if you can up it to 800. How about 1000?

Fiction and memoir writers might spend their two pages on a short scene, a description of character or setting, or even a list of unanswered questions about their story. Nonfiction writers can use this time to build research facts into interesting prose, or develop anecdotes to illustrate a theory.

It's important to make sure revising time doesn't replace fresh writing. If you find yourself wrestling word choices, try a freewrite to get the creative flow moving again.

Anne Lamott, author of the modern classic on writing, *Bird by Bird*, has an empty one-inch photo frame on her desk. When she sits down to write, it reminds her "all I have to do is to write down as much as I can see through a one-inch picture frame." Once you start with enough fresh writing for this short assignment, you may find yourself easily writing more.

Don't worry if it's any good—we often can't tell when we're producing writing that's fresh. We don't have the perspective because we're too engaged. Plenty of time for the editor self to judge that later.

Your goal is simple: two pages, every day, with depth and meaning. You'll be amazed at how quickly they become enough to make a book.

Making a Brainstorming List

John, the journalist mentioned earlier, kept a list of topics to write about in case he wasn't ready to begin on a section of his memoir. This list insured he always had something to write about every day that was relevant to his memoir.

From John's memoir about growing up on a farm:

    red flannel shirts with leather elbows
    miscarriage
    John's disgust with spuds

Uncle S. and his smelly pipe
laughing too hard at the dinner table
rain on dirty windows

I recommend all book writers start keeping a brain-storming list. It is the key to connecting your current life, your interests, passions, fears, and hopes, with your book. It enlivens the material with you. And best of all, it keeps you writing regularly.

Brainstorming lists are simple and very personal. Here are four samples, from books by myself and other authors:.

From my novel about a family of painters *(Qualities of Light)*:

how skin feels, brushed against on a summer night
flying at dusk
summer painting studio
sketches of a young boy asleep in a hospital
spilling tea on purpose

From a book about activism and the environment:

growing tomatoes
bad soil
trees in a winter orchard
argument with farmer about chemical sprays
muddy boots at the back door
cows' breath on a cold morning

From a children's book about pirates:

throwing up over the side of the lifeboat
neighboring treehouses
a mother dying
secret passwords
eye patch—not seeing for twenty-four hours

From a poetry chapbook about cancer:

baldness
needles and veins

Naugahyde recliner chair
jar of wrapped colored candies
poster of Swiss alps
sleeping with the dog

Brainstormed ideas don't have meaning at first—not until they're written about. As E.L. Doctorow said, "It's like driving a car at night. You never see further than your headlights, but you can make the whole trip that way." Like images caught in headlights as a car passes by, or like notes taken from a dream fragment, certain phrases or words encapsulate complete scenes you'll develop later.

Note: For the list to work, you need to write enough to jog your memory.

Keeping a brainstorming list is an ongoing task. I suggest adding to it at the end of each writing session. Use it throughout your book journey. The last few pages of my writing notebook are reserved for my list, where it's easy to locate. Some writers start a computer file for their lists, adding one or two new items every writing session.

It's important not to censor your list or eliminate topics that don't seem to "fit" the book. This is not the time to decide. Often your Inner Critic is talking you out of a delicious clue from the right brain: an insignificant image that finds its way to your list may become the very thing you need to bring emotion to an otherwise dull scene. In the brainstorming lists above, the odd mention of "eye patch" led to the exact impression this writer needed of what it might be like to be captured in a dark cave. Her sensory memory of being patched for twenty-four hours when she scratched her cornea lent credibility to her fictional scene.

"Laughing too hard at the dinner table" brought a poignant memory of a last holiday with a brother who died—important for one writer's memoir.

"How skin feels, brushed against on a summer night" led me to the pivotal love-making scene in my novel, which takes place in a darkened cabin at night in mid-August.

Add to your list at every opportunity—every day if you can, just a few ideas. It will become fuel for your journey. And there will never be a shortage of topics when you sit down to write.

Exercise: Brainstorming List
TIME NEEDED: ONGOING

---

1. In your writing notebook, begin a list of possible topics you could write about—what could become a scene, section, or small moment in your book? Each week, add three items every day.

2. Allow yourself to include things that don't seem to fit, like a color, image, snapshot memory, dream, desire, smell, favorite meal. Use your own special shorthand and descriptions to jot these ideas down. Choose image-rich words, if you can, so your imagination will be triggered when you read them. The most successful brainstorming lists immediately put the writer into a scene full of senses.

3. Each time you sit down to write, choose one of these—whichever jumps out at you—as the subject of your fresh writing.

Add to your list at every opportunity—every day if you can, just a few ideas. It will become fuel for your journey.

Value of "Necessary Boredom"

If product is the production of pages, our internal process is what we think and feel about our writing, how much interior space we give it.

Dorothy Allison, author of *Bastard Out of Carolina* and other fiction, spoke in an interview about "necessary boredom." If it's present, she said, then she has enough intensity in her head for writing. As I thought about this, I realized the truth of it: when I have too much going on in my outer life, there's no internal space to dream. When I am working well with my internal process, there's not only time set aside for the writing, I have enough space internally.

In short, a balanced writing life asks us to put aside the tendency to fill our lives with unnecessary drama and replace it with necessary boredom—a very difficult task in modern times. Most people juggle their daily schedules like a three-ring circus: family, work, household, community, financial, spiritual, and other responsibilities too. These are not the issues I'm addressing here. It's how much more we pile on because of our fear of facing the silence and emptiness inside when we aren't busy—that vital emptiness that allows creative thoughts to surface.

As a book writer, I've had to discipline myself to put aside unnecessary drama in my outer life and put that drama into my pages. If writing is a priority in your life, if you are truly committed to writing your book, you need to find enough inner stillness to capture original ideas.

Unfortunately, perhaps, this is not something another person can structure for you. Each writer explores stillness in a different way. For most authors I know, it involves time alone to disengage from our over-stimulating outer lives in order to find out what is waiting inside. Yes, it's hard to disengage sometimes. The adrenaline rush of a busy life fuels our choices, and stillness feels boring. Kids, family, work, and home dramas are real concerns without augmenting them with more drama than need be. Ask yourself, *How much am I inviting, just to avoid the risk of creating?*

Your Internal Process Produces Pages with Meaning

Singer Bruce Springsteen once said in an interview, "I feel like to do my job right, when I walk out onstage I've got to feel like it's the most important thing in the world. Also I've got to feel like, well, it's only rock and roll. Somehow you've got to believe both of those things." Artists need this viewpoint of ordinary. "It's only rock and roll," is one of my mantras to keep the drama under control.

Process becomes ordinary too—not a phenomenon but a necessity in our writing routine. We take time to nurture the internal creative rhythm because we know it produces pages with meaning. Like healthy breathing, it becomes almost invisible to us after a while. But it begins with commitment of regular and steady internal time to our creative journey. Good product is what emerges from this internal time; it is measured in the pages we produce outwardly.

The marriage of the two gives your writing meaning to a reader. How? When your book intersects with your life, it naturally addresses your passions and interests, the fascinations and obsessions that fuel you creatively.

To me, Dorothy Allison's "necessary boredom" just means this: Instead of living outwardly on the edge, use that "edge" internally to produce creative fuel. We'll explore more of this in the next chapter.

We'll look at that big question: How do I make room for internal process time? It takes work and thought and planning. It takes giving yourself permission to leave the house for an hour and go to a library to get away from the endless pressure of a household full of laundry, dishes, and bills. Or choosing to ignore emails, to not visit Facebook, to turn off the television.

If your mother calls every day with a non-emergency update, you may let voicemail take the calls and return them at all once. Risk her asking, "Where were you?"

You know where you were. You were writing your heart out.

Instead of living outwardly on the edge, use that "edge" internally to produce creative fuel.

6

FILLING YOUR WELL

When Walter Wellesley "Red" Smith said "There's nothing to writing. All you do is sit down at a typewriter and open a vein," he was talking about the vulnerability a writer must bring to the page.

Writers struggle with this vulnerability. How much of their lives should be on the page? How much will being present and immediate with their writing impact their having a normal, functional life?

This chapter explores various writing myths, the most important being that, in order to create really meaningful work, writers must live on the edge—not just with their writing but with their lives. They must be financially distressed, alcoholics or addicts, unable to maintain love or friendships, and stay closeted away from family and society. Yes, many writers in the past have lived these myths. But doesn't a writer have other options?

How do we find that balance where inspiration, meaning, and originality can happen—where we can work in relative comfort, producing a regular number of pages, and live as responsible members of a community? How can we tell when we're walking safely along the edge of art and when we're about to fall over it?

How can we tell when we're walking safely along the edge of art and when we're about to fall over it?

Walking That Edge

Some writers ridicule this quest for a balanced life. "It's so hard to get into the creative space," they lament, so they lean on drugs or alcohol to capture the right mood. Or they say, "Once I'm writing, I can't afford to leave," as they remain holed up for days, weeks, even years.

This strikes me as unrealistic.

Fortunately, there are an equal number of working writers who believe in having a dedicated writing practice to woo the muse. They agree the muse will not wait for anyone, but they've learned she can be as responsive to routine as to extremes.

The dedicated practice we explored in chapter 3 is key here: It allows a writer to set aside a time to go to the edge of creativity, forget herself in the wrestle with the words, to write what she needs to write. A writing practice trains her to surface cleanly from her allotted creative time—with finances, health, and relationships intact.

My entire writing life—and I began publishing in the 1970s—has tested this quest to find and maintain creative balance. I get as swept away as the next writer, but I thrive creatively in a life of good relationships, enough money to live comfortably, a peaceful place to sleep each night—a healthy body, mind, and spirit.

I admire the work of many writers who weren't balanced at all—and reveled in it. They wrote amazing books, poems, essays, and stories while near death as alcoholics, drug-addicts, all-night party-goers, lonely people unable to sustain any friendships or love relationships. But it's not my path. And it doesn't have to be yours.

Letting Go of Magical Beliefs

In her brilliant memoir, *A Year of Magical Thinking*, Joan Didion describes the aftermath of her husband's unexpected death, how she soothed herself with a year of magical thinking: aligning his shoes just so in the closet, ordering the bills in his wallet, in case he returned. A part of her believed these rituals and ceremonies would make the impossible come true: her beloved husband's death would be reversible. In her memoir, Didion writes how her rational mind came up with rituals and superstitions and magical ideas to fend off going insane from the uncontrollable pain of grief.

Many writers resort to magical thinking when faced with pain in their book-writing journey.

This magical thinking surfaces whenever we feel over-whelmed by our own goals and expectations. Instead of adjusting the plan or goal, we malign ourselves as bad writers. If you don't believe me, recall your last diet or exercise plan. Maybe you followed it perfectly for weeks. Then a crisis at home caused you to skip your workout or eat ice cream from the container.

"I've blown it big time, might as well stop," you tell yourself. And you stop. When the blocked day, week, or month leads to "I'm never going to get the momentum back, and I might as well stop now," this is also an alarm sounding. Remind yourself that it's unrealistic to blame yourself that way. Unless everything is absolutely perfect, you're not going to be able to write your book? Not true. A functional writing life is about adjusting and accommodating, making changes as we go. It's not an all-or-nothing lifestyle.

A writer who successfully finishes a book expects and allows for the unexpected: getting a winter cold, kids home from school, the dog throwing up on a manuscript, computer glitches, frustrating delays in research.

Cultivating Interruptions

One evening I was working on a new novel, writing a difficult section I couldn't get ahold of. I finally put it aside in discouragement and went to sleep.

Around midnight, I heard something moving through the house. I got out of bed, turned on lights, but I couldn't locate anything or anyone. We live in the country, so there are often tree branches brushing the roof or animals scampering through the attic, but this noise was indoors and close by.

The disturbance continued for two nights, starting around 10:30 p.m. and stopping near dawn. Nobody got much sleep. We scouted, found nothing. Until the third evening, when I decided to stay up really late trying to write and finally saw a little face peering from the top of my studio bookcase. It was a flying squirrel, watching me and my writer's block.

This magical thinking surfaces whenever we feel overwhelmed by our own goals and expectations. Instead of adjusting the plan or goal, we malign ourselves as bad writers.

As the squirrel and I chased around the house, other members of my family woke up and joined in. I'd lure it into one room with a trail of pecans. It flew down the stairs, way too fast to catch and take outside. We finally got the idea of leaving a window open. We pulled out the screen, and the squirrel left.

For those three nights, nobody except the squirrel got much sleep. I was exhausted and annoyed that my routine was interrupted.

But the morning after the squirrel's departure, when I sat down to work on my book, I had tons of new ideas. I couldn't write fast enough.

This gave me a new perspective on the unexpected. I began to ask myself: Do creative people get stuck in routine? Is following the map always the best way? I started cultivating interruptions, especially when I was stuck.

So here's another way to look at your book. Your book is a tasty soup that defies logic sometimes. It demands a pinch of imagery and metaphor, a dash of imagination that only comes from the right brain. And when combined with a good base of structure, plot, and logic from the left brain, it reveals both inner and outer story. Because of this, the unexpected often brings the exact nourishment your book needs.

Cultivate serendipity, welcome interruptions. Instead of grumbling about having to change your plans, look for blessings. Appreciate the flying squirrels in your life.

Five Ways to Stop All-or-Nothing Thinking

These five simple steps work well to create balance, to overcome or outwit writer's block.

1. Embrace Creative Multi-tasking

Multi-tasking has gotten a pretty bad rap. Legions of burnt-out high achievers of the eighties and nineties lived on the adrenaline high of multi-tasking and it will certainly wear out anyone if it becomes a habit. But I discovered it brings welcome stimulation and perspective and lets me avoid the all-or-nothing syndrome. I just train myself to jump subjects.

I learned this in one of my painting classes, when I was struggling with a still life I wanted to kill. Nothing was working; everyone else in the class seemed to be doing beautifully. I happened to be standing next to an empty easel, so I moved my still-life-in-progress to it and started a new painting.

When I took a break, the abandoned still life caught my eye. Suddenly, because I hadn't been glaring at it for hours, I saw what it needed.

I spent the rest of the class toggling between them and produced two good pieces. When I paint at home now, I often set up two canvases at once. My two easels, side by side, let me get unstuck. I switch often. When I come back to the other canvas, the break has refreshed my eye. I see with new enthusiasm the subject that bored or frustrated me minutes before. I now do this with my writing.

I open two documents on my computer and toggle back and forth. While my mind's solving one problem, an idea comes for the other piece. Toggling from a freewrite to a revision keeps me engaged, surprisingly alert, and free of magical thinking.

2. Flex Your Routine

Writers who completely avoid structuring their writing time often never complete their books. There's a deep fear of routine in many creative artists.

No one stays the same throughout the long process of writing a book. Assume you are going to change as a writer. Make your writing structure flexible enough to change as you do.

When I first began writing seriously, routine caused me great anxiety because I thought I had to stick with plans. I thought routine was terribly uncreative—what if an intriguing detour emerged? Could I follow it and still produce a finished piece of writing? Now I know detours are often helpful, but only within a dependable routine to reorient me when I need to remember my original purpose for writing.

> Writers who completely avoid structuring their writing time often never complete their books. There's a deep fear of routine in many creative artists.

I now hold a loose structure around each writing session, showing up for my planned time, producing pages, reviewing my goals. I'm now willing to stay committed, but also willing to vary my routine.

3. Use Your Life

A *New Yorker* cartoon shows a man sitting on a screened porch in front of a typewriter. Crumpled pages litter the floor. Everywhere are dogs—big dogs, tiny dogs, panting dogs, sleeping dogs. The writer's wife stands in the doorway to the screened porch, hands on hips, exasperated at her obviously blocked spouse.

"Write about dogs!" she tells him.

What's on your plate? What are you grappling with right now in your life? Maybe you can use it to unlock the block, get you back on the page. Writing about the ordinary, the life in front of you, will help you reconnect to yourself, restore inner balance, and get you back to your book.

4. Force Yourself to Have New Experiences

The opposite of fear of routine is obsession with it. If we're not writing, the job is to write regularly. If we are writing about the same stuff, we could be caught in a rut. Too much repetition can lead to creative blocks.

If this happens, you need to (1) recognize it, and (2) force yourself to go out into the world so you have something new to write about.

When I am repeating myself, it may be that the well has run dry. Or life has become too fast to look deeply. I'm living on the surface without time to think, to find the original in myself.

Julia Cameron's *The Artist's Way* suggests choosing a brand-new place to go for an hour, solo. Use the time to fill the creative well, open yourself to new experiences, expose your senses to something that nurtures in a new way.

Cameron spoke of how regular creative outings were the hardest task she proposed in her book. People loved writing morning pages, doing the other activities, but resisted these dates with their inner artist. Exposing yourself to something completely out of your normal life or to your own inner life—without the speed of distracting activity—can be frightening, but things held at bay suddenly come forward. In a good way.

Some outings to consider: visit a new museum, take a walk in a never-explored neighborhood, go for a hike.

5. Keep Filling Your Well

The writing life requires intimacy with your own self. Intimacy is about getting close and letting go of what stands between you and your subject.

If your writing feels repetitive or dried up, if you aren't writing regularly, consider the level of intimacy you have with your book topic. Are you bored with it? Is it connected with your life? Consider filling your well.

I polled published authors: how did they fill the well? Many suggested activities fostering internal slowness. See below.

If your writing feels repetitive or dried up, if you aren't writing regularly, consider the level of intimacy you have with your book topic.

WAYS TO FILL THE WELL

Make a collage of something you'd love to have in your life—a quality or experience.

Page through an art or photography book.

Listen to music, especially music you don't know well.

Visit a museum and sketch a picture or eavesdrop on a conversation.

Memorize a poem.

Take the dog out for a long ramble in a new place.

Clean a closet or a desk drawer.

Visit a farm stand, pick wild blueberries.

Nap, contemplate, meditate, pray.

Keeping Your Life Going—While You're Writing

When I was in college, I had to declare a major by my sophomore year. I was interested in two majors: painting and the Russian language. I liked both, but painting was my passion.

I remember the day the head of the art department stopped me in the hall and very strongly suggested that it would be a shame if I wasted myself on Russian. But the myth of the starving artist, the alcoholic writer, the irresponsible painter was too strong in my consciousness. I opted for the Russian major, went on to get a Master's degree, and taught for a year at university before I left that career for the arts—where I really belonged.

Back then, I didn't know how to have it all: the arts I loved, integrated with a balanced creative life. Many writers are afraid of losing their "real" lives if they take time out to write a book.

If you have this confusion, consider the exercise below, inspired by Jennifer Louden's excellent book, *The Life Organizer*.

It asks for two lists. As you write them, see if they help you find your edge, the place on your personal tightrope where you can walk and still maintain a balance.

Exercise: My Life and My Writing—
Minimum Requirements
Time needed: 1 hour

1. For thirty minutes or so, write about your personal life in each of the areas below. Consider your minimum requirements to feel happy, balanced, and healthy. How are you doing in each area? Add any others that are essential to your well-being.

    ✓ **physical** (getting enough sleep, regular exercise, eating good food, keeping healthy)

✓ **emotional** (time for relationships with your family and friends, enough self-care, enough private time)

✓ **job/finances/career** (meeting your work commitments, bringing in enough money, keeping up with your savings goals)

✓ **creative life** (learning and growing, exploring creatively, staying current with your interests)

✓ **spiritual** (practicing your faith, having enough private time with yourself, serving in your community)

2. Take twenty minutes to explore what you need to have in your life, to get your book written. Be specific, referring to the Five Fundamental Practices on page 39:

   privacy

   time

   feedback

   supplies

   resources

   good, working equipment

   flexible schedule

3. Compare the two lists. Does one neglected area on the life list also show up in the writing list? For example, no privacy?

4. Starting small, choose one area from the life list and one from the writing list that could improve.

5. This week, begin one small change.

Be prepared for reactions as you make changes: There may be comments from family, friends, even your Inner Critic. If this happens, go back to your lists and review the changes. Consider the pay-off—in terms of your health, happiness, and longevity, as a writer and functional human being.

7

FINDING THE BEST
FORM FOR YOUR BOOK

Here's how it goes: You decide you must write the memoir of the ten years that shaped who you are today. Your story starts after your parents' divorce, when you lived in eighteen different places including one month in your mother's car. Describing all these moves comes together pretty smoothly at first. The pages pile up.

When you begin to write about your mother, and how she quits her tenth job in three years because her alcoholism got noticed once again, you stop. A fear clogs your throat. And an enormous case of writer's block sets in.

A writing friend counsels you. She tells you it will pass.

"Of course it will," you snap back.

But your mind is saying you will never be able to write this story until your mother dies. You don't get along so well, but you don't wish for her to die.

The book idea gets shelved.

In my experience, it's rarely over for most writers with an important story to tell. Strong book ideas don't stay on the shelf. After months of trying not to think about it, the time will come when you sit down with your idea again, even though you can't stop seeing your mother's face in your mind, her hurt voice—"How could you tell that story?"—haunting you.

You talk with your writing friend. She comes up with a brilliant idea: Why not make it a novel?

Writing the story as a novel is much easier. You change the story's location, your mother becomes your uncle, you become a teenage boy instead of an eight-year-old girl. Suddenly you are writing—a lot! The story emerges fresh and interesting on the page. Your paralyzing fear of telling family secrets is gone. So is your writer's block.

Writing the story as a novel is much easier. You change the story's location, your mother becomes your uncle, you become a teenage boy instead of an eight-year-old girl. Suddenly you are writing—a lot!

Some writers would say the story wanted to be a novel all along. Others would say you caved. Who's right? A lot of writers would tell you there's an inherent form to every book, and it's just up to the writer to find it. Mark Twain was one of those. He said, "There are books that refuse to be written. They stand their ground, year after year, and will not be persuaded. It isn't because the book is not there and worth being written—it is only because the right form for the story does not present itself. There is only one right form for a story, and if you fail to find that form the story will not tell itself."

Finding Your Book's Best Form

Helpful feedback from other writers is one way to find your book's best form. Another way calls for some investigation. You need to go to the library or your local bookstore. Your job is to find out what's out there. You need to see how other writers with a similar book idea found their form. Did they make a mystery, a romance, a literary novel? Perhaps an essay?

The form must not only fit the book, it must fit you. It must serve what you, as a creative artist, need to express in the world. "An organic structure is aligned with who we are and what we have to say," says writing teacher Natalie Goldberg. "It is not disconnected from ourself. If a form isn't organic, I think a great struggle ensues—the writer tries to stuff her being into a costume that doesn't fit."

In other words, if you ignore this task and don't find the best form, it will influence the entire writing process. In my experience, it's like an underground river coursing beneath a building, one that eventually gets too big to be ignored and could potentially flood your project. So while your book is still in the planning stages, approach the search for its form as one of the essential steps on the journey. Finding the best form for your book involves two steps.

First, you explore the possibilities of classification, what genre your book will take.

Second, you look at how your book will physically appear in print or other media, how it will be used by the reader.

A Brief, Subjective Overview of the Genres

A book's genre is the category it is assigned by bookstores and publishers. The main genres are nonfiction, memoir, creative nonfiction, biography, long-form fiction, short fiction, young adult and children's, and poetry.

There are many more genres available to authors than fifty years ago. Memoir, for example, has raced upon the scene in the past ten years and now has its own section in many bookstores, separate from its parent "nonfiction." And graphic novels, once relegated to the children's section, are a new phenomenon and shelved with fiction or in their own genre.

Below is a quick tour of the major genres. As you read, think about where your book fits best.

Nonfiction

A large catch-all genre for informational books that has quite a few subgenres: art, writing, nature, body/mind/spirit (self-help and personal development), how-to, medical, diet and health, business, gardening, and many others. Think of *The Seven Habits of Highly Successful People* (Steven Covey) or *The Artist's Way* (Julia Cameron), two nonfiction bestsellers.

Most nonfiction books present a place, community, culture, or other topic in depth. Nonfiction asks the writer to be a good researcher who uses trustworthy source material. The writer might be an expert or be writing with an expert. Or perhaps the writer has developed a good idea or theory to share.

Nonfiction is different from creative nonfiction (see next page), but it does require good storytelling skills—careful pacing, engaging anecdotes that illustrate the topic, even dialogue and action.

Nonfiction books vary widely in number of pages. It's a good idea to research your specific nonfiction genre to get up-to-date information.

Most nonfiction books present a place, community, culture, or other topic in depth.

Biography and Memoir

A popular subgenre of nonfiction focuses on a person's life if it is a biography or on your life if it's a memoir.

Both are truth-based books.

A memoir must tell your truth as accurately as possible. Memoirs concentrate on a specific time or event within your life, and this time or event's effect.

Biography is based on careful research and accuracy to the facts of a person's entire life, although the writer can bring in multiple sources with differing viewpoints (friends, colleagues, relatives). Biographies are often done in collaboration with the person being written about (if they are still alive) or with the approval of the subject's family or estate. Unauthorized biographies do not have that kind of approval.

A popular subgenre of nonfiction focuses on a person's life if it is a biography or on your life if it's a memoir.

Creative Nonfiction

Another type of nonfiction, harder to define, is an exploration of a nonfiction topic from your unique point of view. The narrator's opinion or perspective is essential. This exploration through a subject or a collection of short pieces (essays) linked by common theme sits between memoir and informational nonfiction. It can touch both.

Many forms of creative nonfiction exist today, from Annie Dillard's *A Pilgrim at Tinker's Creek* to Rick Bass's *Winter*.

Another type of nonfiction, harder to define, is an exploration of a nonfiction topic from your unique point of view.

Graphic Novel

A relative newcomer to mainstream publishing, graphic novels were once called comic books and had only a young audience. Now adults read them for their engaging and often edgy stories. A popular example is Ariel Schrag's *Likewise*.

They are often action-oriented—maybe because only a limited number of frames can show people just talking before a reader wants to move forward with something happening.

Graphic novels tell a story in pictures with captions. Illustrations are as important as words.

Graphic novels tell a story in pictures with captions.

Novel

Long-form fiction. A novel can be based on a true event (sometimes called "faction") or be completely made up. It must dramatize an event, describe the people involved in the event and how they changed from that event.

Novels are grouped into two categories: entertainment literature (sometimes called genre fiction, which includes mystery, thriller, horror, romance, true crime, western, sci-fi and fantasy) and literary fiction. Entertainment literature most often features the plot as the most important aspect of the story. Literary fiction most often features character-driven stories. Rules about what makes up this genre are being broken all the time—an example might be Anne Carson's *Autobiography of Red* which has tiny chapters and resembles a very long prose poem.

A novel can be based on a true event (sometimes called "faction") or be completely made up.

Short-Story Collection/Story Cycle

Short stories can be grouped into a collection or a story cycle, where the stories are linked in some way. In a story cycle, the stories might take place in the same community, concern one family or group of characters, or occur around one big event.

What makes this genre different from the novel? In short-story collections and most story cycles, each story is a chapter, complete in itself, and can stand alone.

In short-story collections and most story cycles, each story is a chapter, complete in itself, and can stand alone.

Children's and Young Adult (YA)

Fiction, nonfiction, memoir, biography, and almost any other genre fit into the children's and young adult (YA) categories, but they all have one thing in common: the book is age specific and the audience is not adult.

The genre ranges from read-to-me books to chapter books to children's books to teen stories. Children's books are usually for readers ages nine to twelve. YA books, for readers ages twelve to fifteen, straddle the pre-teen into teen years. Note: If your story requires drawing or illustrations, you do not need to supply them—the publisher will find a suitable illustrator.

Children's books are usually for readers ages nine to twelve. YA books, for readers ages twelve to fifteen, straddle the pre-teen into teen years.

A collection of poems, loosely or carefully linked together by theme (such as "light") or subject (such as "growing up with war hero grandfather").

It's essential to do careful research about your audience's reading level, topic interest, and language. Make sure the story is geared toward the right age group. Word count varies a lot in this genre.

Poetry Chapbook

A collection of poems, loosely or carefully linked together by theme (such "light") or subject (such as "growing up with war hero grandfather"). The poems are arranged like chapters and create a flow for the reader.

Chapbooks average thirty to fifty poems and are usually less than fifty pages.

Inventing Your Book's Structure

Memoirist Abigail Thomas tells us in *Thinking about Memoir*, "There is no hard and fast rule about structure; you can invent your own." That's the fun of finding your book's form.

Explore the many ways your book can be put together—don't just consider a perfect-bound 6-inch-by-9-inch trade-size paperback. Modern books contain sidebars, exercises, tip boxes, recipes, images, photos. Some have wider pages, blank sections for note-taking, spiral binding so they lay flat. They contain pockets and pop-up images.

They are packaged as decks of cards, present games along with the text, or offer workbooks. Interactive books (such as children's books where the child can interact with the story, change a character's experiences, change the ending) are becoming increasingly more available.

Here's one example: Many years ago, J.P. Tarcher began publishing a new form dubbed "the Inner Workbook." It combined traditional nonfiction text with wide margins so the reader could take notes. Julia Cameron's 1992 release of *The Artist's Way* was an inner workbook. The only limit is your imagination (and the publisher's willingness, unless you publish yourself).

Exercise: Fun Forms for Your Book
TIME NEEDED: 40 MINUTES

---

1. Spend an afternoon looking over your personal library. Survey your favorite books.

2. What interests you about their layout, size, number of images (photos or art), or amount of white space? Make some notes.

3. Then take a trip to a bookstore. Find the section where your book might be shelved. Look at the forms of the published books. Are there wide margins? How are the chapters laid out—with sidebars or boxes or exercises? Are the chapters titled or just numbered?

One of my students, intent on creating uniform-sized chapters for her nonfiction book, was amazed to see that modern books vary widely in chapter lengths—with short and long chapters all in one book. What new ideas can you come away with?

Talking with Your Book

Many writers believe their books take on a certain "consciousness," becoming more than just something inside the writer's head. Ever hear of an author saying a character spoke to him? Or a writer reading over her work and not remembering she wrote it? All of this points to the somewhat out-of-body experience of book writing. Consider the idea of a book talking back to you about its best form.

I've conversed with all my books-in-progress. The notion that books can talk back has helped me with every book I've written. Call it your subconscious, the universe, or some higher part of you—but if you ask the right question and put your skepticism aside, you often get something that surprises you and will enhance your writing.

Ever hear of an author saying a character spoke to him? Or a writer reading over her work and not remembering she wrote it?

Exercise: Interview with Your Book
TIME NEEDED: 40 MINUTES

1. Pretend you're a reporter. You're going to interview your book. List some questions you want to ask your book about its form, content, goals. You can start with something nonthreatening, as you would if you were a real reporter. Ideas from my class are below, or you can make up your own:

   What do you want to tell me about yourself?
   What form suits you best?
   Who is your readership and how will they access you?
   What are you most eager to say?
   What are you most afraid to say?
   What genre are you?

2. Put aside skepticism and imagine the book answering you.

3. Write down everything it says—no matter how odd, silly, or irrelevant—again, no censoring.

4. Whenever the book runs out of things to say or you get too uneasy about the answers, switch to a different question.

5. Keep going until you get something that surprises you.

The goal of this exercise? To tap hidden parts of yourself as a writer, parts we often censor.

If you maintain the attitude of anything-can-happen, if you let go of your linear self, you can find out a lot about your book and your partnership with it. I come back to this exercise whenever I get stuck or can't see the way forward. Each time I try it, I am willing to be surprised by the results.

Remember as Mark Twain said, "There is only one right form for a story, and if you fail to find that form the story will not tell itself."

When the writer finds out what form the book wants to take, it can make the book-writing journey a more gracious and pleasurable experience.

8

LETTING YOUR IDEAL READER
HELP YOU STAY THE COURSE

Do you know who your ideal reader is? What age is that reader? Are you writing primarily for women over fifty? Boys under fifteen? What kind of person is he or she? Someone who loves fishing? A tennis pro? A bored child? Is your language, tone, and style going to engage this particular reader? Is the pace of your narrative going to bore her? Make her want more?

If you're thinking of being published, if you want your book to be read by more than your close friends and family, you have to consider these questions. If you want people to turn the page, you have to consider the reader.

Your agent will. Your publisher will.

It's time in your book-writing journey to get to know your reader. You need to find out who you are writing for.

Write for One Person

Many writers begin by writing for themselves only. After a while, they start imagining others reading their words. Some writers are thrilled to think of readers poring over their pages. In my classes I've encountered many writers who feel their books are on a mission to touch another person's life. Or they have a story they can't wait to share with as many people as possible. I've also met writers who are terrified at the idea of being read by the outside world.

Balance is best gained by thinking of one reader. Writer Kurt Vonnegut says that by keeping one reader in mind (in his case, his sister Alice), he felt free to write. "Anything I knew Allie wouldn't like I crossed out. Everything I knew she would get a kick out of I left in. . . . Allie was funny in real life. That gives me permission to be funny too." Vonnegut went on

Many writers begin by writing for themselves only. After a while, they start imagining others reading their words.

to say, "A story written for one person pleases a reader, dear reader, because it makes him or her a part of the action."

"Write to please just one person," he added. "If you open a window and make love to the world, so to speak, your story will get pneumonia."

As a beginning writer, I didn't like this idea of writing for one idealized reader. If I put attention on this reader, wouldn't I lose track of my own voice in deference to the reader's needs? Wouldn't my uniqueness, my creativity, collapse? It took publishing many books before Vonnegut's advice made sense. I know now the logic of this approach: one sympathetic reader can help shape and focus your work, and also keep you moving forward, because as you work on your book idea, you can imagine asking your ideal imaginary reader, *What would you need here? More time to digest the idea? More information? More character or more plot?*

Start by visualizing your ideal reader—maybe modeling her or him after someone you know—and begin a dialogue with this person. It's not so far-fetched. Think of it as another point on your book map, to keep your book on track as it develops. You can change your reader's profile as you discover more about what you really want to write, but keeping the reader in mind keeps the writer from getting too self-absorbed. It really is unreasonable to think that a total stranger would take time to read your book, even if it's fascinating to you, without being invested in its story. So how do you do this? By delivering a benefit.

Many writers are so wrapped up in their own words, they forget to ask, *What benefit will the reader get from my book?*

True Partnership with Your Reader

Please don't think this means keeping yourself out of the equation. Remember the exercise in chapter 1 where you explored the reasons you're writing this book? Your own needs are as important as the reader's or publisher's. But not more important.

Many writers object to this. "Isn't this selling yourself out?" one student asked me. "Seems like I'd be compromising my creative flow if I paid the reader more attention than my own process."

But good books become the reader's journey too.

When I was twelve, I read *The House of Thirty Cats*, and the story touched me so deeply I had to tell the author. I wrote a thank-you letter to Mary Calhoun. Much to my amazement, Ms. Calhoun wrote me back. She said it was great that I loved her book, because her readers were so important.

Books that stay with us, change us. They may have meaning all our lives. Prolific writer Ursula Le Guin says, "If a book told you something when you were fifteen, it will tell you again when you're fifty, though you may understand it so differently that it seems you're reading a whole new book."

So don't be a writer who thinks only of herself and her small world of words. Don't be someone who just pays attention to the beauty you're creating on the page and ignores the person who might read that page months or years from now. A wonderful feeling of expansion comes to your book journey when you begin to think outside of pleasing only yourself. If you pay attention to your reader now—before you get too far into your book—it will actually help you write a better book.

> Books that stay with us, change us. They may have meaning all our lives.

Exercise: Who Is My Ideal Reader?
TIME NEEDED: 2 HOURS

Put attention on your ideal reader and write whatever comes to mind as you think about the questions below.

1. What's my ideal reader's approximate age?
2. Is my ideal reader male or female?
3. What's my reader's education level?
4. What's her or his income level?
5. Does my ideal reader have a career or profession?

6. Does my ideal reader have health concerns?

7. Any interests and hobbies?

8. What are my ideal reader's biggest life concerns?

9. What kind of books does my reader read?

List any other details about your reader that you can think of. Then write for fifteen minutes about the final questions:

What need will my book address, what question will it answer for this reader? Is there anything I need to add, approach differently, take away from my book as it is now, in order to really speak to my ideal reader?

Introducing Yourself to Your Reader

If you're not sure who your ideal reader might be, grab your writer's notebook and visit a bookstore. I do this whenever I get too wrapped up in my own words and lose sight of my reader. So when I need perspective about who my book might be helping, I go to a big bookstore. I go on a weekend when many people shop, and find a chair near the section where my book, when published, will be shelved. I sit and watch.

As I watch people browse, I take notes on their appearance, race, gender. I make guesses about their economic background, educational level, profession, family history.

When I get home, I reread my notes and try to get clearer about my ideal reader, imagining the need or questions that reader would bring to my book. I ask myself, *Why would this person read my book?*

As I mentioned in chapter 1, readers buy books for one of three reasons.

WHY READERS BUY BOOKS

- entertainment
- inspiration
- information

It's a happy thought if your book fulfills more than one of these reasons. But be sure you're aware of at least one, because it'll shape the trajectory of your book-writing journey.

A children's book writer told me about the realization that came to her after she began to "talk" on paper with the ideal reader of her new chick lit book: "I started out believing I was writing for older adults. As I wrote, I realized my ideal reader was younger, perhaps in her early twenties. I knew my book would speak most to her. She's the one who most needs this story. I changed my book's focus entirely, adding sections that were tailored to this reader's understanding. I also found that knowing my reader gave me sustainability for the times when the book-writing got hard. She motivated me to finish." This writer spent regular time asking her ideal reader questions—especially when she got stuck with a chapter or scene.

Like Vonnegut imagining his sister Allie's reactions, this children's book writer visualized "Stella," new kid in the workplace, living with her first serious boyfriend, contemplating buying a house. What would Stella need to hear, want to know? She renewed her acquaintance with her reader by visualizing Stella picking up the chapter she was working on, imagining her satisfaction (or frustration).

One day, if you try this, you won't just be imagining things when your reader nudges you and says impatiently, "Hey, I'm waiting for that chapter!" and you'll continue to write because someone cares.

One day, if you try this, you won't just be imagining things when your reader nudges you and says impatiently, "Hey, I'm waiting for that chapter!"

Exercise: Ideal Reader Research
TIME NEEDED: 2 HOURS

1. Imagine yourself in a comfortable chair at your favorite bookstore.

2. You're sitting near the section where your future book will be shelved. In your imagination, see your book on the shelf, its face out to the world.

3. Enjoy the feeling of seeing your book, your name, your cover in that imaginary setting.

4. Now imagine a reader coming up to the shelf.

5. This reader picks up your book and skims the back cover, reads the inside flap and the table of contents.

6. Study this person. Take note of anything you "see" in your imagination.

7. Ask this person, "Why is my book resonating with you? What question does it answer for you? What need does it satisfy?"

8. Open your eyes and write down everything you can about this reader.

9

WHAT YOUR BOOK WANTS TO SAY: WRITING THE PREMISE STATEMENT

In my book-writing workshop, I had my students play a game. I asked them to craft a one-sentence description, called a "premise statement," for their most favorite book.

This isn't as easy as it sounds. They had to get to the essence of the book's story, figure out what it was trying to say, then whittle this down to twenty words or less.

Our favorite premise statement came from a heated discussion about Frank Baum's *The Wizard of Oz*. The result was this:

> **Dorothy travels to the magical land of Oz and discovers there's no place like home.**

I imagine this was very close to the publicity line MGM Studios chose when the movie first came out in 1939. It's a good premise statement because it appeals to both children and adults. Kids love hints of an outer adventure, the travel to the "magical land of Oz." Their parents are comforted by the reason for the journey, to discover "there's no place like home."

In short, the outer and inner story.

A Premise States the Inner and Outer Story

A premise needs to contain your book's outer and inner story. Outer stories are easier to figure out than inner stories because they're more visible. As we learned in chapter 2, the outer story is always the main event that is externalized in action. It's what happens in your book or the main information you're delivering via research, facts, opinion.

In our premise for *The Wizard of Oz*, the outer story is represented by this part: "Dorothy travels to the magical land of Oz." Something happens: Dorothy goes on a trip. Do we

A premise needs to contain your book's outer and inner story.

103

need to add where she travels from? Where she travels to? What about the companions who went with her?

As my class distilled the premise to its essence—with heated debate about whether the Tin Man, the monkeys, and different witches should be included—we decided these "extras" were important players but Dorothy's travel was the main event, the outer story.

The inner story addresses the meaning of the main event, topic, or opinion—and how it changed the characters. In *The Wizard of Oz*, the inner story is the second part of the premise, where Dorothy "discovers there's no place like home." This is what she learns from her adventure.

Inner story touches on what is realized as an effect of the outer story. Inner story can be stated in the premise very directly. It can also be hinted at, as in some of the examples below from my students:

Bel Canto by Ann Patchett (novel)

Premise: Unlikely alliances form when guests gathering at a birthday celebration are captured by a terrorist organization that holds them hostage.

Outer story: terrorists invade a birthday celebration

Inner story: unlikely alliances form

The Duke of Deception by Geoffrey Wolff (memoir)

Premise: Growing up with a shifty father, a son learns that the guilt of betrayal lives in the soul of the betrayer.

Outer story: growing up events

Inner story: learning about betrayal and guilt

Housekeeping by Marilynne Robinson (novel)

Premise: In soul-scouring Fingerbone, Minnesota, the inadvertent actions of an aunt change the lives of two sisters, forever separating them physically, but not from their longing for each other.

Outer story: what the aunt does

Inner story: two sisters' longing for each other

Middlesex by Jeffrey Eugenides (novel)

Premise: When a girl learns she is born intersex (as both sexes), she has to decide whether to continue living as a woman or be true to herself and live as a man.

Outer story: being born intersex

Inner story: journey to be true to self

The Nurture Assumption: Why Children Turn Out the Way They Do by Judith Rich Harris and Steven Pinker (nonfiction)

Premise: Maverick psychologist fights the establishment to show why your child's peers will influence him and change his future to a greater degree than a parent ever can.

Outer story: research showing how peers interact

Inner story: anecdotes showing how the child develops

Proust and the Squid: The Story and Science of the Reading Brain by Maryanne Wolf (nonfiction)

Premise: A revolutionary discussion of how reading makes the brain more efficient, and the sobering evidence of what happens when the brain doesn't learn to read.

Outer story: research about reading and brain

Inner story: stories about the effect of reading, and not being able to read, on a child's life

White Oleander by Janet Fitch (novel)

Premise: When her mother is imprisoned for killing her lover with poisonous oleander flowers, a young girl has to raise herself and finds out about the allure of beauty and the strength needed to overcome its power.

Outer story: the imprisonment of the mother

Inner story: discovery about beauty and power

It's often easier to notice inner and outer story in another author's book, and through such analysis you may

It's often easier to notice outer and inner story in another author's book, and you may get more perspective on a premise statement for your own book.

get more perspective on a premise statement for your own book. Use these questions to get started:

> Where does this story happen?
> What's the main topic or theory?
> What action is taken?
> What is the effect of the action?
> Who is the main player or narrator?
> Who has power over whom?
> Who changes the most?

If you're trying a premise for a collection—a poetry chapbook, series of essays, or short-story cycle—choose one section you especially like. Write a premise for that section. Broaden it to see if the same theme echoes in the other poems, essays, or stories. Then try writing a premise that speaks for the whole collection.

To your reader, your book's outer and inner story should act like baking soda and vinegar put together in a jar. Do you remember this experiment from high-school chemistry? How together they start to foam? Apart, these elements are neutral. Together, they are volatile.

The Premise Always Changes

Because a book's inner story can take a while to surface, premise statements nearly always change. They change even more frequently if you're working on a novel or memoir.

In one of my classes, a writer, after months of writing about the invalid mother who raised her, discovered her book was really about her relationship with her prickly grandfather. She grew in understanding about her book and discarded her initial premise of "Growing up in 1940s Mississippi, a young girl who loses her mother when she is four, finds herself again when she reunites with forgotten family." The premise became "After losing her Southern Belle mother to disfiguring cancer, a young girl finds refuge in her grandfather's gruff love," which was much more aligned with her new focus.

A novelist who began writing a story based on his sojourn in a small west Texas community changed the location to Mexico when he went to live there for a year. His premise changed as he changed. The novelist kept the same theme of finding home in a foreign community, but with totally different characters and setting.

An essayist, intending to focus his collection on what he'd learned through his relationships with his children, ended up discovering what he really longed to write about: namely, how his move to a small European country revealed different fathering practices that changed how he fathered his own son.

Every premise statement evolves to reflect your real book, as you discover new topics for that book. How is each new direction connected with your book? When the premise doesn't match, either the book reorients or the premise adapts.

A working premise is dynamic; it changes as our understanding of our work changes.

A writer in my class, a botanist writing about his large collection of bonsai plants, wondered how the premise statement could be used for his nonfiction book. His book focused on growing bonsai as an art form using unique techniques he had discovered growing his own bonsai. He came up with this premise: "Learn to grow bonsai and bring the ancient Japanese art into your home." It was a good premise—it included the event (growing bonsai) and the effect of that event (bringing art into your home). So he went forward, using the premise as a guide.

Weeks went by. He had written a hundred pages, mostly about gardening techniques. But then during some research, the writer came upon a history of Japan in the twelfth and

A working premise is dynamic; it changes as our understanding of our work changes.

thirteenth centuries. He read how growing bonsai became a meditative practice among Buddhist monks. He wanted this new information to connect with his book topic. But how?

"Learn to grow bonsai" reflected growing techniques. History and the inner story of bonsai growing—how the monks used it as a symbol of refinement and enlightenment—wasn't his stated focus. Was this new material relevant to his book? It didn't match his premise statement. His interest in bonsai plants hadn't diminished, but this serious sidetrack grabbed his imagination. What to do? In his confusion, the botanist's book languished.

One afternoon, he was talking with a fellow classmate who also loved history. The friend suggested a way to combine the two ideas in a new premise: how ancient Japanese practices affect bonsai growing today. The new premise helped the botanist rework his book. He included thirteenth-century Japan and the Zen Buddhist influences on botany and how those influences continue to impact bonsai growing.

With the new premise, the writer regained his enthusiasm and saw how to marry his new-found fascination of Japanese Zen Buddhism with his love of botany.

Your Book's GPS

John Gardner, author of *The Art of Fiction*, said that writing a book was "like heading out over the open sea in a small boat." He added, "It helps if you have a plan and a course laid out." Like a good GPS, your premise statement will help reorient you whenever you get off track. That's because as you write more and more, your manuscript gets harder to contain in your head. Without a reminding focus statement, it can become hard to remember what you originally wanted to write about.

But since book writing is a journey, your book's premise statement will change each time you discover more about your topic. Plan to rewrite your premise statement quite a few times during the book-writing process, at minimum:

1. When you first get an idea for a book
2. When you've completed your first draft and begin revision
3. After you revise—before drafting your query letter to submit to an agent or publisher

Fear of Definition

Writing the premise and discovering an inner and outer story can feel risky to some writers. That's understandable. A good premise statement causes us to go deeper into the book we're writing.

Premise statements ask you to define your story, make connections between your life and your writing, and learn things about each that you might not know—or might not want to know. This exploration can trigger the Inner Critic, who often doesn't want to go there. It prefers writing safely, unemotionally, in a way that will not reveal your vulnerability on the page.

In *Thunder and Lightning*, Natalie Goldberg writes, "The nearer I get to expressing my essence, the louder, more zealous that belittling voice becomes. It has been helpful to understand it not as a diminishing parent but as something universal, impersonal, a kind of spiritual test. . . . It is my signal to persevere and plow through."

Perseverance is essential. If writing your book's premise strikes fear in your heart, then try going at it in a nonthreatening way. Trick your Inner Critic by writing outside the main arena of your story.

If writing your book's premise strikes fear in your heart, then try going at it in a non-threatening way.

Exercise: Writing Outside Your Story
TIME NEEDED: 30 MINUTES

---

1. Briefly describe a place that is in your book but not central to it. For instance, if the story takes place in a hospital operating room, choose the cafeteria. It's key not to focus on the place that is the most important.

2. Do the same with one person in your book who is not central to it (the ER nurse, not the patient).

3. Describe an event that takes place, but not the main event.

4. Write anything that comes to mind about the effect of this event.

5. Ask yourself how the person you listed above features into this event. Are they a witness, a participant? What is this person like? Who has power over them, whom do they have power over?

6. Look at the information you've gathered. Using it, write a premise about this "outside story."

When my students try this, they usually get some useful results. The premise written about their "outside" story gives them clues about their book's main premise. One writer hadn't been able to write her book's premise directly—it was too overwhelming. But the exercise helped her realize another level of the book's premise because the smaller premise had the same qualities of inner story as her main book idea. Writing outside the story gave her the way into understanding the essence of her bigger story.

It is a useful trick to soothe that Inner Critic. You're telling the Critic, "We're not doing anything really important, so take a vacation for an hour."

How to Use Your Premise

Once your premise is drafted, print it out. Draw or paste relevant images on it. Put it above your writing desk or in your writing notebook.

Look at it often.

As you plan, write, and develop your book, you'll come back to the premise. You'll check its accuracy as you change your book's focus, as you research, as you explore new areas.

A premise's guidance system will help you reorient as your book idea meanders around inside the head and heart. In the early stages of writing your book, a good premise will also help you focus on the various topics your book will address—and find what is missing.

> **USE THESE QUESTIONS TO HELP EXPLORE THE PREMISE STATEMENT FOR YOUR BOOK:**
> 1. Who or what is causing the most trouble for the reader, client, or main character?
> 2. What do they long to change?
> 3. What do they fear most?
> 4. Is there a realization, choice, or transformation occurring in a town or community?
> 5. Where in the book does this first appear?
> 6. How else could this be demonstrated?
> 7. What's the most important action that shows transformation?
> 8. What changes from beginning to end?

10

THREE-ACT STRUCTURE: CREATING THE MAP OF YOUR BOOK

Writers who approach book writing as expanded short pieces are in for a surprise when they begin to structure their first manuscript. I know because I was one of those writers. As a newspaper columnist for twelve years, I loved writing short and sweet. It fit my creative impatience. I loved the forced closure of a column's limited length.

When I was asked to write my first book, I thought, *How hard can that be? I'll just take my ideas and expand them.* But as I soon learned, my book evolved from a handful of short linked pieces to dozens and dozens of pieces. It was near impossible to hold the structure in mind anymore! A visual map was required. I needed a new way to organize the unwieldy collection of islands that made up my manuscript. That's when I discovered the beauty of the three-act structure.

I learned that any manuscript could be divided into three sections, each holding certain keys to the story. I realized I could work on these sections independently, letting myself complete one part before tackling the next. It made structuring my manuscripts, in any genre, much simpler than I imagined.

Suddenly the planning part of the book-writing journey became manageable.

A visual map was required. Enter the three-act structure.

Three Acts Force You to Organize and Choose

Organizing material into three acts is an ancient idea. It's been used for centuries by many writers in many literary genres. Ancient Greeks used it to order their poems and plays. According to the Greek philosopher Aristotle, the three-act structure works because it imitates the essence of how most real-life action unfolds, namely with a beginning, middle, and end.

Aristotle also said that if you infuse emotionally arousing incidents into the three-act plot, the audience will then experience an enriching emotional cleaning or "catharsis."

In *The Writer's Journey*, screenwriting teacher Christopher Vogler took Aristotle's idea and analyzed dozens of films, showing how many of the most successful use the three-act structure. Vogler then adapted Joseph Campbell's *Hero's Journey* analysis of myths to further inform how the three acts need to proceed. We'll explore each of the acts in this chapter, starting with Act 1.

Open with Energy: The Purpose of Act 1

Act 1 introduces the primary question or quest of a story. What quest will be interesting enough for the reader to follow? Act 1 sets this up in the first chapter. Usually, an illustrative anecdote or scene presents this question or quest, often via the primary dilemma (conflict or challenge) the book will address.

Act 1 also gives us the primary environment of the story—the main setting or place it all happens. A hospital? A kitchen? The backyard? A small town? A riverboat?

We also learn who is struggling with this question or quest. In nonfiction, it might be the reader herself—as in a self-help book—or it might be a political party, a vanishing culture, a library foundation. In memoir, it's often the author. In fiction, it's the main character. As John Truby, screenwriting guru, says in *Truby's Story Structure*, the basic question is "Who is fighting whom for what?"

Act 1 usually introduces us to the main helper, mentor, or ally—whether person or concept—within the first few chapters, after the dilemma is presented. Think of the classic quest: there is always someone who helps the hero in dangerous times, the teacher or wise person who shelters him, the voice that guides the way. A helper can also be a belief that will assist in finding an answer to the question the book asks.

Sometimes, Act 1 will also present what Joseph Campbell named "refusal of the call." This is a temporary setback that keeps the main character or narrator from really starting out on her quest.

In the final chapter of Act 1 there's often some parallel action or discussion or moment that echoes what was asked or started in chapter 1. This creates a very satisfying loop for the reader, a sort of recap of what they've read so far—not in obvious ways, but as a parallel moment. For instance, love letters received in chapter 1 of Act 1 could be reread in the final chapter of Act 1.

Lastly, Act 1 must leave us with a greater problem or question by its end, enough momentum to propel us into Act 2, the middle of the book.

Act 1 must leave us with a greater problem or question by its end, enough momentum to propel us into Act 2, the middle of the book.

Act 1 must
1. Introduce the primary quest or question
2. Set up the primary environment of the story
3. Introduce who is struggling with the primary quest or question
4. Welcome the main helper or mentor
5. Present refusal of the call
6. Create a loop for the reader between the opening and final chapters of Act 1
7. End with momentum into Act 2

Exercise: Imagining Act 1
TIME NEEDED: 30 MINUTES TO 1 HOUR

1. Line up seven large Post-It notes on your desk.
2. Close your eyes and drift into the creative imagination. Ask yourself, *Of all the ideas I have come up with for my book so far, what's the strongest possible opening?*
3. Jot it on the first Post-It.
4. Close your eyes and ask yourself, *What possible*

ending for Act 1 would echo that beginning chapter idea?

5. Jot it on the last Post-It.

6. Now imagine the steps in between. Fill in each Post-It with an idea that might logically track from the ending you imagine to the beginning you imagine for Act 1. Add more if needed.

7. Go back to any notes you've made for your book's opening chapters. Compare what you just came up with and the ideas you originally had. Which is strongest?

Keep the Momentum Going: Act 2

As a professional editor, I've worked on hundreds of manuscripts, some that became books, some that didn't. I find that the reason a manuscript doesn't keep my interest is often due to a poorly planned Act 2.

Books are huge projects. A writer can easily get tired—even bored—with his manuscript at about the midway point, then race through it to the more interesting climax, otherwise known as Act 3. But if tension and complexity isn't accelerated with skill in Act 2, readers won't stick around for that climax.

I visualize Act 2 as the bridge that connects my opening with my ending, the only element holding my readers up in the air for ten, twenty chapters. It must be solid. If it isn't, my book will collapse.

I often tell students to examine Michael Cunningham's *The Hours* to see how Act 2 is built. In this complex story of three women in three eras, revolving around the biography of Virginia Woolf and her writings, Act 1 sets up strong dilemma and characters who are trying to live and find truth and beauty within these dilemmas. By Act 2, things are dicey. Virginia Woolf has backed herself into a life corner and clearly must take action; her 1940s counterpart, Kitty, books the motel room and pockets the sleeping pills; the modern-day poet Richard sits on the windowsill over Manhattan. Three possible deaths, with impending impact for a lot of people they will leave behind. Will they go through with it? If not, what will happen instead?

Act 2 deepens the problem, propels us into the grand finale, and because of this, Act 2 is often a bit harder to plan than Act 1. It takes more thinking, asking yourself to consider how you might deliver a new or deeper understanding of your story or material. Act 2 addresses big questions, like: In what way is the question or quest presented in Act 1 manifesting in a more complex way? Are the main characters or narrators evolving as they respond to the question or the quest? How is the main question being answered—or not? Is the action of Act 1 taking on new meaning as the story progresses? What bigger test is being imposed on the characters, what deeper challenge is the book's material suggesting, as a take-away?

What bigger test is being imposed on the characters, what deeper challenge is the book's material suggesting, as a take-away?

Act 2 must
1. Take the reader toward a deeper mystery, a darker cave, a bigger question—and suggest a coming change
2. Provide tests and new systems to explore
3. Deliver a surprise or new perspective
4. Deepen the narrator's relationship with the main allies in her life
5. Foreshadow the final crisis

If you'd like to try your skills at discerning Act 1 from Act 2, try the fun exercise below. Locate a movie you love and watch it again from a writer's point of view. You can learn a lot about the three acts this way.

Exercise: Movie Research
TIME NEEDED: 45 MINUTES PLUS MOVIE VIEWING TIME

After you watch your movie, answer the questions below:
1. Where does Act 1 stop and Act 2 begin? Is there a precipitous moment, when things are newly in question, or when the main characters,

having solved one problem, are presented with an even greater one?

2. Where does Act 2 take us as viewers? What greater challenge or question is presented?

3. Where does Act 2 end? What are we experiencing by this point in the story?

Act 3—Are You Ready to Finish Your Book?

One summer long ago, I took a writing course at the University of Iowa. My instructor shared a concept new to me: "earned outcome." An outcome is earned, he told me, when the ending of a story makes sense to the reader. That only happens because the writer carefully places hints along the way.

Viewing Act 3 as an "earned outcome" means laying a trail the reader can follow unerringly toward the ending you're designing. This is most easily done by working from the end backwards, going back through chapter ideas, asking if each thread brought into the ending actually weaves, unbroken, back through the book.

Act 3 must give a sense of satisfaction. We've traveled somewhere, we've been thoroughly engaged. Good books leave us musing, still a little (or a lot) in love with the story we've just encountered, excited about the ideas we've just heard.

This is the result of well-planned beginnings and middles, but especially a carefully designed Act 3. Act 3 ties up any loose threads from Acts 1 and 2, bringing it all to a reasonable conclusion.

Act 3 must
1. Bring about an unexpected but anticipated change
2. Take the story to a final level, often via a twist
3. Reveal the true alliances
4. Tie together any loose ends (use that gun that appeared on the mantelpiece in chapter 3)
5. Present a final test—how to apply what's been learned so far

6. Revisit the beginning chapter, echoing the primary question or quest

Looking at your book from the end and working backwards lets you see how each act contributes to your reader's experience.

Remember that the three acts in your book need not be equal lengths. One may be longer than the others. It all depends on what effect you are trying for, what helps your reader have the experience you intend for that section of the story.

The exercise below is very helpful as you begin mapping your book. It lets you make each act strong and sure. It's very common to frontload the book, with too much given away in Act 1. When you do this exercise, you might discover that you can shift scenes to Act 2 or Act 3, creating better pacing of your story—and an easier journey for the reader.

Looking at your book from the end and working backwards lets you see how each act contributes to your reader's experience.

Exercise: Planning via Three Acts
TIME NEEDED: 2–3 HOURS

1. Ask yourself: How could my book be divided into three sections? Where are there natural breaking points?

2. Imagine yourself in your ideal reader's point of view. On paper, brainstorm what you would like this reader to have experienced by the end of Act 1, the first section of your book. Maybe you'd want the reader to feel full engagement with the characters or topic you're presenting, an understanding of the basic dilemma, and a strong sense of the setting of the story by the end of Act 1.

3. Now do the same brainstorming for Act 2. This is the middle of your book. What would you

imagine a reader needing to experience in this middle section, in order to read on?

4. Now go back to the topic brainstorming list you made in chapter 5. Look at this list and begin to designate topics for Act 1, Act 2, or Act 3. Ask yourself what connects best with your reader's desired experience for each act.

5. Review your notes from the exercise on page 117. Ask yourself where you would like your reader to be by the end of your book. Do you want to leave the reader with a certain feeling about the main character's change, the major events and their effect, the setting and its part in the story? For example:

   ✓ Understand and be ready to try a new idea?

   ✓ Know something different about the world?

   ✓ See deeper into family dynamics?

   ✓ Believe a certain event could not have been avoided?

   ✓ See a different side of things?

6. Working backwards, brainstorm three things that would have to occur earlier in your book, to earn this outcome.

Once you understand the outcome you wish for, you can trace the pathway to it, working backwards. This is actually easier than it sounds, if you use an organization tool called a storyboard. We'll explore storyboards in depth in chapter 11.

11

STORYBOARDS: MAKING SENSE OF YOUR BOOK'S STRUCTURE

A new book writer, Joan, was an accomplished quilter. After her beloved aunt's death from breast cancer, Joan began writing a book about the family. At the same time, she decided to sew a memorial quilt to honor her aunt. It was interesting to watch Joan structure both projects.

From having sewn dozens of quilts, she knew how to piece one together. She decided to make the quilt out of squares cut from a dress, a pair of jeans, and other favorite items her aunt wore when she was alive. Intrigued, I asked Joan to bring her squares to class.

When Joan spread the squares on the table to assemble her design, I couldn't imagine how the mix of colors and textures would make a unified whole. Fabrics from fifties dresses and Calvin Klein jeans didn't blend at all when they were just pieces. But Joan confidently placed them side by side. She then mapped her quilt ideas on paper, first creating a visual diagram that pulled together the disparate parts via one unifying fabric that echoed colors in each square. Once sewn together, light and dark, pattern and solid wove into a harmonious yet startling whole.

Because she had planned well, the finished quilt was extraordinary. Joan's skill—and her love for her aunt—created a tribute that spoke of the fresh, unexpected quality of the raw moments of a person's well-lived life.

When it came time to structure her memoir, Joan was nervous. I told her that in fact she was already a seasoned pro. The storyboarding tool I then showed her and my other students in class is quite similar to how Joan mapped her quilts.

Once sewn together, light and dark, pattern and solid wove into a harmonious yet startling whole.

Although she wasn't sure the random pieces of her book could ever come together in a logical way for anyone who didn't know her family, using her storyboard she succeeded in stitching her life moments into a cohesive picture.

So here it is: the last step of planning your book. This is where you create a visual map, a storyboard. You'll use what you learned about the three acts to get an overview and design the next stage of your journey.

Your storyboard will help your linear self feel organized and your creative self feel heard.

How Storyboards Work

Many years ago, I was hired by a small press in the Midwest for an all-day "storyboarding session." The book's subject was already decided. Our team was hired to brainstorm a visual map, a storyboard, showing what the chapters would cover and the best order of topics.

On one wall of the meeting room was an enormous whiteboard. The session leader drew a series of big blank boxes, one representing each chapter-to-be. First we brainstormed a huge list of possible stories, ideas, topics, and moments for the book. Then, looking at the list, we suggested a possible order for these items. The leader placed the items in the storyboard boxes, using a shorthand that would easily lead us back to the original idea for that topic. For instance, "Jerry's discovery of his health problem" referred back to a long story about one of our clients who was to be in the book. After the storyboard was assembled in rough form, we read it end to beginning to see if the topics tracked well. Adjustments made, the "book" was sent off to be written by in-house writers.

Years later, I watched a screenwriter organize his movie for filming via storyboard. He told me most movie ideas are diagrammed this way before shooting, to work out possible kinks and group similar location shots to save money.

Storyboards are invaluable as layout guides. They quickly tell what's working and what's not.

Exercise: Studying Storyboards
TIME NEEDED: 2–3 HOURS

1. Choose five favorite books in your book's genre.

2. Look over the tables of contents to check out each book's organizing system and make some notes in your writer's notebook. Are they chronological or do they move back and forth in time? How are the topics arranged—beginner level to more advanced, or random?

3. Look at the opening chapters. Write your observations: Where does the first section of backstory appear? How long is the backstory?

4. Now look at the first act. See if there's any pattern to how the chapters are put together. For example, if the book is nonfiction, look at the frequency of anecdotes or exercises, where they are placed in each chapter. What patterns work for each chapter?

5. Now consider your book. With what you've learned from the five favorites, what idea comes as a way to organize your material?

Using a Storyboard to Organize Your Book

It's impossible to hold the vision of your book in your head, even with an outline or good notes. You can't see the overview—the book's best organization—when you've created it as separate scenes, islands, or moments. Because your linear self will unconsciously create patterns in your manuscript, using the logic of plot, chronology, topic, and timeline, you'll often wind up with something fairly boring. A linear approach often neglects the inner story. A storyboard allows you to play with other options.

As you see each section unlinked from its chronology, you can also see its subtler connection with other parts in

A linear approach often neglects the inner story. A storyboard allows you to play with other options.

your book. The inner story is realized.

Are you ready to get an overview of your book's structure? Start by reviewing "Imagining Act 1," the exercise on page 117 of chapter 10. The exercise asked you to line up seven Post-It notes, write the beginning and end of Act 1, then work toward the middle. This is a great way to ease into trying a storyboard.

Although you'll eventually storyboard all three acts of your book, I've found it's easiest to begin storyboarding with the first and last chapters. You create bookends for your story, then work toward the middle. Again, this is a less logical process than outlining, but the result is a more organic overview of your book.

Viewing Your Scenes in a New Way

Gaby was writing a novel. Before she came to my workshop, she'd written about a hundred pages, five chapters in all. She loved her first three chapters. But the book was developing in a new and exciting way, so the first chapter didn't seem relevant anymore. Three scenes made up her first chapter: (1) a one-page description of a town port before a storm, (2) two pages of backstory telling where the narrator learned to sail, and (3) a five-page fight between narrator and mother. Chapter 2 detailed a sailing race that had happened the day before.

When we began storyboarding, I asked Gaby to print out chapter 1 and cut it apart to form three original scenes. Although writers hate to break up what they have written, even if it's not really working, they often see stronger arrangements when the scenes are not welded together. This is a good first step for storyboarding.

Gaby took scissors and cut chapter 1 into the original three scenes, and chapter 2 into two separate scenes, one on the boat and one on land. Chapter 3 was the sailing accident, all one scene. She didn't need to cut it apart. It all took place in present time with the same people and no flashbacks.

When she looked at the pieces separately, she immediately saw that chapter 3 was the strongest opening. It was dramatic and engaging. It was a perfect beginning for Act 1 on her storyboard.

I asked Gaby to take Post-Its and make little titles for these scenes, then arrange them on an 18-inch-by-24-inch posterboard, to start her storyboard. She could choose either the "W" or linear layout to play with (see page 134). Over the next week, she worked through her brainstorming list of topics, plus the rest of her 100 pages, making Post-Its and arranging the scenes in a new way. Although there was still much to fill in—to write—she loved having a map that worked for her book. When she brought it to class and shared it with the group, they were very enthusiastic.

Gaby's biggest discovery was the opening chapter, which contains what's called the "triggering event." A triggering event must be an outer action that launches the quest (fiction or memoir) or an anecdote that illustrates the question the book will address (nonfiction). It triggers the book's forward motion in Act 1 (see chapter 10).

Gaby's entire book changed because of this new beginning scene. She continued to have these kinds of important realizations as she storyboarded. She now keeps her storyboard near her writing desk and lets it evolve as she writes more sections of her book.

A triggering event must be an outer action that launches the quest (fiction or memoir) or an anecdote that illustrates the question the book will address (non-fiction).

Exercise: Step One of Your Storyboard
TIME NEEDED: 1 HOUR

1. Print everything you've written so far.
2. Take scissors to your pages to separate each scene: the trip to the grocery store, the conversation with the ailing mother, and the grandmother falling down the stairs all are separate scenes. A section that combines different aspects of piano instruction—sections on fingering, reading music, and rhythm—gets cut into three.

3. Look at what you have, in its separate pieces. Consider the most dramatic and interesting opening for your book. Gather the scenes or moments that might make chapter 1.

4. Take a break, then come back and assemble a possible last chapter from scenes or moments. See if you can view each section unlinked from its chronology—and consider stronger arrangements.

After you fill in the rest of the storyboard, you can go back and check each transition. Do the chapters hook together organically? Adjust wherever you find an awkward segue, fill in what's missing, note what you still need to write.

If your writing process itself is quite emotional—if you're writing a story that touches something in your own life, a trauma or event that is still fresh—storyboarding can provide a framework to organize the emotion behind the events as well as the events themselves. You might find yourself intuitively arranging scenes by their subtext, or underlying meaning. Teresa, a novelist, told me, "Storyboarding forced me to think in a logical, sequential manner about the images that were so close to my heart. It helped me stay focused until I could see a book developing."

Dori, a nonfiction writer, had already identified significant turning points she needed to include in her book; writing them as islands gave her the freedom to develop each segment without getting overwhelmed with the overall process. But storyboarding let her weave these moments into a bigger picture. "It helped me find the story that really needed to be told," she said, "rather than the story I was hiding behind."

The beauty of a storyboard is that it allows this kind of discovery. Because it is fluid, compared to an outline, it lets you work forward or backwards, filling in missing pieces as you discover them. Although you are working with a structuring tool, storyboarding actually frees the nonlinear right brain to think more creatively, because you can move parts around as you learn how to forge the ideal pathway through your book. Maybe chapter 5 will become chapter 1. Maybe the other way around.

Storyboards also reveal that serendipitous inner story, the meaning behind events or facts and theories. Since inner story emerges indirectly, since it can't be forced, a rigid structure smothers it. Storyboards succeed because they are organic. They evolve. But you still have to decide what you're really writing about. That's the other beautiful aspect of storyboards. They make us choose.

Storyboards succeed because they are organic. They evolve. But you still have to decide what you're really writing about. That's the other beautiful aspect of story-boards. They make us choose.

Exercise: Cue Cards for Your Storyboard
TIME NEEDED: 2 HOURS

1. Once you've cut your writing into islands and arranged some scenes into possible first and last chapters, the next step is to create a cue card for each section of writing, using Post-It notes.

2. In a few words, describe each island on one Post-It note. For a novel, you might note the place, event, motive, main players, time, and theme each scene addresses. For a business book, you might write a few words about the theory or idea of this section, the anecdote used to illustrate it, the research you're citing, the interview topic. (Because your cue card will remind you, you no longer need the actual cut-up manuscript pages. Cue cards are much easier to maneuver than three hundred pieces of paper.)

3. Begin to play with your cue cards, arranging them in different ways. Consider them both logically and intuitively. Respond to nudges your right brain delivers—how one section might pair well with another, even though they occur at different times in the book's chronology.

Creating the Storyboard

To set aside some dedicated time for your first storyboard, sometimes it helps to take a "storyboard" retreat, away from family and work, as my student, Prill, did.

Prill had already published a successful nonfiction book when she began using this storyboarding method to approach her first novel. She was having fun with it, writing at least a page of material (often much more) every single day, but then she hit a wall.

"My manuscript felt like a hodgepodge," she told me, "and I started losing heart." So she gathered up four colors of Post-It notes, a large pad of presentation paper, and her computer and took herself to Martha's Vineyard for a week of reflection and storyboarding.

"I went through each section," she said, "and consolidated and labeled them, much as one would label a scene in screenwriting. Then I gave each scene its own Post-It note. Next, I arranged these on my presentation paper—using one page of presentation paper per act of my three-act novel." Not only did her storyboarding session help Prill discover that she "had an entire novel," but it was "complete with two related sub-plots and some interesting twists."

Whether Martha's Vineyard or a corner of the local library, it's not a bad idea to reserve dedicated time for this step of storyboarding. As Prill did, gather yourself a simple storyboarding kit: one sheet of large presentation paper, such as posterboard or foamcore (about 18 inches by 24 inches); a package of Post-It notes to make cue cards; your islands to date; and your topic brainstorming list.

Be sure to leave your Inner Critic at home.

Exercise: Step Three—Assembling Your Storyboard
TIME NEEDED: 3–4 HOURS

1. Start with your cue cards (Post-It notes) from the exercise on page 131. Begin sticking them onto your storyboard. Use either diagram from the two on the next page. Place chapter 1's cue cards on your storyboard first.

2. Next, consider your ending chapter. Ask yourself, *What do I want to leave my reader with? What key understanding, realization, or moment wraps up my book most effectively?* Find the cue cards that most represent this ending moment—your best guess for now. Place these on your storyboard, following the diagrams on page 134.

3. Once you have placeholders for your beginning and ending, work through the rest of the cue cards, arranging them in an order that flows from the first to the last box of your storyboard. It's all up to you. Play with the order, rearranging the cue cards as if you are working a giant jigsaw puzzle, until you experience that "ah-ha!" moment where your book feels—like a book!

4. Don't worry if you see holes everywhere. There will be missing sections still to write. Jot down any ideas for these sections (as you discover them) on their own Post-It notes. Place these on your storyboard where they naturally occur in your story. Leave blank cue cards as placeholders for holes you have no clue how to fill yet.

As you storyboard, as you allow new ideas and patterns to come through, you may suddenly notice a big piece of your story is still missing. Peter, working on his first novel, said that storyboarding "exposed important issues that were difficult to see in isolation." Another student, David, used storyboarding

Set aside some dedicated time for your first storyboard. Sometimes it helps to take a "storyboard" retreat, away from family and work.

MARY CARROLL MOORE

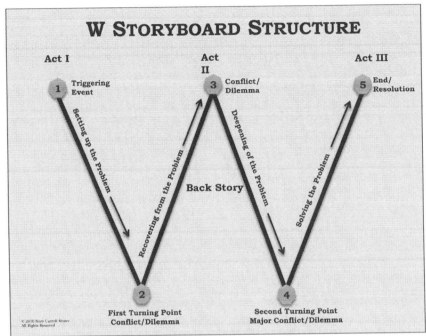

See chapter 14 for more information on the W structure.

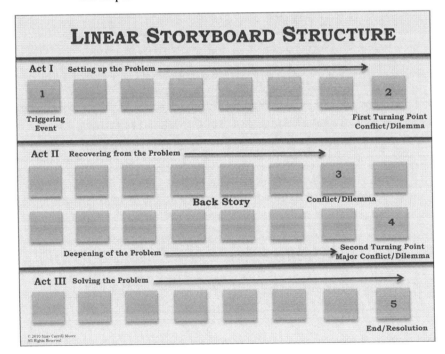

to give his scenes a litmus test of worth in his book. "If I can't summarize the scene in a few words," David told me, "I rethink its purpose. Storyboarding lets me ask myself, *What is the value of this scene to my overall story?* and it identifies the gaps." David saw where his story lagged, where he had possibly spent too much time (or too little time) on a particular moment even. "It helped me identify areas where character development is lacking," he added, "where scenes didn't flow as they should."

Have fun with this task. Customize your storyboard to fit your creativity. Add cut-out photos from magazines to describe characters or landscape. Find a form that works for you. One nonfiction writer storyboards with a clothesline strung along one wall of his office, cue cards pinned to the line with colorful plastic clothespins. A memoirist splurged on a large metal bulletin board and cuts apart sheets of magnetic backings for business cards to use as her cue cards. A sci-fi writer creates her storyboard with PowerPoint slides. I often use a bulletin board and tacks. The board hangs above my desk and I stick it full of Post-It notes in various colors—blue ones for sections close to revision stage, green for ideas partially developed, yellow for sections still to write.

I've also discovered it's really fun to storyboard with another writer or writers' group. Spend an afternoon, listen to great music, ask each other questions. An after-storyboarding feedback session is often helpful, but respect each writer's storyboard. Each shows the uniqueness of their book, the potential to reach a reader.

Storyboarding is the best way I know to organize disparate islands into a flow your reader can easily follow. It's a foolproof method that lets you chart the small movements you've crafted for your story, forming them into a bigger whole. As Kenneth Atchity says in *A Writer's Time*, "The dream is on the horizon, the stepping-stone is directly in front of you."

> Customize your storyboard to fit your creativity. Add cut-out photos from magazines to describe characters or landscape.

IDEAS TO OVERCOME STORYBOARD BLOCK

✓ Create multiple storyboards if you have more than one era or point-of-view character. Eventually, combine them onto one storyboard to see how they intersect.

✓ If you're stuck on the first chapter and don't know how to begin your book, go back to chapter 10. Reread how to dream Act 1 and discover what it must contain.

✓ Post your storyboard near your writing desk.

✓ If you're stuck on the last chapter and can't imagine how to end your book, do a ten-minute writing exercise exploring this question: *What do I want to leave my reader with? What could possibly happen in my book that would make a satisfactory ending?*

✓ Revise your storyboard often during the planning and writing stages—whenever you need help seeing your book's emerging structure.

✓ Be willing to move your Post-It notes (cue cards) around—that's why we use them. The storyboard is a flexible map. Don't try to get it perfect the first time—it's supposed to change and evolve as you work on your book.

Fear of Storyboarding

As you immerse yourself in diagramming your book via a storyboard, don't be surprised if you feel a somewhat uncomfortable shift in perspective. The book is becoming a reader-centric structure, and the storyboard is often the first time writers see their book from this viewpoint.

Fear and resistance may creep in. Ask yourself what you're holding on to with such a death-grip. Are you worried you won't have the writing skill to translate your inside dream into an outer book? Are you afraid to let others into your private world? These are understandable concerns since storyboarding is the first real, reader-focused system your book has encountered. But it is an essential step to let your book communicate to others.

Early book ideas are like those raw fabric squares of an unpieced quilt, surprising, colorful, and nonlinear, but not yet forming a cohesive whole for anyone to see but the quilt-maker who holds the vision of the completed quilt.

There's a necessary mourning period during storyboarding as the writer must let go of the endless possibilities of an unformed book idea and begin to "fish or cut bait." Storyboarding requires us to choose, discard, and structure. So it's normal for fear and frustration to surface as you do this task. If sorting through the piles of written material seems overwhelming, if you feel you'll never be able to get them organized, review your premise statement from chapter 9. Steep yourself in the simplicity an overview can bring. If you hate losing your options, pamper your right brain with a freewrite.

But also acknowledge that you will need to close a door at some point, if your book is ever going to be finished. Fear and its companions (inertia, procrastination, irritation, and negative self-talk) are natural during the storyboarding process. Acknowledge them and keep going.

Tell the fear that you're still preserving your golden idea; you're just creating a form for it so that others can enjoy it too.

Steep yourself in the simplicity an overview can bring. Tell the fear that you're still preserving your golden idea; you're just creating a form for it so that others can enjoy it too.

Congratulations! You've Completed Part One of the Book-Writing Journey!

Storyboarding is the final step in the planning stage of your book. Now you have a complete map to guide you as you start writing the first draft.

It's rare in our creative lives that we take time to celebrate an accomplishment, and this is certainly a moment to do so. Write yourself a letter of congratulation for all you've accomplished in these past weeks or months. Write about how far you've come in your understanding of your book—its inner and outer story, its premise statement, its structure—your ideal reader, and yourself as a creative person.

And be sure to plan some fun time for yourself as a rest and reward. Ideas from my students include:

✓ A spa day

✓ Flowers

✓ A trip to a favorite sporting event

✓ Two hours with just me and my journal

✓ A concert

✓ A trip to an exotic place

✓ Weekend fishing at the lake

✓ Dinner out with friends or partner

✓ Reading a great book someone else wrote!

PART TWO

WRITE:
MANIFESTING YOUR BOOK'S
INNER AND OUTER STORY

WRITE:
MANIFESTING YOUR BOOK'S
INNER AND OUTER STORY

Writing is taking what you learned in the planning and exploring phase, and turning it into a real manuscript draft. It's an exciting step! Using visual maps such as your storyboard, you'll find a flow that enhances the book's story and material.

Your book is taking form. You can see it manifesting in real pages, stacked high on your writing desk.

In the writing stage, you will start to move out of a writer-centric view and begin seeing your book from the reader's point of view, considering not just the events but also the meaning of those events and how they speak to a reader.

You will emerge from this stage with a solid manuscript draft, cohesive and exciting to the reader, ready for fine-tuning.

12

SHOWING, NOT TELLING: HOW TO USE THE TWO SIDES OF YOUR BRAIN

A student in my class, Samantha, was writing a difficult passage in her memoir, recounting the effect of her father's death on her family. In a chapter dealing with the day after her father died, Sam described sitting in the kitchen with her aunt, watching breakfast cleanup, trying to absorb the grief that had descended on everything. But the writing wasn't delivering the emotional punch Sam felt it deserved.

"It's a really important moment in my story," Sam complained to me, "so why do I feel like I'm writing it from another room?"

When I read the draft, it did feel as if Sam was absent from the "room" of the scene. Rather than experiencing the moment with her readers, she was observing it from a predigested distance.

I asked Sam to write out a list of details about her aunt's appearance that morning. She wrote: *messy hair, clothes didn't match*, and *she picked at her fingernails as we ate breakfast*. She added these in, good details to describe an upsetting moment in someone's life, specific and real. But Sam's passage was still not vibrant with the impact of grief. It wasn't a "felt" emotion, only a thought.

"Perhaps it's because you're telling us about her," I suggested, "and you need to show her to us."

Showing and *telling* are familiar terms to most writers, but many have no idea how to put them into practice.

I asked Sam to close her eyes and put herself back into the moment at the kitchen table the morning after her father died. "Watch your aunt move around the room, cleaning up from breakfast," I said. "Pay attention to any particular details you notice about the setting; note the tension, journey

Pay attention to any particular details you notice about the setting; note the tension.

145

back into the intimacy of that moment. Be open to what might appear that was forgotten in the writing."

It took focus. It took some bravery—because this wasn't an easy event to remember. Eventually Sam jotted down four things:

1. *A rotten smell came from the garbage can.*
2. *My aunt's lilac sweater was buttoned funny, odd because she was a good dresser, a fashion maven.*
3. *Her hands shook—they were so unsteady, she dropped a glass in the sink.*
4. *She left the glass pieces in the sink.*

When Sam wrote this last item, tears came into her eyes. She was now "in the room" of the scene, fully present with the emotion that had been eluding her.

The glass pieces remained in the sink all morning—and sun from the window made them sparkle enough to catch the attention of anyone coming into the room—thoroughly demonstrating the emotional shattering the family felt. This bit of "shown" story released the memory and its potency for Sam. She wrote furiously that week, reworking the scene and expanding the image. She wrote about how it bewildered her, at eight years old, that no one cleaned up the glass. Finally, Sam recalled that she herself had found a small hand broom from under the sink and took on the task.

It became a powerful scene in her memoir because she allowed herself to feel the intimacy and vulnerability of real in-the-moment grief.

She successfully moved the memory from telling to showing.

Show Demonstrates, Tell Describes

Showing is a demonstration of emotion through specific sensory details—sight, sound, smell, texture and temperature, taste. Anton Chekhov reminds us, "Don't tell me the moon is shining; show me the glint of light on broken glass." Telling backs away from such intensity; it summarizes the feelings from a distance. Showing places the reader squarely in it.

Telling demands reflection, an almost-intellectual assessment of what happened. Showing dies with intellectual language. It relies instead on words revealing externally felt sensations from all five senses.

Telling is usually safer for the writer. It's not as raw. To show well, my student Sam had to be willing to travel fully into the moment and re-experience it. Sam said little about the meaning of the glass left in the sink. Because the "showing" was so accurate, a reader caught immediately why the glass was a strong sign of the family's grief.

Gateways to Emotion

Robert Olen Butler, author of many stories and novels, talks about this in his book *From Where You Dream*. Butler advises us: To deliver emotion in its purest form, don't dilute it with even the tiniest bit of interpretation or lack of specificity.

Butler proposes that emotion can be shown in five ways. Using these, I was amazed at how effectively they transformed my writing by revealing how to show, not tell. Here is a checklist for how I've used his terms and ideas in my own writing for an emotional punch.

To deliver emotion in its purest form, don't dilute it with even the tiniest bit of interpretation or lack of specificity.

- Details about sensations inside the body (goosebumps on arm, itchy ear, tight throat)
- Specific gestures or expressions seen in others (tearing a small paper napkin into bits, jiggling foot)
- Specific memory from the past
- Fear, anticipation, or a desire projected into the future
- Sense selectivity (when all but one sense goes away during moments of extreme emotion)

During this second stage of book writing, whenever I need to change a scene to more "showing," I will go through

Butler's list and ask myself how I can bring in one of these.

Sam used the third one—memory—and the specifics of the broken glass left in the sink.

Showing and Telling—Which Is Best?

Writers wonder when, if ever, it's good to use telling instead of showing. Students in writing classes and English comp courses are warned to always "Show, don't tell." But that's not always best for every genre.

While showing is a good tool to enliven your work and bring in emotion, it also highlights and intensifies. So, like any other tool, showing can be overused.

Memoir writers who try to show all the time can deliver an exhausting ride for the reader. Pacing is key. Backing away from the emotional moment every now and then to tell the meaning of that moment gives the reader a welcome break from intensity. In the example above with the broken glass, Sam did just that. She told us the meaning several chapters later, perfect timing for a segue into telling that was brief but quite effective because it slowed the pace, allowed us to pause and reflect with the narrator about the effect of the death.

In nonfiction, telling is predominant. But it too needs showing. Nonfiction uses anecdotes to show. For successful anecdotes, most modern nonfiction writers employ the same tools as a novelist: setting, action, dialogue. All show. Research, facts, information is telling—necessary but not always easy for a reader to absorb straight up. Anecdotes close the distance. Author Malcolm Gladwell is a master at this; check out *Blink* or *Outliers*.

Showing is important—because showing engages the reader's imagination. Once the imagination is hooked, the reader can absorb why something is important and how it applies. So it's not always "show, don't tell." You have to choose well, based on the effect you want. Telling puts us in a restful, background state; showing makes emotion come strongly to the surface.

Scan the chart below to see how to use these tools in ways appropriate to your genre.

If you want the intensity of showing:

- Use more sensory detail—smells, sounds, sights that place us in the location.
- Give us the sensations a person is experiencing in his or her body to demonstrate emotion.
- Show gesture or movement to demonstrate emotion.
- Use dialogue and action rather than summary—put us in real time with people doing and saying things, rather than telling us what they are doing or saying.
- Use specific words rather than general terms—"Jenna's rusty 1959 Cadillac," not "Jenna's old car."

If you want the restful distance of telling:

- Summarize action and dialogue.
- Write from a distance of years or from a narrative overview.
- Generalize rather than using specifics—"the lot was filled with old cars" rather than "the lot had three blue 1964 Caddies and two red Studebakers."

Showing brings intimacy. It asks you to be present in memory and scene.

Key Emotional Moments

To accurately use telling and showing, you first need to know what effect you want from each passage. This requires a maturing of the writer's viewpoint on her story. You no longer use a certain passage in your book just because you love it and can't bear to change it.

Moving to the reader's viewpoint means being objective and asking: *What do I want to deliver?*

First find the most important emotional moments in your book, the sections where threads of your theory and method come together or where the character realizes something; in other words, where the turning points are. They may appear in each chapter or only at the end. If you're not sure where to find them, look for places where your own feelings well up as you're reading your story. These may be peak moments.

Do you want the reader to feel as if she is in the same room as this story, very immediately present in it? Showing delivers that effect. Using the tips from the "showing" list above, refine these moments.

Now examine the sections where you've used telling. Are they appropriately balanced for your book's genre? Are these really places where you want the reader to linger and think about the ideas from a distance?

Showing brings intimacy. It asks you to be present in memory and scene. The exercise that follows, lets you practice writing sensory details, then expand that into your own reactions as you write, paying attention to your writing's effect in your body, heart, and mind.

Exercise: Showing via Memory
TIME NEEDED: 40 MINUTES

Switching between sensory memory and physical, present-time body sensations is great training to develop intimacy with your writing. Try this exercise repeatedly for best results.

1. Find an event from your childhood, one that evoked strong emotion.

2. Set a kitchen timer for twenty minutes. Write about this event. Focus on using the sense of sound as much as possible. Your writing may encompass the other senses, but really hone in on how things sounded, as much as you can recall.

3. Now continue writing about the event, but add the sense of smell, keeping the emphasis on these two senses. The writing may feel mechanical as you try this, but don't let that critical voice stop you. Also, don't interpret, just create as strong a sensory experience as possible. Write for ten minutes by the kitchen timer.

4. Stop writing. Close your eyes and perceive your breathing, heart rate, tightness of muscles, any fatigue. Do you feel irritated, bored with your writing, sad, angry?

5. Open your eyes. Write about these physical sensations for five minutes or longer, feeling the sensations in your body as much as you can, rather than intellectualizing about them.

6. Next ask, *What* don't *I remember hearing during this childhood event?* Asking yourself this question often brings back memories you may have forgotten—or wanted to forget. Write for five minutes.

7. Finally, ask, *What was I afraid of smelling during this childhood event?* Write for five minutes.

8. Finish the exercise by writing how you feel now, looking back on this event. What has changed in your perception?

Listening to the Whole Self

Jess is a smart and polished lawyer who was a dedicated student in my writing classes. After hundreds of law briefs and legal articles, she was attempting a novel, a love story. She had crafted a hundred pages, but she hated what she'd written so far. What was wrong?

We looked at the chapters she had created from her scenes, following her storyboard's map (see chapter 11 for a refresher on the storyboarding process). The basic story idea was good, the plot interesting and well structured. But the writing was way too linear for a love story. Written law-brief style, with romance plugged in, using dry language that sparked no emotion in a reader, even the writer herself was uninspired by it.

But Jess was one persistent woman. She was committed to her story. She knew she had a great book idea. The problem, we realized, was with her writing. She needed to learn how to show, not tell. Training her to listen to the creative side of her brain wasn't easy. It bucked her natural preference for logic and analysis, for telling.

I proposed a plan to loosen her up.

> *Pay a lot of attention to the senses—taste, touch, sound, smell, sight*
>
> *Go on solo outings to places inspiring these senses and take notes on what you see, smell, touch*
>
> *Begin a touch journal—jot down what things feel like*
>
> *Read novels and short stories that are strong in images*
>
> *Watch romantic movies instead of the documentaries you prefer*
>
> *Begin having fresh flowers in the house and eating home-cooked food*
>
> *Take long walks and afterward write down favorite images*
>
> *Listen to music—different kinds than you usually listen to*

Jess was dubious. She cited no time for walks, music, flowers. She said I was asking her to change her life.

Yes, I told her, I was asking her to change but not her life, rather her very left-brain approach to life. I told Jess to get a copy of *My Stroke of Insight,* by neuroanatomist Jill Bolte Taylor. In this short but stunning memoir, Dr. Taylor reveals how after a sudden left-brain stroke shut down her left brain, she learned what it was like to operate just from the right brain.

For hours after her stroke, Dr. Taylor was aware only

of what the right brain delivers—sensory details, images, wholeness of being. In the bliss of right-brain beingness, she was barely able to save her own life. Her left brain, which is home to ordered, logical thinking—the kind necessary to pick up a phone and call 911—had been all but annihilated by the stroke. It would take years of rehab to bring it back to life. Dr. Taylor had to learn all over again how to read, to add, to make decisions. This dramatic experience of losing her left-brain functions changed Taylor's entire approach to living. She slowed down, did less, but much to her surprise found she enjoyed life more.

As Taylor says, we tend to use more of one side of our brains. We need both.

This is especially true for writers. We often miss the full potential of our book-writing journey by not tapping into the right brain. Our manuscripts develop primarily from the voice of our dominant hemisphere, which for most of us is the left. Blind spots appear on our book map because of this, creating unnecessary roadblocks on our journey. We get stuck easily.

Alone, neither the linear left brain nor the image-rich right brain can create a complete book. Using the whole creative self delivers both coherent structure and emotional engagement. Both sides working in concert turn every book into a more complete vision.

Jess took up the challenge of freeing her right brain. The newly embraced creative self began to speak up. Her writing changed. Novel scenes, very good ones that packed an emotional punch, emerged.

I didn't predict the next event, but I wasn't surprised. Jess fell in love. She sold her practice, and she and her lover moved to another country. Falling in love is very much a right-brain activity. A person in love suddenly appreciates detail, especially sensory detail. Love changes your perceptions about everything.

Using the whole creative self delivers both coherent structure and emotional engagement. Both sides working in concert turn every book into a more complete vision.

I thought that was the end of Jess's novel. But six months after her move, a chapter arrived by email. I couldn't believe the difference. Here was real romance! The writing made my heart jump.

She was listening to the right half of her brain—and it changed not only her writing but her life. To date, the book is still in the works. It's going to be wonderful.

"Share this story with your classes," she emailed me. "If someone like me can make this change, anyone can."

Do you have to fall in love to change your habitually left-brain approach? No. You just need to be willing to accept the parts of your self that don't make logical sense. Learn to balance the strengths of the organized left brain with the whimsy of the right. Learn to structure your wild imaginings so you really communicate your book's message.

Which Side Do You Favor?

As book writers our first task is discover which side is taking up the most room in our creative process. Asking good questions can help you learn which side you are favoring, and which you are ignoring.

GOOD QUESTIONS

If you are **naturally ordered** in your writing, ask questions that propel you or your character into awareness of senses, which comes from the right brain:

What did it smell like?
What sounds did you/she/he hear?
What time of day was it?

If you tend toward the **meandering and random,** ask questions that track time sequence or logic, which comes from the left:

> *What happened right before this?*
> *What will up the stakes right now?*
> *What could happen next?*

Our second task is to train ourselves to use both, to switch readily between them, using our whole creative selves and making our books publishable.

How many writers are able to seamlessly switch from ordered to random and back again? It often depends on how we approach our daily lives, how fluid we can be. When I surveyed my book-writing classes, writers were visibly uneasy at the idea of such fluidity. (Let's not forget our culture is very left-brain oriented.) "My material is way too emotional to access all the time," said a new memoirist. "It's a wild animal; I have to keep it contained." A skilled essayist and mother of three said, "I stay in left brain to survive. If I let myself get dreamy, I get instant chaos at home. I want to write this book but not if it means giving up control of the rest of my life!"

This is not about giving up anything. It's about opening up to more, it's about trusting the part of your creative self that gets less air time. If you're naturally organized, keep the left-brain control, the structure—it's essential. Just add in the beauty your nonlinear right-brain self can contribute. If you're one of the rare right-brain dominant, then you will need to learn to embrace a structured writing system that can help bring order to your freewheeling words.

Freewriting: Training to Use Our Whole Brain

Natalie Goldberg's book, *Writing Down the Bones*, burst upon the writing world in 1986 with the concept of freewriting—short, regular writing sessions on *random* topics to keep us from getting stuck in any one place.

Freewriting can produce surprisingly good material, especially for writers whose left-brain dominance makes

How many writers are able to seamlessly switch from ordered to random and back again? It often depends on how we approach our daily lives, how fluid we can be.

open-ended, non-structured writing hard.

What is a freewrite? Well, it's writing for a set amount of time with no "official" goal in mind. It's writing for writing's sake, like vocal warm-ups for singers. There are two parts to a freewrite. The first is creating a list of "prompts." These can be anything that strikes your fancy: the sun setting over your backyard, your dog's nose, the meaning of the word *righteous*. Prompts are exactly that—anything that will prompt you to write. You can also use your brainstorming list (see page 65) to relate the freewrites to your book in some way.

Ideally you want your prompt list to be wild, goofy, unusual. I often use sense memories—something I remember smelling, tasting, or hearing—to jumpstart my freewrites. "Sense memories are a way to anchor us in the present," Goldberg says, "and to open the past, to connect with it in a physical way, making it real and vivid. They help cut through our 'official story,' the one we've made up about our lives and told over and over until we've created a shiny impenetrable veneer over the authentic truth."

When I am working on a new book, I create a prompt list of memories, images, ideas that are relevant to my book. I keep an ongoing list of prompts in my writer's notebook (this is part of my brainstorming list). In class, when we do freewrites, I tell my students they can create a list of prompts on the spur of the moment or think of things from their books. For example, if your book is set in the Midwest, your prompt list could be thunderstorms, pie, prairie winds.

Once you have your list of prompts (the list can be two items or twenty), pick one that sparks something in you. Now set your timer to twenty minutes and write anything you feel like about that prompt. The writing could be a poem, a series of sense memories, a scene, an anecdote. The point is not to *think* about what you're writing about. Just go with the flow of what comes out on paper.

Don't be too surprised if while you're writing, your Inner Critic chides you into thinking that this freewriting is "stupid," or a "useless waste of time." It's not. The Inner Critic often pops up when we are learning something new. It doesn't want you to be uncomfortable or, heaven forbid, do something that might be foolish. Thank it for its consideration, but keep focusing on the words.

When a topic feels too intense or you can't think what to write about, make a list of irrelevant words: *red horse, silver soup spoon, credit card, bank teller, gangster, great aunt Tilly, surly waiter.* Pick one and write about it. Usually it will meander back to your story. You'll know you've hit the jackpot if, during a freewrite, the writing gets tense or emotional, and your Inner Critic gets even more agitated ("What are you writing *that* for?"). Or you get body symptoms such as boredom, restlessness, irritability, or sleepiness. This means you're accessing the less-used side of your creative self. A very good sign.

Keep going. Keep using that new muscle, and it will get less stiff over time. You're building trust with a part of yourself that's been ignored or perhaps denigrated.

Writing from the whole creative self involves surrender, being a beginner with what you don't know, and allowing the change to become natural. As memoirist Abigail Thomas says, "a lot of writing consists of waiting around for the aquarium to settle so you can see the fish."

When I am working on a new book, I plan at least one twenty-minute freewrite session a day. Freewriting brings more authenticity to my writing; it helps whenever I get too linear and close-minded—too left-brained. For example, when a character or place in my book feels boring and predictable, freewriting lets me leap into my whole self—and I end up with ideas I couldn't see before. Sometimes part of a freewrite goes into my book, but usually they remain in my writer's notebook.

My freewrites are raw and unshaped, but they deliver the fresh images and ideas I desperately need to kick-start my book writing. Writer Eudora Welty spoke about, "the need to hold transient life in words" because there was "so

Writing from the whole creative self involves surrender, being a beginner with what you don't know, and allowing the change to become natural.

much more of life that only words can convey." We can capture this fleeting beauty of our inner landscapes through the amazing tool of freewriting.

How Freewriting Transforms Your Writing

In chapter 1, you met book writers working in different genres. Here's how freewriting helped three of them transform their manuscripts.

David's Story

David's concern that his family would read his memoir stopped him cold just as he got to the most emotional scenes. Even after he realized how his fear was holding him back, David still felt shut down while writing his memoir.

Freewriting each day, using prompts of any random memories (images, objects, sensations from his childhood), relaxed David's left-brain control. He wrote about his grandmother, a southern transplant who raised him on their New England farm. He wrote about cows in the barn. Each freewrite surprisingly revealed the core emotions of his book—his tangle of love for his clan, coupled with his ever-present eagerness to escape their craziness. Freewriting brought the emotion out, without David's left brain even suspecting.

Linda's Story

Linda wasn't sure how to draft the autobiographical stories she'd decided to include in her self-help book on relationships. She felt stuck. How could she access the more free-flowing memories she wanted to use?

Her freewriting sessions explored this question in stages. First on her prompt list she explored the main topics of her book, by diving in to her own beliefs about "communication," "silence," "anger," and "giving space." Then she began freewriting memories that were connected to these abstract topics. She wrote about her own challenges with anger, how she learned to give space to her friends, and the way silence works in love relationships, even how the techniques in her book helped her.

Linda slowly accumulated a collection of good right-brain images and vignettes. She ended up inserting pieces of her freewrites in her chapters.

Margo's Story

Some writers have the opposite problem. They suffer from right-brain dominance. They rarely have writer's block, as long as they are allowed exploration without limit. But trouble arises when they begin to structure their books. They have a hard time creating an order out of all their free-flowing content.

But freewrites can help them, too. Remember Margo from chapter 1? Margo liked her loose, rambly writing style. Her mystery scenes poured forth easily, but she couldn't find a way to tie them together, especially in the middle chapters. I suggested she read through ten scenes and look for anything they had in common. She found three things: a city bus, a certain minor character, and rain. I asked her to dedicate a few writing sessions to these topics, freewriting anything that came to her about them.

What emerged was an unexpected connection between the three things. Margo inserted these newly found connections through the slumping middle of her book, and it created a natural structure that still allowed her right-brain looseness. But now it had a welcome path the reader could easily follow to stay engaged with Margo's material.

Think of freewriting as a way to bridge the two sides of your brain. It strengthens whichever side you don't use very often. It lets you practice moving back and forth between these two creative parts of yourself, the linear and nonlinear.

Freewriting Also Gentles Intensity

Sometimes a book idea strikes and it burns to get out. You find the time and just write, letting it run. I wrote three hundred pages of scenes for my first memoir in forty-five days; exhausted but happy, I took a break. Then I began organizing the pages into a first draft. After I finished, a funny

Think of freewriting as a way to bridge the two sides of your brain. It strengthens whichever side you don't use very often.

thing happened.

Reading the pages was instantly discouraging. Many scenes were dry, dull, more telling than showing, more information than inspiration. By sticking with the facts, I avoided the emotional recall. What had gone wrong? I realized that my memoir was essentially about traumas too intense for me to write effectively about.

I went back to my brainstorming list of possible topics for my book, looking for prompts that were outside the story's trauma. I wanted sweetly sensory prompts, such as how leaves look in summer, melting ice cream, my grandmother's favorite chair, African violets, even the smell of new motor oil.

I wrote freewrites for twenty minutes each day, picking one of these prompts each session. It took about ten different prompts before the fear subsided.

I thought the freewrites were simply an exercise, but surprisingly quite a few of those ten freewrites made it into my published memoir in some form. Sometimes I only used one sentence, sometimes a whole paragraph, but it was often enough to enliven a dead chapter or pull together loose threads into a better structure. Freewriting tapped a deeper source of creativity, perhaps because it relieved me from having to be linear and organized.

But what was really amazing about those ten days of freewriting was that it let me meander around my story, writing outside of it, until the intensity gentled and I was no longer afraid of writing the more traumatic scenes.

Writers need to explore, as Natalie Goldberg says, what has "brought us to our knees" in life. But since such explorations can go deep into our psychological and spiritual make-up, it can feel very risky, shameful, and overwhelming. "The secret of the creative life is often to feel at ease with your own embarrassment," says director and screenwriter Paul Schrader. "Some people like racing car drivers are paid to take risks in a more concrete way. We are paid to take risks in an emotional way."

Freewriting Tips

✓ Freewriting needs to be completely open-ended. Write whatever comes, in whatever form— phrases, dialogue, run-on sentences, even lists of random words.

✓ Set a kitchen timer. Work in ten- or twenty-minute segments.

✓ Don't judge yourself if you can't "get it" at first. If it seems silly. It is—that's the point.

✓ Keep the pen moving. If you can't think of what to say, write about that. Random stuff that doesn't make sense in the moment often leads to gold by the end of the freewrite.

Resources for Freewriting Prompts

Listen to Me by Lynn Lauber

Old Friend from Far Away by Natalie Goldberg

Story Matters by Margaret Love-Denman and Barbara Shoup

Tell It Slant by Brenda Miller and Suzanne Paola

Thinking about Memoir by Abigail Thomas

What If? by Pamela Painter and Anne Bernays

Word Play, Word Power by Kimberly Snow

Writing Down the Bones by Natalie Goldberg

13

ARE YOU A CONCEPT, EVENT, OR IMAGE WRITER?

The short-story writer, André Dubus, described writing as having vertical and horizontal moments. In an interview for the anthology, *Novel Voices*, he spoke of the challenges in his first novel, *The Lieutenant*: "I'm not sure I knew how to bear down then. . . . I was writing what I call horizontally, making scenes go. In my forties, I switched to writing vertically, trying to get inside a world and inside a character."

Have you ever driven long distance through the Midwest of the United States? The horizon stretches forever, across a landscape that is flat and predictable. I loved driving the endless prairie roads when I lived in Minnesota and took summer trips through North and South Dakota. But I longed for a little variation in the unending peace of the grasslands, which sometimes had me struggling to stay awake.

When I reached the western edge of these states, and the mesas and mountains began to rise, my heart thrilled. I always looked forward—after three days of flatness—to the Badlands. The newly vertical landscape provided more tension and interest, a happy contrast to the sleepy time spent knowing exactly what was around each turn in the road.

Just as the variation of landscape excites a long-distance traveler, unexpected moments charge your book with energy, suspense, and tension. If we adapt Dubus's terms, these vertical moments could be external—a suspenseful plot twist, such as the final scene in an emergency room when a patient is flatlining—or internal moments where a character makes a life turn and we, as readers, witness the profound change.

During a vertical moment, the reader is tense and engaged, whether the plot is taking us around mountain switchbacks past high overlooks with breathtaking scenery

Just as the variation of landscape excites a long-distance traveler, unexpected moments charge your book with energy, suspense, and tension.

or through a teary acknowledgment of truth. These moments are shown to us, and we're placed right smack in the middle of them, on the edge of our seats.

In books, you need both vertical and horizontal moments. You need the passage describing a quiet bedroom at sunrise, the light coming through in filmy curtains, as well as the lover driving away. A resting moment of setting can serve as an essential prelude to the action happening in the next moment when someone turns the ignition and leaves forever. Same with the slower moment of two people taking a long walk on a beach, easy with each other, discussing a trip they're about to take where some event will change their lives.

Few writers can keep the edge required for vertical writing throughout an entire book. That's good, because most readers don't want to stay on that edge for three hundred pages. Even in suspenseful writing, we need moments to catch our breath and reflect, to think about what's happened, to figure out what it means in the bigger picture of the story.

A balance is required, and finding that balance comes now during the writing stage of your book journey.

The Difference in Later Drafts

In early islands, writing tends to be predominantly horizontal. We're still telling ourselves our story, warming up to our subject. Essentially, we are spending time describing what we *would* write, rather than writing it. Scenes are likely to be reflective, interior, and told rather than shown. It's a very natural process of getting to know our own material on the page.

Often, this early writing is not yet vibrant enough to let a reader really engage in the moment of each scene. It's a bit like watching a slide show of someone else's vacation. To us, the images are full of emotion, very alive because we hold the complete picture and sense of them in our minds and hearts. But to a reader, they do not yet live fully on the page. They do not evoke an emotional response in anyone else.

As writer E.L. Doctorow said, "Good writing is supposed

to evoke sensation in the reader. Not the fact that it is raining, but the feeling of being rained upon." How do we take what we know and infuse it with immediacy and excitement?

We need to revise toward the high-energy writing that a reader demands from a book. We need to take the reader with us on that vacation.

Concept, Event, Image—Balancing Elements for Your Writing

When we write flat we go unconscious. We think we're deep in our story but the writing feels a bit dead. It's not always easy to figure out where too much horizontal writing occurs, where you've unconsciously gone into a distant room in telling your story. The reader will know it immediately. The writer has to work to see it.

Feedback from a writers' group or writing class can locate some dead spots, but unless it's delivered with much encouragement for what *is* working, early-draft feedback can just as easily stop the process. I've seen many a writer abandon his book after the first draft, just from a casual remark about a flat piece of writing.

A much surer way is to learn to use a balance of image-rich prose, some reflective or conceptual passages, and lively events that illustrate them. This combination brings both vertical and horizontal moments to your writing. It adds necessary opposites: emotion to overly intellectual sections, sensory detail and imagery to ungrounded settings, events and action to places where not enough happens, necessary pauses of reflection to let a reader realize meaning.

So first I'll ask: What kind of writer are you, most naturally? A concept, event, or image writer? Do you enter your book via your fascination with the concepts, thoughts, and ideas about the subject? Maybe you find yourself most involved with the plot, always considering the next event. Perhaps you are first drawn in by a single image, a moment in a particular setting, your story's atmosphere.

> Learn to use a balance of image-rich prose, some reflective or conceptual passages, and lively events that illustrate them. This combination brings both vertical and horizontal moments to your writing.

All three are valid entry points to writing your book, but most writers are strongest in one. The trick is to realize this and learn to balance it.

Concept Writers

When writing about an event that's already digested and learned from, most of us use detached language. We summarize; in other words, we condense the moments, omitting more vivid details such as weather, time of year or day, smells or sounds. This is often called reflective, or concept, writing.

Writers who habitually communicate via concepts love this distance, detachment, and overview. They avoid placing a reader directly into an event as if it were still happening.　But the result can be a very horizontal experience.

How do you know if you are naturally a concept writer?

> *You think it through first, then write.*
>
> *You summarize rather than use specific details.*
>
> *You're concerned about not giving enough information.*
>
> *You like big words.*
>
> *You use the passive voice.*
>
> *Your sentences tend to be long.*
>
> *You use a lot of adverbs.*
>
> *You prefer the beauty of abstract language.*
>
> *You can't really see any image in your mind when you read your own writing.*
>
> *There are few events, more thoughts and feelings.*

Concept writers predominate in our culture. As we've gotten more intellectual and abstract, writing has become careful, doesn't quite say what it means, holds back on emotion. Perhaps our tendency toward virtual communication contributes? Or perhaps it's a way to balance reality TV and sensationalistic media. Regardless, conceptual prose, unless used for a clinical or academic purpose, can be distancing.

If you were first trained in business, legal, or academic

writing, you may unconsciously approach your book from concept. Concepts give good information. But they can fall flat.

What to do? Learn about the other two types of writing that follow—event and image. They may seem so foreign, you couldn't imagine using them. But to get published today, you'll need to learn.

Don't worry, you won't have to throw out all you've written so far. Concept writing is necessary in a book—it's just needed in small doses. Used well, it gives time to reflect on what happened and distance from the intense moment. But only if there is enough event and image writing to provide the need for this rest.

Two excellent nonfiction books that succeed in varying concepts with event and image are *The Tipping Point* by Malcolm Gladwell and *The 7 Habits of Highly Successful People* by Steven Covey. Gladwell's book begins with event—a solid situation and setting. This event hints at the emotional impact of the information the writer is about to deliver. If you read these books as a writer, you'll appreciate how often events and imagery are added to make the concepts and theories much more palatable.

Look at sentences and paragraph length in these books—they are also shorter than anything you'd see in academic or business writing.

If your strength is writing about the inner world of abstract ideas, feelings, and concepts, your task is to learn to write events and sensory details that use the external senses rather than thoughts and feelings.

Exercise: Balancing Concept
TIME NEEDED: 2 HOURS

If your strength is writing about the inner world of abstract ideas, feelings, and concepts, your task is to learn to write events and sensory details that use the external senses rather than thoughts and feelings.

1. Make a list of ten things that could possibly happen in your book. Don't overthink this. Anything even remotely possible needs to be

on the list. Use memories of events that happened to you, which could illustrate an idea or concept.

2. Set a timer for twenty minutes. Freewrite (see page 155) on one of these. Make sure you include at least two senses in your freewrite. Let yourself go, relax inside.

Event Writers

Event writers love action. They are often bored with slow-paced writing. They take risks, aren't afraid to share the gruesome, look for suspense. Their writing is about movement, where people are going.

Event writers are vertical writers. They go for the peak moments, often omitting smaller events that lead up to them. Their book sections will chronicle the outer situation, the "who, what, when, where, and how." Their writing puts the reader squarely into the moment—as long as something is happening.

How can you tell if you are an event writer?

Your heart races when you write.

You think setting is boring—and you have no idea how to write it.

Action is everything to you.

You don't clutter your writing with explanations.

You believe in showing not telling.

When you read a mystery, you read the last page first— to see what happens.

In my class, I had a student who worked for a major television station. He wanted to write a novel based on a very nightmarish real-life event he'd experienced when he worked as a cameraman. His scenes, written in bits and pieces during stage one of this book-writing process, were all action. They were exciting, often jarring, but sometimes hard to follow.

Like driving hairpin turns through the Rockies, readers

are exhausted by non-stop action. My student thought stopping to rest would bore his readers, but when he added concept sections, where the main character reflected on the meaning of what happened, the entire story took on a deeper meaning.

Event writing by itself is non-emotional. Yes, it is suspenseful. But suspense is not the deeply felt emotion that gets transmitted to a reader. Suspense is more like holding your breath, then letting it out in a rush. You just feel relief at being able to breathe fully again. It's not a sensation that lingers in the heart and mind. It doesn't change your thinking and feeling. Breathe slowly for five minutes, eyes closed, then open your eyes, look around. I guarantee you'll see things differently.

On the good side, event writers have plot nailed. They just need to slow down and begin to appreciate the stationary moments of a narrative so they can tell what the plot means.

Stephen King, John Grisham, and Sara Gruen are excellent event writers. But watch how Gruen's characters in *Water for Elephants* or Grisham's hero in *The Firm* take time out to think over what's happening (concept) or how skillfully these authors depict sensory setting details—such as weather, lighting, smells, and sounds (image). Small moments like these give us welcome rest from the intense activity of event.

Exercise: Balancing Event
TIME NEEDED: 2 HOURS

If your strength is event writing, your task is to build skills in writing concept and image.

1. For the next week, record five impressions of smell and five impressions of sound every day.
2. Find a poem you like. Write down what you think about it, what it means to you.
3. Take a look at *Ten Poems to Change Your Life*. The author, Roger Housden, does a terrific job of explaining the meaning behind each poem.

If your strength is event writing, your task is to build skills in writing concept and image.

Certain writing tasks don't produce manuscript pages or exciting scenes, but they greatly improve your writing by fostering new inspiration and ideas to balance the sheer verticality of events. Event writers often need these because they bring "discovery" to the writing process.

Take freewriting, for example. It asks you to be open to what presents itself in the moment—not what is planned or already known. Freewriting feeds the imagination, and scenes from freewrites enhance your manuscript's emotional depth. Meaning will come to an event writer as he takes sidetracks, tries artistic-inflow activities such as making a collage, writing to music, reading, or freewriting.

Start a dream notebook. Record sensory impressions while waiting at a train station or doctor's office. These will help you fill the framework that your event-structure builds. They'll help whenever you find yourself getting bored or frustrated with your writing, or if you fear going deeper into a subject.

Image Writers

Image writers are the poets. They appreciate the five senses—sight, sound, smell, touch, and taste. Everything is evocative to them.

Image writing is sometimes called lyrical writing because it uses metaphor, or words that symbolize something bigger than they are. Used well, metaphors transmit emotion and meaning beyond the conceptual level.

How do you know if you're an image writer?

You've written a lot of poetry.

People have called your writing lyrical or vivid or painterly.

Setting is key to you.

You find it hard to write action—something actually happening.

You love long sentences about the scent of peeled oranges or a view of russet leaves in sunlight.

A poet in my book-writing class spent so much time choosing each word that she crafted only a few poems per year. Each was a carefully constructed still-life painting. It took her a long time to work her way through building a book, but eventually her poems were organized into a chapbook that was published last year.

To balance her tendencies as an image writer, she worked event and concept into her poems in small amounts. In writing about breast cancer, she added the feelings in her body as her lover stroked her now-bald head. This tiny event, one or two lines, gave the reader an action to ground the image in place and time.

Examples of image writers are Virginia Woolf and William Faulkner. Some readers find their image-dense prose hard to swim through, but study how they use imagery; their prose is like reading a gorgeous poem.

Exercise: Balancing Image
TIME NEEDED: 2 HOURS

If you love lyricism, imagery, the subtle, sensory, and multi-layered, your task is to place this sensory detail within a concrete event that reveals its conceptual meaning. To do that you must separate from the moment of imagery and tell us what that moment signifies.

1. Make a list of possible events that could happen in your book—go wild with this!
2. Pick one event at each writing session. Write two pages that put us in that event.
3. If you find yourself avoiding writing the actual situation, veering again and again back into the setting or atmosphere, keep trying to make something happen.

If you love lyricism, imagery, the subtle, sensory, and multi-layered, your task is to place this sensory detail within a concrete event that reveals its conceptual meaning.

4. If your characters are inward-looking, have them walk, run, or do something active. Use active-voice dialogue.

5. Or, to stretch your concept writing, pick an image in your writing and write about what it means to you. What does it symbolize?

How Structure Balances Concept, Event, and Image

Many writers dislike structure. But structure creates a framework for both your book and your writing life—no matter if you're a concept, event, or image writer.

Structure holds up the form of your book as well as the structure of the writing itself: chronology, pacing, balance of dialogue and action. In my classes, I can recognize a writer comfortable with structure because she wants to know the number of pages to shoot for. She is at ease with outlines, charts, storyboarding—essential tools for manifesting a book.

If you run from any schedule about starting and completing a piece of writing, you run the risk of creating writing that never comes together in book form. You skip the essential task of editing, continue to expand because it's more fun. You love daydreaming about your book, you love exploring and researching, but this can get in the way of finishing your book.

You can't complete a book without structure tasks. It would be like trying to put wallboard on a house without any framework to nail it to. Structure is essential to help you move forward when you're stuck in too many islands (see page 24) with no sense of how they make up a manuscript. It gives you steps to take, concrete ideas. It also gives welcome objectivity during overwhelm.

Notice how the storyboard you worked on in chapter 11 created a form for your book, how it condensed and focused your writing process. Setting a daily writing schedule is another structure task, as is line editing (as opposed to revising) and other discipline-driven activities. It's time to learn to use structure whenever you find yourself feeling spacey, overwhelmed, or wondering where your book is going. Choose from the list below, offered by writers in my classes.

STUDENTS' EXAMPLES OF STRUCTURE TASKS:

Stop writing on the couch and set up a better desk.

Clean the clutter—or at least the desk.

Forge agreements with family members for sacred writing time each morning.

Buy a new laptop that teenage children can't use.

Storyboard chapters into more logical sequence.

Transfer files into organized folders on your computer.

Break your book into individual chapter files so it's easier to move chapters on your computer.

Passion: The Real Reason You're Doing This

Learning to add new elements to your writing is hard sledding. To add in concept to an event novel takes work. Your original passion can get lost. Don't let that happen.

Passion addresses the creative urge to express, the need that each writer has to outflow to the world. Its tasks focus on that need to manifest something new.

Passion revitalizes a project, especially in the later stages when it can be so easily abandoned out of boredom and familiarity. Julia Cameron's *The Artist's Way* addresses passion and how to get it back.

Criticism from others and self-doubt from the Inner Critic wipe out passion very quickly. Support is essential to keep it alive—finding feedback to positively mirror your creative efforts, keep you confident and believing.

If you wonder *Why am I writing this book?* you may need to get back your passion for the project. If you need help

Passion revitalizes a project, especially in the later stages when it can be so easily abandoned out of boredom and familiarity.

recalling your passion, consider some passion tasks to let you explore the ever-changing reasons you are doing this project and whether you are expressing your voice in the most authentic way.

PASSION TASKS

Write a dialogue (on paper) with your book.

Write a letter to Inner Critic to get it to settle down.

Make a mock-up of your book cover.

Make a collage of any book chapters that aren't working.

Make a collage of your goals about your book.

Write about why you *don't* want to write this book— even why you hate and fear it.

Cluster or freewrite about what you have read in *Your Book Starts Here* and how it could help your writing.

Find a different writers' group—one you can flourish in.

List thirty things you love in your life to remind yourself of your passion.

Wear brighter colors—not black.

Do you relate to any of these tasks? They come from a diverse group of writers of all backgrounds, cultures, education, and skill levels.

Maybe one of these tasks will interest you and you will try it for yourself. It is hard work to change your writing habits—to learn to add image if you're a concept writer, for example, or to add event if you're an image writer. Passion tasks can help.

The goal is to develop all three aspects in your writing

life—concept, event, and image—and to have all three moving through your writing process all the time.

14

PEOPLE IN CONFLICT: HOW DILEMMA DRIVES TENSION IN YOUR BOOK

As you write your book, following the map of your storyboard, you'll be considering three elements that are the primary anchors for any story: the dilemma, the players, and the container (the story's main environment). We'll spend the next three chapters exploring these, with dilemma being the first.

Dilemma is the problem your book solves, whether it is how to plant a bonsai garden or who killed the victim in a murder mystery. Dilemma, also known as the dramatic arc, forms the path of your reader's journey through your book. Without strong dilemma, there's no story.

One of my students, Chris, was writing the story of her grandmother's life, but she wasn't happy with the slow pace of her book. When we studied Chris's storyboard, there were many lovely moments; however, few of them showed conflict. Her grandmother lived an interesting life, which she had written about in family letters, but something was missing—the dilemma that drives a story. It all seemed too perfect, Chris told me.

I suggested she make a collage of her grandmother's life, from what she knew about her. Her grandmother died when Chris was nine, but she'd been Chris's primary caretaker until then. Chris went through the letters again and old family photos. Then she put these documents aside and turned to her intuition.

She gathered a stack of magazines and spent an hour tearing out any images that spoke to her of her grandmother's life. Then she arranged them on a large sheet of paper. This is when the central dilemma began to reveal itself.

For some reason Chris pasted a beautiful garden next to

Dilemma, also known as the dramatic arc, forms the path of your reader's journey through your book. Without strong dilemma, there's no story.

a car accident, then a fallen bird near a sunny kitchen. Why the opposing images? She tried to recall conversations about her grandmother's past, before her marriage. Were there secrets she didn't know about?

Chris decided to call up an elderly aunt and interview her. Chris learned that her grandmother had an illegitimate child when she was very young, and that child was given up for adoption. This explained the persistent sadness Chris always felt from her grandmother, and the disjointed collage images suddenly made sense. Chris now knew the central dilemma of her grandmother's story and how she could write her book around it.

Most dilemmas arise from external circumstances thrust upon a person. An external dilemma nearly always leads to an internal dilemma, and if you have both, it strengthens the book even more. Chris's grandmother was forced to give up her baby—an external dilemma. Her life-long feelings of guilt were her internal dilemma. Together, they created a life of unresolved conflict always festering beneath all the gardening, cooking, and bird-watching.

Where does dilemma in books come from? As I mentioned above, external dilemma comes from circumstance forced upon someone or a choice that person makes that affects her life. External dilemma comes from outer change, not outer stasis. To write your book's external dilemma demands that you, the writer, look at what might be missing. What's been lost? What has happened to your narrator or characters, either beyond their control or because of a choice they made in the past? Chris's grandmother's external dilemma led to an internal dilemma— the secrets she carried caused her life to always feel off kilter, and this is what Chris discovered as she made her collage.

Internal dilemma can also be the instigating force in a book's action. For instance, say a character desires something he can't have without breaking the law or hurting someone else. This is an internal dilemma. He can try to live with this unmet desire but it messes up his life. In literature, the internal power of an unmet desire usually forces action, which creates external dilemma so the plot moves forward.

Each player on the stage of your book must have something they desire or long for or fear. The greater the desire or fear, the more momentum it creates and the more likely it will drive the person to do something risky. This leads to a dilemma, and on it goes in good stories.

Holding your characters or narrator in stasis does not a story make. But dilemma can sometimes be downright uncomfortable to write. It requires us to tolerate risk, deal with conflict—even if it's only on the page.

It requires us to face our own fears.

Why Dilemma Reveals Character

Dorothy Alison, a novelist and short-story writer known for her gritty tales about life in the rural South, says a writer should always write the stories she is "most afraid of." Because dilemma makes a writer confront her deepest desires and fears, it reveals her inner nature, her beliefs, her values. Dilemma forces our characters to choose: to run or fight or play dead—and we often live this out as well.

Good dilemma presents an unfolding array of choices and changes in literature. Characters—and the writer—will learn about themselves as they make these choices and face these changes.

Dilemma can rarely be hidden away. It will leak out through unconscious action. This is true in life, and also true in literature. Our actions show the dilemmas inside us; it's the writer's job to let this leak out on paper.

If you don't believe me, think about the old parental maxim, "Do what I say, not what I do." Watching what Mom or Dad did under stress teaches much more than listening to their words. In books, too, we learn a character's values by watching what they do, not what they say. The dilemma is revealed through action.

Dilemma can rarely be hidden away. It will leak out through unconscious action. This is true in life, and also true in literature.

It's time to look closely at what's at stake in your book. How strong is your dilemma? Is it still being held too tightly inside, unable to reveal itself through action? Have you looked at what unmet desire drives your story?

Dilemma in Three Acts

In chapter 10, we explored the classic three-act structure used by many writers during the planning stage of their books. I recommend revisiting this three-act system during the writing stage because it will help you doublecheck the strength of your book's dilemma by looking at its "rising" and "falling" action.

Rising and falling action is best understood if you think of a giant W.

Act 1 is the first leg of this W. Something happens to trigger the action at the beginning of the book, to set the need. This triggering event is presented in the form of a question or a quest, and it begins a falling action that moves down the first leg of the W.

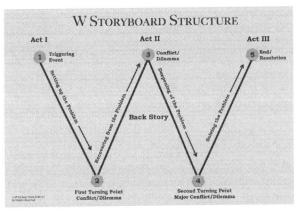

For a more expanded version, please turn to page 134.

Joseph Campbell's *The Hero's Journey*, a classic definition of mythic structure in storytelling, says that the first part of a story is where the hero faces the initial crisis (the triggering event) that propels him into action and things tangle soon after.

In Act 1, dilemma must continue to escalate—otherwise, why would we read on? Knowing this, you need to study your storyboard's Act 1 for sufficient obstacles that enhance your book's dilemma. A great example is the fairytale. The opening chapters always set a hero on a quest. But very soon the hero learns that the quest is much more dangerous or more difficult than imagined. This is the falling action, and it accelerates the momentum, eventually driving the story into Act 2.

It's important to choose your islands (see pages 115–17) carefully when writing Act 1. No one sits around drinking coffee and thinking great thoughts during a falling action. There's no time. Things are speeding up. The falling action of Act 1 is very much like a rollercoaster taking its first big swoop downward.

So first doublecheck the triggering event, the beginning of Act 1's falling action. Ask yourself, *Is the dilemma presented immediately and clearly? Is it big enough to propel the entire book?* Remember that a triggering event should be an externalized action without which the story would not happen.

Your second place to check for sufficient dilemma is at the end of Act 1, the bottom of the W. Sometimes called the "first turning point," this is where something changes. Things literally bottom out. From the triggering event which started this journey, we reach, at the bottom of the W, a point of no return. The tension has increased but now there's a bit of a pause to assess what to do next.

Act 2 contains the next two legs of the W, a rising action that cranks the rollercoaster up a steeper slope (feel the tension building!), a tiny pause, then another falling action that drops us to the second turning point, the second bottom leg of the W.

Often the first chapters of Act 2 contain hope—so you need to choose islands that show a new level of understanding, or a new clue, or a new friend. We take time to regroup and gather strength.

But soon the action changes, things get worse again

Is the dilemma presented immediately and clearly? Is it big enough to propel the entire book? Remember that a triggering event should be an externalized action without which the story would not happen.

and tension builds. New complications take us to the end of Act 2, the second turning point, where we encounter a crisis of greater magnitude than any other moment in the story. Things really fall apart now. The tension is intense, with a sense that there's no way out.

Look again at your storyboard to see if you have these turning points in place. Does your peak of the W show a change from hope to complication? Consider the islands you've chosen for the peak of Act 2. The dramatic action should change now from hopeful (rising) to oh-no! (falling). If these islands are not located in the exact center of Act 2, that's perfectly fine. The W doesn't have to be symmetrical. One leg can be longer or shorter—each book's story will determine that. But make sure you have some peak in your W, some change to show things are getting more complicated as we slide down to the second turning point.

Does the second turning point at the end of Act 2 contain the worst moment in the book? If not, then think about ways you can show the dilemma worsening. What complications can you add to heighten the tension? Make sure what you are revealing feels much more complicated than at the first turning point.

The final leg of the W moves us into Act 3. It is an upward movement, another rising action that takes us to the end of the book. In some genres, there's a crisis in Act 3, a final battle that's propelled by the second turning point. In others, something unexpected is revealed, a new level of understanding brought to light, that lets the dilemmas of your book be resolved. Act 3 is a big exhale of tension, and it usually delivers a new level of clarity about the story or subject. This is where your characters realize how much they have grown, and how overcoming all those dilemmas earned them their insights. (Editors call this the "earned outcome" we talked about on pages 120–21.)

I like using this W to check my storyboard. I can immediately see whether there's enough dilemma in each act.

Just considering the five main points—the triggering event, the first turning point, the peak of Act 2 where the "rising" action changes to a "falling" action, the second turning point, and the end—gives me plenty of direction on correcting the dramatic arc of my book.

Raising the Stakes in Your Story

What happens if the storyboard doesn't show enough dilemma at these key moments? Then the writer must turn to her characters and raise the stakes in their stories.

I was struggling with dilemma in my second novel when I came upon a great technique for raising the stakes. I often make collages of difficult characters, because my right brain can help me get to know them if I use images.

One of the images in my collage for my rather bland character, Kate, was a photo of a woman wearing a wedding dress and running alone through a mock doorway in an empty field. The image was a strange choice but it grabbed me. I didn't know what it was telling me about Kate, but it did show she was indeed in conflict. I studied the collage for a few days, trying to figure out Kate's big problem.

Then I came across an article written by legendary New York acting teacher, Uta Hagen. Hagen is a proponent of the Stanislavsky method and coach to generations of successful actors such as Geraldine Page, Jason Robards, Jr., and Matthew Broderick. Actors under her tutelage get into a character's longings and desires via two different doorways. First they consider the external person; they search out a character's motives by looking at the external aspects of that character's life. The actor might pay attention to the character's shoes, as does Alec Guinness. Second, they study the internal thoughts and feelings of the person they'll be playing. They might take the character to a therapist (as Sir Laurence Olivier liked to do).

So I made a list of possible questions I could ask Kate, using this two-part approach. As I imagined Kate answering my therapist questions, I learned she was on the run (the run-

What happens if the storyboard doesn't show enough dilemma at these key moments? Then the writer must turn to her characters and raise the stakes in their stories.

ning woman) from her marriage (the wedding dress). This led to good questions: What was keeping Kate bound to her current life? Why did she want to run away from her husband?

I looked at the actions Kate takes throughout the book, and I saw a problem immediately. Kate only *thought* about how unhappy she was. I didn't have her *do* anything about it. This made her character flat. I brainstormed ways to increase Kate's external dilemma. A good idea came: What if she wasn't able to escape? What if she had an illness that kept her bound to her unhappy marriage?

As I added these islands to Acts 1 and 2, Kate became a much stronger character. Moreover, the book deepened as her dilemmas deepened. As if floodgates had opened, I suddenly had enough material to write many more scenes.

The image of the running woman became my compass to keep conflict in Kate's story, and I used the external/internal dilemma questions each time she seemed to get too safe. Most of us know that when a person faces danger or conflict, we see what that person is made of. High stakes bring out hidden needs, as well as hidden strengths.

As I said before, dilemma reveals if a person will fight or run or freeze.

Even if you're writing nonfiction, you will need to consider dilemma. Every genre of book delivers a question to be answered, a quest to be followed, a wish to be fulfilled. Growth comes whenever we face the unknown and take a risk, even if it's not the life-threatening risk of hunting down clues in a mystery. Your book must present the challenge of change, the fulfillment of new opinions, new skills, new understandings.

Exercise: Raising the Stakes in Your Story
TIME NEEDED: 2 HOURS

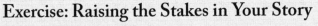

1. Choose a character in your book who feels distant, too safe, even bland. Take a look at these two lists of questions.

External Research Questions

What do you like or dislike about your
looks?

How do you feel about your age?

What five things are in your refrigerator?

What are your favorite shoes? Why?

What is your least favorite article of cloth-
ing?

What sort of work do you do? How do you
feel about it?

What's a favorite possession that you'd
never let go of?

What's your favorite music? When do you
listen to it?

Internal Research Questions

Who or what in your life first broke your
heart?

What do people who know you think of
you?

What or whom would you eliminate from
your life?

What do you wish never happened to you?

What's a secret you hide?

What is so painful you can't let it go?

What makes you so happy you can hardly
bear it?

2. Pick three questions from each list. Write
down how the character might answer these
questions. If you are writing about someone
real, research the answers so they are accurate
and true to life.

3. Do any of the answers give you a new insight
on possible (and as yet unrevealed) conflict?

Every genre of
book delivers a
question to be
answered, a quest
to be followed,
a wish to be
fulfilled.

Maybe you are suddenly aware of a desire or longing that person hasn't mentioned before.

4. Freewrite for twenty minutes about how this new understanding could increase the conflict in that person's story.

Look for answers that contradict each other: this is gold for writing dilemma. For instance, if one of your characters says he has no pain in his life, no one who ever broke his heart, but in the same breath talks about a woman who once told him he wasn't very smart, go deeper. Two answers that challenge each other hint at something unresolved.

Who Is Fighting Whom for What?

Another way to raise the stakes in your story is to ask yourself *who* this person is fighting and *what* they are fighting for. What do they want, and what stands in their way of getting it? On page 116, I mentioned John Truby, Hollywood screenwriting guru, and his wonderful question, which I recommend to all my students who need to raise the stakes in their stories: *Who fights whom for what?*

One of my students, Matt, was writing a thriller. Despite a compelling plot idea, Matt's storyboard fell flat. In class we doublechecked the five points of the W. Only the first triggering event in chapter 1 had enough conflict; Act 2 was disturbingly peaceful for a suspense novel, causing the middle of Matt's book to really slump.

I suggested that Matt list the name of every major and minor player in one column. Next to each person's name, Matt would write down *who* this person was fighting and *what* they were fighting for, using John Truby's question.

It was surprisingly hard! Matt could answer these questions only about his villain, his favorite character in the book. All the other characters, including the protagonist, came up blank.

As we talked, I realized that Matt liked these characters way too much. He wasn't letting them get into trouble.

So I took a different tack. I asked Matt to scan the list and begin pairing up characters as dance partners. Then imagine these two people having a conversation. What argument could evolve? The goal was to leak out tiny moments of conflict. This exercise really worked. Conflicts started coming fast as Matt visualized these players tangling with each other as they danced a tango.

Externalize the Action

By asking Matt to create an external action—a dance—it became easier for him to imagine dilemma. This is because it's hard for the mind to sense dilemma if it's not dramatized, or made external. We learn about characters by watching them move around their worlds.

Dilemma is rarely believable if it's passive—thought about, talked about, put in letters or emails, or discussed on the phone—without any active outer risk.

As you externalize the action in your book, you can complicate dilemma beautifully. You can see if there are any characters who are stalled between what they want and what they think they should have. A great example of this is Ann Patchett's award-winning novel *Bel Canto,* whose main character is a Japanese businessman who loves opera. For his birthday, he and other elite guests are invited to a private villa where a famous opera singer will entertain them. The businessman is more than a little in love with this opera singer, but his desire to get closer to her is not something that can be realized unless some outside event happens, a dilemma that will force change—in this case a terrorist take-over of the villa during the recital.

Once the businessman and the opera singer are trapped, more action gets externalized. He sees the opera singer every day, in difficult situations. Emotions begin to play out, because desires are spoken aloud. This is typical during trauma—witness the deep friendships and sudden romances of wartime. Patchett took characters who were safe in unexpressed

As you externalize the action in your book, you can complicate dilemma beautifully. You can see if there are any characters who are stalled between what they want and what they think they should have.

interior worlds and forced them into a dilemma in the outer world. If she hadn't, there would be no story.

My student Carol is writing a self-help book for women who do too much. Carol's ideal reader is a generous soul, a people-pleaser who spends her days doing for others. Carol was like this too, and that's why she is motivated to write this book.

Carol's book contains some great anecdotes, as most modern self-help books do. For Carol's triggering event, she chose an embarrassing and true story of one of her clients who got "caught" tending to herself instead of a sick friend. The shame that resulted caused the woman to completely turn her back on her own needs for many weeks, until she got sick herself. Act 1 contained a series of stories like this, as well as good information about the mindset of people pleasers.

In Act 2, Carol's book slumped. She only had low-key scenes with little external action. It was pretty easy to build the rising action—stories about women who would simply sneak away by themselves to get some peace and privacy, hiding with a good book and a glass of lemonade in their bedrooms. But the falling action, which brought us to a bigger turning point, was more difficult.

I suggested Carol look for stories that showed a woman about to burst from being too contained for too long. Yes, the first story showed someone getting sick. Did Carol know of anything worse that had happened when needs were really repressed?

Carol thought of a story of her own: a serious confrontation with a neighbor, who called Carol for a committee favor on a morning when Carol's son was suspended from school. She remembered how she blew up at the woman. Although it was embarrassing, it beautifully demonstrated what happens when two desires clash—the desire to maintain the aura of being everyone's helper with the extreme need for privacy to cope with personal pain. When desires clash, there is surprise, drama, action.

Carol's willingness to include this island made a big difference in the overall depth and credibility of her book. If you're in a similar situation, take a clue from Carol's story. Don't feel your conflict has to be highly shocking to be effective. It just has to be unexpected. "The important thing in writing is the capacity to astonish," says writer Terry Southern, a screenwriter who worked on films such as *Easy Rider* and *Dr. Strangelove*. Shock is "a worn-out word," wrote Southern, but astonishment always makes for good literature.

Don't feel your conflict has to be highly shocking to be effective. It just has to be unexpected.

Fear of Writing Conflict

Each time I moved, my writing changed dramatically. When I relocated to the Midwest, I lived with the politest and most self-contained people I'd ever met and my writing became calmer, with less conflict on the page. Then I remarried and returned to the East Coast where I grew up. Suddenly I was writing more dramatic prose.

I realized that each location I lived in was teaching me a different aspect about conflict.

I wondered if it was just me, but I began to see it in my writing classes too. When I teach at a writing school in the Midwest, I notice a hesitancy to brawl on the page. I have to prod the "not nice" into these polite writers' outer stories, helping them face the less pleasant aspects of memory; I have to encourage them to challenge their characters.

When I teach in Westchester County, near New York City, it's the opposite. Few are shy about outer conflict; in fact, I find I need to nudge them to drop the drama and go deeper into the internal twists of character.

If you are reluctant to raise the risks in your story, consider where you live, where you grew up, the family you are in now or the family you came from. How acceptable or unacceptable has it been to express conflict outwardly in your life? Is that standard mirrored in your book?

Try to become aware of conflict in your day-to-day life.

Observe how it appears in the world around you. Notice how people in your family, community, and work place deal with it. Do people have open arguments in stores and other public places? Or is everyone very nice outwardly but seething with road rage once they hit the commute?

Our environment directly affects our preferences about writing conflict. The exercise that ends this chapter will help you with this—hopefully, you will discover a whole set of conflict-writing skills that will benefit your book.

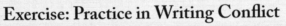

Exercise: Practice in Writing Conflict
Time needed: 2 hours

1. Make a list of potential conflicts that could be brought out in your book. What kinds of trouble could people get themselves into? If you're writing fiction or memoir, list desires and difficulties for each of your main characters. For nonfiction, make a list of possible problems that readers might encounter and how your book solves or addresses them.

2. Pick one problem and write about it. See if you can create a scene where the person faces this problem.

3. Now spend a few minutes with your writing notebook. Ask yourself how the conflict writing felt—did you notice anything in your own body as you wrote? Tense shoulders? Headache? Put those sensations into your characters.

15

WHO *ARE* THESE PEOPLE? GETTING TO KNOW YOUR BOOK'S MAIN PLAYERS

The 1990s saw a sudden rise in a certain kind of book: one-page stories offering a moving anecdote about life. Jack Canfield and Mark Victor Hansen's *Chicken Soup for the Soul* series was the most notable. Since the first *Chicken Soup* book launched in 1993, over 100 million copies (200 titles) have been sold. These inspirational parables appealed to an unmet need in American readers—and soon worldwide.

What is this need? Maybe it's simple: These stories are about people doing ordinary things but learning extraordinary lessons.

Why did they sell? Maybe that's simple too: Readers love reading about people who overcome challenges.

If dilemma contributes momentum to books, writing about vivid characters, real or imagined, builds empathy and emotion. We love to study the lives of others. How are they losing weight, playing the cello, solving the crime, surviving or leaving the marriage?

It's hard to publish a book these days if you don't include stories about people.

In every genre, people now populate books. Years ago it was common to read nonfiction books, say on the then-current financial upswing or down surge, written in abstract, academic prose. Now most nonfiction books, even the driest tomes, include vignettes or stories about people interacting with the nonfiction subject.

So one of your hardest jobs as a writer is to convince readers that these people are real, whether the "character" is you at thirteen, a fictional war hero from 1918, or a client sharing her experience of divorce.

The secret to writing vivid players on the stage of your

One of your hardest jobs as a writer is to convince readers that these people are real, whether the "character" is you at thirteen, a fictional war hero from 1918, or a client sharing her experience of divorce.

197

book is demonstration. If you demonstrate, rather than describe, the reader enters the room willingly, interacts with your players, makes them part of her own world. Have you ever heard a friend say, "You'll love this book. The story stayed with me for days"? It's usually because of the characters.

In this chapter we'll explore the basic steps to writing good characters. We'll learn how to create an emotional arc for each person in your story, and how this emotional arc travels through the book, building connection with the reader.

But first you, the writer, need to get to know your characters well. Even the most obscure ones.

Your Major and Minor Cast

One of my students, Lisa, is midway through her novel set in Italy in the 1920s. The novel's cast rivals an Italian opera's onstage company. There are so many players that Lisa often gets discouraged keeping track of them. So I suggested making a cast list, a comprehensive line up of everyone who comes onstage during the entire book.

Lisa listed fifty-two characters, which included bit players such as the local innkeeper in the village where the story takes place.

Good, I told her. Now rate them according to how often they appear onstage as well as how influential they are in the story. An uncle in America, who sends money to the family, is lower in rank than the woman from the village who comes every day to clean and cook. Lisa narrowed the cast to ten major players and fifteen minor ones, the rest being seen only in passing.

Compared to short pieces of writing—an essay, an article, a short story—books are marriages as opposed to one-night stands. Marriages require that you know more than a person's name, where he works, the color of his eyes. You need to know moods, longings, and fears; what he keeps in the refrigerator and goes to when stressed; what kind of music he loves and his favorite ice cream. Major players in the cast need more attention than minor players, but all of them must be known fully by the writer of their story.

I asked Lisa to put a star by the names of any characters she was haunted by, obsessed with; the ones who were following her around in her head.

She immediately picked four.

What about the others? I asked.

"You mean I have to get to know *everybody* on that level?"

Yes, I told her. Otherwise, the reader will wonder why they are in your book.

Even minor players count. Why? Because of what they tell us about the main players.

Minor players are sometimes called "foils"—and I think of the shiny patina of aluminum foil which reflects when smooth. Minor cast members must reflect something about at least one main player and often tell the reader new details or aspects we wouldn't otherwise know. I pointed to one of the names on the list: *Mario.* "Who does Mario tell us about?" I asked her.

Turns out Mario was once in love with Flora, the heroine. Mario knows one of Flora's secrets, something not even her family—or her current husband—is aware of. Because of this, whenever Mario walks by, Flora gets tense. Will Mario reveal this secret? It depends on how well his creator, Lisa, gets to know him.

Just like we learn new things about a lover by watching how they interact with friends, family, and strangers, we learn about main characters by watching them interact with other characters in a book. In other words, just as every scene that ends up in your book needs a unique purpose, every player must have a unique reason for being onstage. I asked Lisa to justify the existence of these minor players by asking, *Why did I include this character in my novel? What purpose does he or she serve in my book?*

When I was in my M.F.A. program, I studied the 1960

Major players in the cast need more attention than minor players, but all of them must be known fully by the writer of their story.

classic, Harper Lee's *To Kill a Mockingbird*, looking for how carefully the author depicted her characters. *Mockingbird's* cast is as vast as Lisa's, with about ten main players that all have important roles. Lee is masterful in showing us the motivations of each of these people during intense racial strife. But Lee's many minor characters are also well drawn, such as the family's housekeeper who is not onstage all that often yet still acts as an anchor in the story, filling out our understanding of Scout (the child narrator), Scout's family, and the dilemma of this small town.

Scout becomes real by how she is reflected, or shown, through the eyes of other characters. In chapter 12 we saw how emotional truth—the essential information that shows us a person's real motives and beliefs—is rarely communicated by telling. Better to show it. Mirroring becomes an important way to show what a character is about.

Think of the moment you first fell in love. No doubt, in the beginning you and your beloved isolated yourselves, savoring the intensity. But eventually there was an urge to take your lover out, to see him against the backdrop of other people. You learned something as you watched how he spoke, laughed, ordered a meal; in essence how he treated others and how others mirrored him. Was he kind, interesting? Did other people glow in his presence the way you did? Chances are you learned aspects about your lover that you might never have discovered if you two had just stayed by yourselves.

So it is in books, too. Each character should reflect something about the other characters. We learn a lot about our cast by watching them in their "hall of mirrors." Minor characters exist primarily to mirror the main character. This is not mimicking, but by their presence these characters cause a trait to surface in the main character. That said, if every character mirrors a main character's honesty, the reader grows suspicious, wondering what's being hidden. The goal is multi-dimensional people, just like in real life.

Explore the multi-dimensions of your characters via the following exercise.

Exercise: Hall of Mirrors
TIME NEEDED: 2 HOURS

1. In your writer's notebook, list all the players in your book or story—everyone!

2. Rank them by how much time they have on-stage and how deep their influence on your story.

3. Select one minor character from your list and one major player that are connected in some way. Write down any qualities the minor character brings out in the main character.

4. Find a scene in your book where the minor character interacts with the main character and identify one particular quality in the main character that is brought to light. If you haven't written one, set a kitchen timer for twenty minutes and draft a scene, then develop it to two pages.

5. Repeat this exercise with other minor players.

Writing Beyond What You "Know"

Just as in real life, once we think we know someone well, we have a hard time not taking them for granted. Writers too can get lazy after months of working with the same fictional or nonfictional characters. As you expand your understanding about the people who live in your writing, you may open up to new aspects of these characters, which can bring needed freshness to your book. Looking at your main player through the eyes of someone else can help you see from a reader's point of view, rather than your own.

Linda, a skilled writer in one of my fiction classes, struggled with the point-of-view narrator in her novel. The narrator's name was Brenda and she was irritating and shallow; Linda found her far from fun to write about.

Looking at your main player through the eyes of someone else can help you see from a reader's point of view, rather than your own.

Linda worked on Brenda for months, but Brenda refused to budge from her sullen performance at center stage, making it hard for Linda to move the story along. Linda couldn't jettison Brenda as a major player because Brenda's antics created just enough tension to make the story work. Well, almost work. Something was definitely missing.

As Linda complained about Brenda's stubbornness, I was reminded of one of my own experiences with an unsavory character in my novel.

Mel was the name of my difficult star player. After hearing my writers' group complain about his distance and lack of emotional punch, I was happy to give him up, but like many difficult relationships, there was something about Mel that I liked.

I remembered an interview about Barbara Kingsolver who had just published *The Poisonwood Bible,* a novel where each chapter is told from one of the five different main character's points of view. Before she settled on which character was best, she wrote each chapter from all five characters' points of view. She did this to figure out who was the best person to tell each chapter's story. I decided to do the same with my Mel character. I wrote one of Mel's scenes from his estranged wife's point of view and learned a lot about why Mel was so distant. Next, I tried writing a chapter from Mel's point of view but in first person instead of third. I learned of his loneliness.

By the time I moved back to my original third person, the parts where Mel showed up had many new layers.

When Linda tried this same exercise with Brenda, it helped her soften Brenda's edges. She wrote about Brenda from her mother's point of view, then from a close friend's. As Linda got clearer about Brenda's point of view, a better plot emerged. Brenda now had ceased being troublesome.

Point-of-view exercises work equally well for all genres—fiction, nonfiction, and memoir. As long as you're telling a story, whether by anecdote in a nonfiction book or scene in a memoir or novel, you need to play with point of view. Which point of view tells the story in the best way?

In the exercise that follows, you'll get to experiment with point of view, trying one section of your book from different perspectives.

Exercise: A Different View
TIME NEEDED: 1 TO 1½ HOURS

---

1. Choose one of your characters and write a short anecdote, interview, or scene from his or her point of view. Write the scene in either first person (the "I" viewpoint) or third ("he" or "she"). Don't worry too much about how the scene flows at this point, just try to get the character doing something. Make sure there is another person in the scene, so your chosen character has someone to bounce off.

2. Read through the scene and find an exciting part that pulls you in as a reader. Underline that sentence or section.

3. Start a new page, using that exciting part as the beginning trigger, but this time change viewpoints. Make the scene come from the mirroring character, not your main character.

4. Again, underline the most exciting part, and transfer it to a new page. This time, continue the scene, but switch back to the main character's point of view. Also change voices, go from first to third person, or vice versa—using the point of view you didn't use in step one.

5. After you read all three scenes, ask yourself, *Which is the best story? Why?* Your answer may reveal who should be telling the story. If you decide to stay with your original character, this exercise should deepen your understanding of this character.

As long as you're telling a story, whether by anecdote in a non-fiction book or scene in a memoir or novel, you need to play with point of view. Which point of view tells the story in the best way?

Emotional Arcs

In the last chapter, we talked about dilemmas and how they create momentum in a book, keeping a reader engaged. These outer events, fueled by people's actions, are the essential foundation for reader involvement. But they are only half the reason we stay with a story. The other reason is our fascination with a character's inner life.

A book that is solely based on carefully constructed dilemmas, with each one serving as a plot point, will miss this inner story. There can be no outer experience without some kind of inner reaction. Whether you know it or not, each player on your stage travels along a certain inner trajectory, what editors call an *emotional arc.* Characters begin the book knowing and understanding certain things about themselves and the world. By the end of the book, they have had experiences that have changed them in some way. Usually, they know more. Sometimes they regress and know less, or go back to a less developed state. But always there is inner change and growth.

As you get to know your characters, you can begin to see their emotional arcs. The "internal questions" from chapter 14 can speed this process—asking the characters what they long for or fear, what they dream of, or what they've given up on in their lives. In answering these questions, you'll begin to understand their motivations, what drives them, where they might slip up or stand up heroically and unexpectedly. In this way, emotional arcs can be one of the most exciting parts of writing your book.

When I was writing my memoir/self-help book, *How to Master Change in Your Life,* I interviewed many friends, family, and people who had experienced some kind of change. The stories I chose to include had to pass two criteria: (1) something dramatic needed to occur in that person's life and (2) they had to show considerable change in themselves because of it. If I didn't find both the outer plot point and the emotional arc, I put aside that anecdote.

When I was working on my first novel, *Qualities of Light,* I followed six to eight main players through a summer. It was easy to find their plot points on my storyboard, but much harder to track their individual emotional arcs. So I began character charts for each of them.

I drew a timeline for each player. Above it, I placed the plot points for that person. My main character Molly's timeline listed points like: *brother's accident, first kiss with Chad, meeting Zoe, rescuing Zoe on the lake.* Under each of these moments, I wrote the emotional effect. How was Molly changing because of them? From this, I could trace Molly's emotional arc. In early drafts of the book, I noticed that some plot points contributed little to the character's inner evolution. They got jettisoned in later versions or rewritten to include more meaning.

Emotional arcs are all about meaning—the meaning of the plot to the players. It's the other half of your story.

Start with the plot points on your W, the main crisis points on your storyboard. Find the big things that happen, then ask yourself how they affect the main players. Rethink these plot points; reject or rewrite them if they don't contribute to the players' growth.

Emotional arcs are all about meaning—the meaning of the plot to the players.

When Your Characters *Are* Your Life

In memoir, we're writing about ourselves—that main character is you. Memoir usually is about a time in the past we've digested and reflected upon, accessed meaning from, and are now able to present with some equanimity.

While predigesting our own story is necessary to live our lives, it can create a tale that feels distant on the page. How do you keep the freshness in your own story, when your main character is you and your minor characters are people you know only too well? You need to stay fascinated throughout the book journey, take the reader on a journey of realization as you create your book—by discovering more about your own story with each island you write.

But facing ourselves and our own lives can be traumatic and troublesome, and many memoirists veer away from this level of alertness. If you begin to notice a flatness about everyone on your pages, or your own part in the story begins to feel very scripted, break away from that part of your book. Something is causing a disconnectedness. Sometimes what's going on in your own life now parallels what is going on in this part of the story. You may be going through a personal passage of change, something you have to face before further truth can emerge in your book.

This is not just the case with true-life stories, either. Fiction writers also face themselves in their characters, since most fiction has some autobiographical elements, even if heavily disguised. This parallel can shut us down when the scenes come too close to home.

What to do? Stop writing. Spend some time with your writer's notebook and consider your own life right now—what is happening and how might it parallel what one of your characters is going through?

Getting Close to the Fire

We began this chapter talking about how characters need to approach the heat of circumstances to reveal their true natures. But as we just learned, this heat can also singe us, make us uncomfortable, even make us turn away from our writing.

Over the time you write your book, you'll get more accustomed to this parallel between your characters' lives and your own. You'll begin to notice how, as you write a character getting closer to the fire, your own feelings get closer, too. If the writing makes you uneasy, if you begin to cry or the scene makes your heart race, you'll realize this is a good sign. And a very common experience in writing a book.

It's hard to harvest emotional intensity in a book unless we are feeling it too.

Generalizing characters—real or imagined—is death to

a book. We have to stay open to our players showing sides of themselves we didn't script, we didn't prepare for, that surprise us.

Julie, a nonfiction writer in my class, was collecting interviews from environmental activists. Before she began her interviews, she listed topics she wanted her book to cover. As soon as she began her interviews, she knew her approach was off track. Many of the group of activists spoke about different ideas than Julie had prepared for.

At first, she was annoyed. She considered throwing out the interviews that didn't match what she really wanted to write about. But in truth, those were the ones that fascinated her the most. It was clear to her that her book needed to evolve, to follow the surprises.

As you get to know your book's players, be open to their uniqueness and their differences from what you imagined. Not knowing them at first, you might generalize about who they are. But people are always more complex and unexpected as you get to know them. Likewise, more lurks beneath the surface of each character than we can ever conceive.

We have to stay open to our players showing sides of themselves we didn't script, we didn't prepare for, that surprise us.

Exercise: Values and Vulnerabilities
TIME NEEDED: 1 HOUR

Everyone's always at risk in good literature. So one way to keep yourself open to new dimensions in your cast of characters is to think about what each person stands to lose.

What risks are they facing in your book?

How can their risks bring you, the writer, closer to who they really are?

1. Choose one of your book's main players.

2. Write for five minutes, answering this question: *What's valuable to this person?*

3. Ask yourself: *Is this an outer, tangible item or possession? Or is it something this person could lose emotionally or spiritually?*

4. Make a list of all the things that actively threaten this person, which could bring about this loss.

5. Write two pages where your character faces one of these threats.

16

LOCATION, LOCATION, LOCATION: WRITING THE CONTAINER OF YOUR STORY

Margaret was working on her memoir about growing up in post-World-War-II Mississippi. The story-board worked well: plot points were good and you could track the dilemma of her story. So Margaret confidently took a few pages to her writing group for review.

Feedback was lukewarm. The pages lacked a sense of place, her fellow writers told her. Margaret, confused, came to my class to learn about this mysterious "sense of place."

She didn't want to include moss-hung oaks and sweet tea in her story, she said. The South was old news to her; she was writing her memoir to put it behind her. Thoughts and reflections about what she'd learned since she'd left the South were much more interesting.

When I read Margaret's islands, I saw how brief her acknowledgement of setting was. She did note the ancient oak tree outside her family's home, the stuffed furniture in the parlor, the separate summer kitchen which kept the main house cool in August. But overall, there was an imbalance of sensory road signs. Indeed, Margaret's story could've taken place as easily in New York as Mississippi.

I told her that while good characters initially engage us, and plot twists provide momentum, it is setting that gives the emotional grounding that keeps us involved.

"But most of this story takes place inside my reaction to it," she argued, "in my thoughts and feelings, looking back from my life now." All good, but thoughts and feelings tell more than show. They are abstract. It's counterintuitive, but reflective writing doesn't communicate emotion to a reader, only to the writer who has thought or felt it. I suggested Margaret study the *container* of her story, the environment

While good characters initially engage us, and plot twists provide momentum, it is setting that gives the emotional grounding that keeps us involved.

where it happens, and distill just enough detail to provide the missing sense of place.

Rick Bass, award-winning author of *Winter* and other memoirs, described this sense of place as the small elements that "lay claim to you, eventually, with a cumulative power." Bass said they can be as simple as "the direction of a breeze one day, a single sentence that a friend might speak to you, a raven flying across the meadow and circling back again." A *container* comprises these small outer details, but also the inner landscape of culture, politics, religion, history—the atmosphere of the life in your book. Writing believable container is much more than just adding one or two setting details. It's about creating a strong center that pulls a reader in and lets her fully live in your pages.

Growing up in such a senses-rich location, Margaret felt the South was overblown and overstated. But it was the container that she could—and eventually did—use to beckon the reader into her book. It was only by showing the South in all its over-the-top glory that she was able to reveal to her reader just how suffocating the South can be.

How Does Setting Deliver Emotion?

John was a first-time novelist. As a professional nonfiction writer, he was trying to learn how container functioned in fiction.

In John's nonfiction books, outer setting details were used effectively to illustrate anecdotes. He was accustomed to crafting a minimal environment in his small stories. But as a new novelist, John was not having success with this plug-and-play approach. He felt his descriptions of breezes, sunlight, and birds were stiff, besides being injected into each scene willy-nilly.

So I asked him first to consider why he'd selected these details, why he'd placed them just there in his scenes.

John sheepishly said he was just trying to check "setting" off his writerly to-do list. There was also zero intent to use setting to enhance emotion—which is its primary benefit.

Setting must make sense with the emotional moment you're writing about, I explained. For example, if a character was struggling with a decision, he might notice something in the setting that mirrored his uncertainty. Not the clichéd dark and stormy night, but a small detail like a sweater buttoned the wrong way on an old man he's talking to. Or if it's a really big decision, a tree fallen across a road. A forgotten pan on the hot stove. These details mirror the character's unsettling confusion.

So John began a list of the emotional moments in his book. He began placing small setting details to echo each moment of his main character's emotion. The effect surprised him—there was so much more payoff! We discussed how, if his character just thinks about his decision, it stays in his gut and never reaches the reader's.

The setting is a roadmap for the reader. It emphasizes what we're supposed to be receiving from the scene.

Every book takes place somewhere. Even the most abstract nonfiction book has to have a setting. Writers can't neglect this outer container, the exterior setting, the physical location of their stories—and also how the interior environment is reflected in those outer setting details.

John learned that good placement of shown setting reveals emotion as subtly as a butterfly landing on a late-summer dahlia—without any interpreting by the writer.

A Basic Lesson: Creating Outer Container

Outer container, what is traditionally called setting, is demonstrated via *outwardly perceived* things: the weather, the time of day or night, where a person is physically in a room or garden or other specific location, how light slants against an object or a wall or someone's arm, what smells and sounds surround us. But how many writers omit these details, thinking, like Margaret, that they're boring or slow or unnecessary?

Outer setting details are the first conveyers of emotion to a reader. They set the stage.

> The setting is a roadmap for the reader. It emphasizes what we're supposed to be receiving from the scene.

Few playwrights set their theater productions on a completely blank stage—no backdrop, no furniture, no atmosphere. Much easier for the audience to imagine themselves inside an 1850s farmhouse kitchen if there is a rocker, an old wooden table, a woodstove, and windows with eyelet curtains. So what outer details exist in your story right now? What have you taken time to write in?

Start by viewing what your narrator notices. Describe the seen setting first. Time of day (light, dark), objects, furniture, nature.

Move through each of the remaining five senses, asking yourself what might be perceived. What smells are in this place? What sounds? Add in these details without interpretation, without qualifiers, without telling the reader what the details mean. Write, "The garden was pink and gold and filled with summer light." Don't add, "It was beautiful to Marci."

We already get that. No interpreting required.

Overly Familiar Settings

Annie, a published mystery writer, was working on her latest story set in the Florida Keys. "I'm trying to be more mindful of adding in atmosphere to heighten the sense of being in Key West," she told me. "But one of the things that struck me when I visited the Keys was how familiar it seemed, how much the Keys were like the Jersey Shore town I was born and raised in. The marshy and swampy landscape, riddled with bays and inlets in South Jersey, has long encouraged all sorts of the same activities that take place in the Keys. Even the architecture is similar," she added, "and the tourist trade and the activities are all alike."

Annie wanted to know how she could give her readers a sense of Key West while showing that, for her character, this setting felt so familiar. I told her that even if a character knows the story's setting, from growing up there or visiting, it's important to realize that her reader won't. It's still necessary to place the reader in space, time, weather conditions, hot and sultry or cool and breezy. Setting places a reader firmly in the time of day, the experience of light slanting across the floor, or the way the tropical wind rattles the windows. In Annie's mystery, she could mention the familiarity of it to her character, but she still had to establish setting.

In short, setting lets us get inside the character's head, via what she notices about where she is, how it impacts her, including what she tries to ignore. You can't skip this step of crafting believable outer container. Or else we won't feel your story.

> Setting lets us get inside the character's head, via what she notices about where she is, how it impacts her, including what she tries to ignore.

Exercise: Five Senses for Container
TIME NEEDED: 20 MINUTES

Choose a section of your writing where you want the reader to really get a punch of emotion. Answer three of the questions below. Select one or two sentences that come from the answers and add them to your writing.

1. What does the narrator smell?
2. What does she sense on her skin (air temperature)?
3. What does she hear close to her? In the distance?
4. What three objects are nearby?
5. What time of day is it? How can she tell via the setting (without a clock)?

Drawing the Physical Setting

Another way to get clear on outer container is to really get to know your book's physical setting by drawing it. When I began writing my second novel, *Breathing Room*, I often lost details of the layout of my fictional family's Adirondack farmhouse. Was the father's studio upstairs or downstairs? How far was each bedroom from the others (shouting or whispering distance)? Did the family enter through the kitchen door off the driveway or through a more formal entrance?

As I began creating chapters and moving characters through scenes, I realized I needed a diagram of the building. So I drew one. I added notes about views from the windows, sounds in the hall. It was amazingly helpful, this simple sketch of each floor. It brought back the position of rooms most used in the book. As the story developed, I enlarged the sketch to include surrounding farm fields, greenhouse and barn, and the river across the road.

Perhaps because I am also a painter, I love to use real-life images to spark ideas in my writing, so I added cut-out magazine pictures to my maps. My main character's bedroom had tiny cut-out images that showed her important possessions, her symbols of desires and conflicts, such as longing for someone who might finally understand her.

Along with images cut from magazines, try real-life photographs too. I've written some of my best scenes in memoir and fiction by focusing on setting using photographs that looked like something from my book. Although nonfiction writers don't need to depict the same level of setting detail, they benefit greatly from the orientation of book drawings and diagrams. When I was a food writer, I would not only test the recipe and taste it but also photograph it. The photograph was my main marker for gustatory setting. It brought back details I needed during writing and revision.

If you're struggling with setting, pick up a copy of Winifred Gallagher's book *The Power of Place*, an excellent collection of essays about how where we live, what we love and avoid in our environment, tells the world a lot about who we are.

Exercise: Drawing Your Setting
TIME NEEDED: 1-2 HOURS

Supplies you'll need:
✓ a large piece of paper, posterboard, or foamcore

✓ drawing materials (ruler, pencil, colored markers and pens)

✓ paint, brushes, pastels, colored pencils; scissors; glue stick; and a stack of magazines

1. Choose your story's primary location: a room, building, street, town, countryside.

2. For twenty minutes, write everything you can remember or imagine about this location. Get as detailed as possible. Describe placement of items, position of a building's entrance, number of windows, items of furniture.

3. Take your large sheet of paper and begin sketching your location. Don't worry about being a top-notch artist; just get down what you can.

4. Add anything that came to mind as you sketched. Add these to the drawing.

5. Color your drawing. Now add images cut from magazines; include abstract symbols, anything that helps you visualize your story in more detail.

After you create your drawing, take it to a copy center to be laminated—which is not as expensive as you might think. Or cover it with clear Contact paper or tack to a bulletin board or wall. Some writers like to reduce their drawing on a photocopier and paste the smaller version inside their writer's notebook, to be studied and enhanced as the story grows. Maps help you orient your story, as they helped all the great explorers chart their travels. And what are writers, if not great explorers?

Drawings, diagrams, or maps can also bring out unexpected levels of a story's emotional container as well. Amy, a memoir writer, uses her book's drawing to jar memories. When she drew a map of the town where she lived until the end of first grade, "I was amazed at my child's perception," she says, "at how incomplete things were." Children may only see a

Maps help you orient your story, as they helped all the great explorers chart their travels. And what are writers, if not great explorers?

limited view of place, or they may pick up on aspects adults ignore. Your memoir map can tell you age-appropriate information about your setting and help you dive deeper into forgotten memories, which are part of creating the inner container.

Creating Inner Container

After you work on the outer container, via physical setting details and senses placed for emotional effect, it's time to consider the next aspect, the inner container. You may have decided on what emotional effect you're after. But it's essential not to dumb down your writing by interpreting this for the reader.

Say you're writing about a girl named Joan who is looking at a butterfly on a late-summer flower, and you, the writer, know she's mad and sad because her abusive father just died. If you write: "Joan saw the flower fading and felt sad suddenly, not knowing why," you state the obvious. Instead, try to use the setting to convey how she is actually feeling: "Joan glared at the Monarch butterfly perched on the brown edges of the fading dahlia."

Yes, it takes more effort to convey the inner container by showing versus telling, by deliberate demonstration of the girl's feelings. But it can be fun too. Imagine the girl picking the flower and shredding it in her fingers then leaving those pieces where her mother will find them. Imagine her creating a trail of flower pieces along a sidewalk or windowsill. These might better tell us about the inner container, in this case the confused atmosphere post-funeral.

What would be another demonstration of feeling, in the same situation? Maybe the girl goes outside at the same time each morning to watch the flower, seeing it fade a little each day, eventually dying.

I use two other techniques to write effective inner container, borrowed from the work of Robert Olen Butler in his writing-craft book *From Where You Dream*.

1. Have the narrator feel something in her body, a physical sensation that's felt by the body, not thought about or

observed by the mind. To do this, sit quietly and observe your own body, then try to put sensations into words. "Joan's throat tightened and her eyes stung." "Flashes of heat traveled across her skin." "Her stomach was suddenly hollow." These specific and felt sensations are not interpreted, and because of this, they share specific internal atmosphere and emotion. Since most of us understand what emotion is experienced by tight throat and stinging eyes (sadness) or flashes of heat on skin (fear, excitement), the moment comes alive for us.

2. Write in a brief memory of a similar time, that contrasts or connects in some way with the emotional container now. "Joan remembered her father's hands picking dahlias from the garden, arranging them in a cobalt vase, bringing them to her bedroom. Only three dahlias, but each one perfect." Again, no interpreting. You don't need to add, "He loved her very much." The emotional container hints at some emotion—was he obsessed with her? Was he a control freak?

Hopefully, the reader will read on to find out.

> *Since most of us understand what emotion is experienced by tight throat and stinging eyes (sadness) or flashes of heat on skin (fear, excitement), the moment comes alive for us.*

Exercise: Writing Emotional Container
TIME NEEDED: 20 MINUTES

1. Find a sentence in your book where you've written the "told" feeling or thought, such as "Joan was sad."

2. Close your eyes and imagine how sadness might feel as a body sensation. Write some ideas.

3. Then imagine a memory of sadness in the narrator's past. Write a short island of two to three paragraphs about this memory. Excerpt a few key sentences.

4. Replace the told feeling, using the body sensation and the excerpted memory. See if the emotion is heightened.

Cultural, Intellectual, Historical Container

A subtle step beyond the inner emotional container of your book is the broader universe of the culture your characters live in. Perhaps it's the nomadic life of a Bedouin tribe, the buttoned-down control of a corporation, or the generations-old stability of a family from a small town in Indiana.

Fran, writing her first memoir, was playing with small scenes from her childhood that spoke of the unwritten rules that ran her family life, how the cultural container of her church influenced each person's actions and preferences, including the odor of scorched coffee that often greeted the family coming home from Mass. Jason, working on a non-fiction book about a trip across northern India, added details of village life that everyone but him took for granted: the smells of spices that mixed with the dung in the street, the flicker of nighttime fires, and the rows of sleepers on the rooftops.

What is important in the culture of your story? What setting details tell the reader the most about the beliefs that govern this group of people?

For another writer in my class, the cultural container was sound. She wrote about hiding one day in a darkened room in the family home when she heard someone come in. Because the lights were off, the girl couldn't see who it was—until she heard ice cubes being put into a glass and liquid poured into it, the slow sipping of the drink. It was her mother. The girl knew she would not be welcome if she made herself known. The adult wanted to be alone to drink more than she wanted to connect with a child.

Sound was the vehicle used to convey this moment of setting, not visual details. The room was dark, so there weren't any. And sound (be it the ice cubes in a glass or the forced silence of the adults) was part of the metaphor of this family—with its bounty of secrets that no one spoke about.

In moments like these, it's important to choose what to include and what to leave out, as far as setting details. Nobody rushing to a hospital emergency will notice every aspect of the streets passing by, but the two or three short bursts of detail will inform us about not only the character's state of mind but also the environment in which he lives. If the moment is intense, consider limiting the number of details to a very few—as the writer did in the darkened room described above.

The Meaning of Your Book's Primary Location

In the memoir *Eat, Pray, Love* by Elizabeth Gilbert, the narrator travels through three countries. Because each is well developed with full sensory details, a complete container is created in each location. Each provides meaning to the story, which parallels what Gilbert is learning on her journey: She proceeds from body (Italy), to mind (India), ending with heart (Bali), a map that charts her search for love.

In the novel *Housekeeping* by Marilynne Robinson, the cultural container is the house. Its piles of newspapers and stacks of saved string create a container. The characters are forced to escape this setting—they ignore it, adjust to it, or change it—just as they are forced to deal with the chaos after a death.

When I was first writing my novel *Qualities of Light*, I spread the story over many locations—the family's summer home by the lake and their winter farmhouse, the hospital, a trip to Canada and one to France, the grandparents' home in Minnesota. But I noticed that I was having trouble creating a viable container with so many locations. Studying books like *Housekeeping* showed me the power of simplicity in choosing one location.

First I eliminated all the scenes out of state. Many were not even important to the story, I realized—they drained the emotion away from the main dilemma. Next I asked myself if there were any other locations I could eliminate without damaging the story. Turned out the farmhouse could go too—and eventually almost all of the peripheral settings disappeared. The lake was it. Once I realized this, I could really

> What is important about the culture of your story? What setting details tell the reader the most about the beliefs that govern this group of people?

enhance the emotional effect of it, develop it into a strong theme.

What if your container is not one location, and it can't be helped? Look for the ties between the locations. Perhaps it is the group of people who are traveling together, stuck in one "place" with each other? Perhaps it is a collection of similar objects that guides the story along (boats that cause accidents) or one moving location (the bus in *Little Miss Sunshine*)? Maybe it is even a concept, such as a home's disarray after a sudden death?

You'll need to spend time developing such moving containers, almost until they become talismans that hold enormous emotion for the reader. If you are writing about a medical journey, and you will be including many doctors' offices as settings in your book, pinpoint a specific aspect that is constant, such as the persistent smell of disinfectant or the slippery paper that covers each exam table. This small but constant detail will ground us by signifying the meaning in your book. Sterility or the anonymity of being a patient in so many places?

Container is where your inner and outer story play out. Readers look for it, they need it, and they rejoice when a writer takes enough time to present it well. It's also fun to write, once you understand its benefit to your book.

17

PERILS OF BACKSTORY

magine you are in a darkened theater, watching a movie, enjoying your popcorn. You're so involved in the story that you almost don't hear the hushed footsteps of an usher coming up beside you.

"Excuse me," he says, tapping you on the shoulder. "But management says it's time to move to another movie."

Of course, you grumble. You don't want to leave this great movie you're watching, but what can you do? You gather your coat, brush the popcorn off your shirt, and follow the usher. He leads you to another theater in the multiplex and you sit down. The second movie starts.

It's not bad. You recognize one of the characters from the first movie, but now he's ten years old. Soon, you are as engrossed as you were with the first movie. Popcorn all down your shirt again, you're slouched in your seat, following the action.

This time you hear the footsteps. The usher again.

"Time to move," he says. He leads you to yet another theater, another movie.

Being a good sport, you sit down, watch. And before long, this third movie is just as engaging. The bad guy from the second movie looks a lot like this movie's main character.

When the usher comes one more time to move you, you've had enough. Each movie has been good, but you're getting sensory whiplash from changing stories so fast. And you're becoming really irritated because you didn't really get a chance to learn what happens in any of them, nor how they relate, if they even do.

Welcome to the tricky world of backstory.

Each movie has been good, but you're getting sensory whiplash from changing stories so fast.

225

If poorly done, it's like switching movies in the middle, and you run a big risk: You can annoy your reader unnecessarily and even lose her entirely. If done right, backstory is a great way to provide emotional depth, historical context, and psychological motivation to your book.

Backstory is literally the *back*ground of the *story*. It's everything that happens before the book begins. It's last year, ten years ago, a past war, and yesterday. It's all history. Taken in small bits, it can be extremely useful, but in large chunks—several consecutive chapters or five or six pages lumped together during a tense scene—it can pull a reader right out of your movie.

Why? Because backstory happened then and elsewhere. We're really most interested in here and now, because now is where your story's highest energy resides. This, of course, is your reader talking. It's not necessarily your opinion, as the writer.

So how and when do you integrate backstory into your story, whether fiction or nonfiction, without overdoing it? How do you weave present and past together so seamlessly that it keeps the energy of the present moment as well as the integral information of the past?

Pros and Cons of Backstory

When we begin writing our books, we feel an urgency to catch the reader up. We have a lot of "important information" to pass along. We think this material is essential: If the reader doesn't know that Jane was traumatized as a child, how will she understand why Jane is so careful with her adult relationships? If the reader doesn't know the entire history of the Scout troop, will he get why the boys are intensely loyal to each other?

Maybe, maybe not. But what's more important—to get your reader engaged in your book or to make sure they understand why you are telling it?

I read that *Mystic River* author Dennis Lehane, a master at intense psychological dramas, once said he feels an alarm bell inside go off whenever he begins to write backstory. That alarm forces him to ask its purpose. Books can be beautiful without any backstory, for example Dave Eggers's *A Heart-breaking Work of Staggering Genius.*

Question your need for backstory, Lehane advised writers; don't use it if you don't have to. I agree. But like knowing when and where to use the device of "telling" in place of "showing," I also find there's a positive place for incorporating backstory.

In fact, it's all about placement.

Do You Know When You're Writing Backstory?

Most writers are astonished to learn how much backstory they include. They don't see it as background but rather as necessary information. Students in my writing classes routinely find that over 50 percent of their first draft is backstory.

This makes sense because in the early drafts of book writing we are still exploring our book's topic, still weighing in our minds what belongs and what doesn't. In a sense, we're still talking to ourselves and haven't yet brought the reader into the conversation.

Backstory hides well on a storyboard, but it surfaces when you begin to put together your chapters, and it can weigh down your manuscript a lot.

How do you recognize when you've gone into backstory? I look for these clues:

Summary—*history summarized or paraphrased*

Exposition—*exposing background information we wouldn't ordinarily find out in the organic flow of the action*

Memories—*thoughts, feelings, or real scenes from past*

Flashback—*reliving memories in current time*

Summary means moving from a specific moment in time that's happening right now to an overview of days or years, events occurring more than once: "Jim always drank

Backstory hides well on a storyboard, but it surfaces when you begin to put together your chapters, and it can weigh down your manuscript a lot.

his coffee black" instead of "Jim was sipping black cofee as usual, jiggling his legs under the counter." Or "Each summer we took a picnic to the river on July 4" instead of "From the picnic basket we grabbed our sandwiches while Fourth of July banners floated above the river's edge." When summary is present, the energy dies down a little. When summary is done in backstory, it dies down a lot.

Exposition is sheer information. Some writers feel it's essential. Even Margaret Mitchell in the beloved story *Gone with the Wind* delivers opening chapters full of battle history. But the funniest example of bad exposition I've ever read was the parody of a butler answering the phone and saying, "No, Master Reginald is not here, he's taken the prize hound Axelrod to the track because his sister Jocelyn who usually takes Axelrod has run off with her lover Rinaldo." None of this is information given in context; it's like reading a list of facts about the family and it's done solely to fill in the audience.

Very unnaturally too.

Memories, sometimes called "recollection," are any bits of recall from the past. These can happen as (1) thoughts ("I thought about how Grandma looked the day she died"), (2) feelings ("I felt awful that morning in junior high when my best friend slapped me"), or (3) scenes ("It was January 3, ten years before. I stepped out of the car and inhaled gas fumes.").

Flashbacks are "felt" memories that are usually triggered by a current event. The character suddenly is back in time, reliving a moment of the past and its accompanying feelings. They are often a combination of thoughts, feelings, and scene. Skilled writers only briefly flash back, giving us small but important context for what's happening now. For instance, to make it clear why a man is suddenly crying as he sees a kid being pummeled at a subway stop, you could write this kind of flashback: "Suddenly James was back in the schoolyard, the snow falling on his bare head, the sounds of his best friend grunting as the bullies beat him. At age ten, James hadn't known what to do with the sickening feeling in his stomach, as if he was being punched, too."

We learn a lot about James in this flashback. It's not necessary to write more.

If you can't spot any backstory in your story, give it to someone to read. You'll probably be surprised to see how much you've been using. Then, once your bits of backstory have been identified, you need to learn what kind they are: summary, memories, exposition, or flashback.

As you discover which they are, you can choose to remove, reduce, or consciously use only what absolutely serves the story. This process requires a very detached attitude.

> If you can't spot any backstory in your story, give it to someone to read. You'll probably be surprised to see how much you've been using.

Exercise: Recognizing Backstory on Your Own
TIME NEEDED: 30 MINUTES

1. Choose one of your islands or chapters. Copy it.
2. Read through the copy carefully, highlighting with a marker every backstory section. Cut and paste these into a document labeled "backstory."
3. Read through this new version—the one without any backstory. What effect does 100 percent present-time story do for you, as a reader?

How to Use Backstory Effectively

While I was working on my novel *Qualities of Light*, I decided to ditch all my backstory. I wanted my book to have plenty of momentum, be a real page-turner. After the purge, my manuscript shrank from 120,000 words to 80,000. I had a huge file of jettisoned background scenes.

Fortunately, I knew a wise writing instructor whose theories about backstory weren't as black-and-white as mine were then. A skilled memoirist and fiction writer, she knew how to weave in just enough backstory without burdening the reader. I hired her to read my manuscript and give me her honest opinion about whether it was better without *any* backstory.

She thought the book had much more momentum. It was now "alive and engaging," but it almost moved too fast, she said. There were places where the emotional potential was not quite realized.

So she asked me to try the same writing exercise John took on in chapter 16 (see page 213). I was to list the most emotional moments of my main character's story, the important turning points.

I found fifteen moments in the book where I felt Molly, my heroine, made a big emotional shift. These were times where she realized or faced something important, not an everyday moment but a major one in the story.

My writing instructor knew of my huge backstory file—I'd bragged to her about how much I'd deleted from the manuscript. She suggested I go on a treasure hunt, scanning the backstory file for any memory scenes that might connect to Molly's turning points. I would probably need to substantially reduce the amount of space these backstory scenes took, she warned me. In other words, I'd have to edit them down from the original version because effective backstory for my novel needed to be short, sweet, and fleeting. We agreed that it took three chapters for readers to engage in the present story. Luckily, Molly didn't have many turning points in those early chapters, so I wouldn't bring in any backstory until chapter 4.

I read my backstory aloud, carefully selecting any small bits—one-liners to two paragraphs—that sounded vibrant, that sang especially loud. I found ten good sections. I took those bits and wove them in here and there, making small changes.

It's hard to describe the difference these changes made. There was now a subtle emotional wave that began rising via the tiny spots of backstory, a wave that wasn't there before. I learned how important it is to connect backstory with something big that was happening in present time. As long as I linked my flashbacks and summaries to what was happening in the main story here and now, they made sense in the sequence of action. They weren't a different movie, in other words.

Whenever your main character is facing a turning point, it's natural that she will slide back to another time when this happened and it didn't go well. But this connective tissue must be present. Otherwise, readers will wonder why the narrator flashes back just then, and why to that particular moment from the past.

The backstory will feel as awkward as text pasted in the wrong place.

For Genre Fiction, Not at the Beginning—Please!

Pete, a new writer in my class, was working on a suspense novel. It had a complicated plot that involved a drug company, two murders, and international warfare.

Pete was excited about his storyboard but as he began writing the chapters, he couldn't get the book off the ground. He asked me to read his first three chapters and tell him why.

The first few pages were tense and engaging. A scary boat ride, a narrow escape. *So far, so good,* I thought. Then I hit page 5. And came to a dead stop.

Pete had decided the reader needed to know the history of the family involved, so he packed the next thirty pages with backstory. We never found out if the hero actually escaped from the sinking ship until page 36. When I pointed this out, Pete hemmed and hawed. It came down to this: like so many writers, he felt it was more important that the reader understand *why* he was telling the story than getting them involved in the story.

Wrong move.

I told Pete that it was way too soon to devote precious opening chapters to telling us what happened before the story got going.

As long as I linked my flashbacks and summaries to what was happening in the main story here and now, they made sense in the sequence of action. They weren't a different movie, in other words.

I suggested an exercise. I asked Pete to go through his opening five chapters and remove all the backstory. Don't toss it, just cut it out and paste it into a separate "backstory" file, I told him, leaving the chapters with only present-time action. Then I asked him to read the backstory-less chapters to see if they felt more alive to him.

This small exercise was illuminating for Pete. It showed him the perils of backstory at the opening of a book. He told me, "I honestly didn't know how much I'd used, but now I see why my book felt so sluggish."

A good rule of thumb for most fiction, both genre and literary: It takes a reader about three chapters to get into a book, to become invested enough not to stop. So the first three chapters need to be as high energy as possible. Personally, I try not to place backstory in those early chapters. I want to give my reader all the encouragement possible to stay connected to my characters and their stories.

When Backstory Is Your Main Story

As you weed out your alternate movies—or at least choose which movie is your primary tale, and give it center stage—you may encounter something very unexpected.

A student of mine, who was writing a novel, experienced this when he was working on eliminating backstory in his novel. As he removed it and reread the backstory-less chapters, he discovered they no longer contained the core of his book. This was not the story he wanted to tell. When he looked in his backstory file on the computer, it was all there—the richness of his characters, their motives, the event he really cared about. His backstory was the main story.

If this happens, a writer has two choices. You can either try to rework your present-time story by weaving in short touch-ins with the backstory, or you can choose the second option: switch the book's focus to the backstory and make it the main story.

Exercise: Choosing the Best Backstory
TIME NEEDED: 45 MINUTES

How do you choose which backstory sections to add back in? As novelist and short-story writer Jhumpa Lahiri says, "In writing a story, one must be careful to choose the essential, most illuminating [details]." Backstory is all about how it serves—or doesn't serve—the present-time story. It's all about emotional effect on the reader.

1. First read the backstory sections aloud. Underline the sections, sentences, paragraphs, or phrases that especially speak to you.

2. Look for the most important lines, and incorporate them—huge amounts of text aren't usually necessary.

3. Pay attention to the feeling you get as you read. Does the feeling connect with the turning point? Are you captivated by the feeling that the backstory information conveys?

If you can answer yes to both of these, then you are on the right track.

18

PUTTING TOGETHER YOUR FIRST DRAFT

ate one winter, I took myself on a writing retreat to a New England bed and breakfast which was a converted farmhouse. Since Thanksgiving, I'd worked from my storyboard, adding images and stronger plot twists to individual scenes. Characters were coming alive on the page, I'd accumulated 120,000 words, about 400 pages, but the book still read as a collection of parts, not a unified whole.

The more I wrote, the more it all felt out of control. I needed to piece the parts together. It was time to create a real first draft so I could see what was working and what wasn't.

I'd held off creating a first draft, because I knew once I had fitted everything into a story sequence, it would be hard for me to go back and rearrange. And so for months I'd let myself explore the deeper themes of the story, playing with character motives and plot, and adding images to each scene. But now I was ready for the next step. An assembly task was ahead of me that would help me see the book as a whole. It was time to decide the order of the main events of my book.

I arrived at the B&B, dumped my bags in my room, and went off to explore. Catering to writers, the inn was sectioned into private areas with cozy sofas, windowseats, and writing nooks. Since I was the only one there, my host, a genial man in his sixties, took me downstairs to a large common room, the living room of the original farmhouse. Two overstuffed chairs flanked a fireplace. Snow was falling outside, and the warm room looked inviting, perfect for a day of concentration.

"I'd love to work down here," I told him. My host showed me the outlet to plug in my laptop and told me how to lift out the unusual wooden damper in the fireplace.

For months I'd let myself explore the deeper themes of the story, playing with character motives and plot, and adding images to each scene. But now I was ready for the next step.

237

The common room's fireplace once burned coal. Its damper was a wooden shelf that snugged into the chimney opening and could be lifted out via a metal door handle. "Be sure you take it out," the farmer said as he left the room. "Otherwise, you might burn the house down."

The next morning, I set up my laptop and pulled out the pages of scenes ready to become a manuscript. On the floor in front of the fireplace, I put my storyboard.

First Drafts

First drafts are the first real indication that a writer actually *has* a book. It's a pivotal moment in the journey—and largely determines whether the book will go on to its final stage of revision and publication. If a writer can make it through the assembly of a first draft, the book begins to feel like a whole.

But there is one huge pitfall to watch for: overthinking.

Putting together a first draft must be a completely mind-less, robotic process. Don't think too much. Just complete the process and get all relevant parts into the new document, otherwise your Inner Critic may surface during the process. If you begin to start editing the small bits of writing being assembled into the first draft, you will lose the objectivity re-quired to get through first-draft assembly. Your Inner Critic may start in with:

This is truly awful, you know.

Maybe I'll do a little rewriting now—it can't hurt.

Hey, what's this doing in chapter 1? What about putting it in chapter 6?

This results in a total shut-down. And this is where a lot of writers give up. Don't fall into this trap. (For more on the Inner Critic, see chapter 4.)

I took a look at my storyboard on the floor and went to work on six scenes for chapter 1, as they were listed on the storyboard. I followed its map and located them in my computer, then opened a new document. Following the map, I pasted each scene into the clean chapter 1 in sequence. Done.

Chapter 2 also went pretty smoothly. If I kept with simple cut-and-paste, no editing, my first draft would be ready to print out by lunchtime.

But disaster struck when I approached the islands for chapter 3. I started intently reading the islands. Big mistake. They seemed disgustingly flaccid, horizontal writing at its worst. *What was I thinking?*

Completely ignoring my own rules, I stopped assembling the draft. I began editing the islands, certain I could remain detached and it would only take a few minutes. An hour went by, as I rewrote in an attempt to get the characters to stop their self-conscious dance, tried to ignite some sparks in the story. Nothing improved. The writing actually got worse, although I couldn't see that at the time.

In my writing life, the universe has often conspired to point out mistakes in a dramatic—even humorous—way. After spending an hour revising, I decided to take a break. Still engrossed in the chapter's complications, I went over to the room's fireplace, struck a match and lit the newspaper and kindling, then went back to my seat on the floor.

Dry wood caught immediately, and the fire blazed. Suddenly, the room filled with smoke. The damper!

I grabbed the iron handle, which was hot, reached in, and pulled out the now-smoking wooden damper. I opened all the windows and let the fireplace and my head cool. I stopped revising and went back to cutting and pasting.

By the time the farmer and his wife returned from afternoon errands, the room had cleared of smoke. I had completed my first draft. The damper was only slightly singed. My fingers healed quickly.

I learned an interesting lesson too: Writing a book sometimes requires that you *don't* write.

Completely ignoring my own rules, I stopped assembling the draft. I began editing the islands, certain I could remain detached and it would only take a few minutes.

Honor the Sequence

There's a natural sequence of steps in writing a book. There's a time to write, a time to assemble, and a time to revise. If you follow this sequence, it will help you avoid unnecessary run-ins with the Inner Critic. Writers who don't follow it, who try to combine these steps, don't usually finish their books. Often they start revising before they should. Revising asks the writer to step back, become analytical, and essentially stop the organic flow.

I had to train myself to honor this approach. It was hard because I love the heat of a story, which often only emerges in final revision. I really enjoy revising. I get more juice from fixing small problems, like which tense to use, while conveniently ignoring more global ones, such as issues with character or plot. These are the slower parts of book work, and it requires trust on my part to not meet the revision needs until the draft is finished.

But when the writing is frustrating, it's easy to go for the pleasurable sidetrack of revising too soon. Sitting in that common room, struggling with my chapters, I didn't see that most of my struggle came from wanting to rush the process.

As a teacher, I often wondered why so many writers gave up before completing their first drafts. I realized it's because the first draft assembly is a turning point in the book-writing journey that contains hard work and not much romance. The writer has to be willing to live with the imperfect and uninspired writing that's all too visible as she pastes in the sequence of islands written months ago.

Here's the lesson I learned that day when I almost burned down a farmhouse inn, because I neglected a very basic step. There's a time in the book-writing journey to be purely mechanical, to make sure all the steps are done right, to remember the obvious. Don't be tempted to revise your work before it's time to revise, or you will lose track of what's right in front of you. You need to be OK with what Anne

Lamott, author of *Bird by Bird,* calls the "shitty first draft."

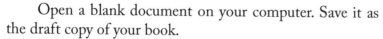

Exercise: Assembling Your First Draft
TIME NEEDED: 2–3 HOURS

Open a blank document on your computer. Save it as the draft copy of your book.

1. Locate the files you've created with your writing for this book. Don't worry about how they are arranged. But do make sure they are labeled with key words, so you can do a global computer search for them easily, e.g., "attic scene," "interview with Bob."

2. Spread out your storyboard on a work surface.

3. Using the cue cards on your storyboard, search for the first piece of writing.

4. Select it.

5. Copy and paste it—*without reading it!*—into the blank document. Save it.

6. Continue to do this with all the cue cards for chapter 1 on your storyboard.

7. Keep going—continue with chapter 2, 3, 4, all the way to the end of the storyboard.

8. Print out a double-spaced copy, with title page and your byline (By_____).

Please! Don't read over your first draft yet. Give it a rest, do something else. You need time to get objective, to relax the Inner Critic. Celebrate your achievement but also refrain from showing your first draft to your spouse or partner, kids, or even your writers' group. First drafts are nowhere near ready for other eyes yet. It's the Inner Critic who is urging this unwise action.

Please! Don't read over your first draft yet. Give it a rest, do something else. You need time to get objective, to relax the Inner Critic.

During the first-draft assembly, most writers notice big holes in the manuscript, ones not caught on the storyboard. Rather than filling them now, simply list them in your writer's notebook or in the margins of the computer file, as sidebar notes. You can also put the questions and concerns in parentheses after the moment in question. This helps you gain the detachment you'll need to take your draft into revision. Some of my notes look like this:

Add more here.

What happened to the beach house? Can it come in
  again?

What's Chad's deeper reaction here?

Don't try to solve the problem now. Just get through the assembly task, print out your manuscript pages, stack them on your writing desk or wherever you can admire them from a distance.

That night at the inn, I went out with friends. I had a great dinner, knowing that my manuscript was resting.

How Long to Let It Rest?

I let my manuscripts rest at least a week, two if I can. The best way to do this is to get away, physically, from the book. I take walks, see friends, go to the movies, let my brain regain balance. The goal is to get some distance.

If I can't stand not writing during this time, I give myself regular freewrites. But I let myself only write outside my story, about something else going on in my life, about my hopes and dreams for this book, about my fears.

Most professional writers I know take a complete break after first draft assembly. It's healthy, it keeps them out of trouble with this tender stage, and it allows them to refresh and fill the creative well. But they don't wait too long. It's important to gain enough objectivity to revise well, but not so long that you lose momentum for your book.

How will you know you are ready? Read through one chapter as a test. If you're able to scan the pages *without* thinking it's God's gift to readers everywhere or it's the worst writing ever done and you'd better stop now, then you are good to go. If you begin reading and find these two reactions coming to mind and heart, stop, put the pages back down, take more time off. Why is so much time needed? Because it takes time to make the switch from writer to reader.

The First Read-Through

You think you're ready? OK, then, now's the time to travel on your final stage of the book-writing journey. Set aside a couple of afternoons, a whole day if you have the stamina. This is one of the longer exercises in this book, but it's essential for moving forward.

Exercise: Objective Read-Through
TIME NEEDED: 6–8 HOURS

---

1. Find a comfortable place to settle in with a regular pen, a yellow highlighter, and your printed first draft.

2. Begin reading the draft from start to finish. Don't skip around—be a reader now, not a writer.

3. Whenever you find a spot where you're happy with the writing, where you're completely engaged, make a checkmark in the margin with your pen.

4. Whenever you find a spot where your attention wanders, make a slash in the margin with your yellow highlighter.

5. Whenever you notice poor chronology, changing verb tense, facts without continuity (a red car becomes green), or other problems make a slash in the margin with your yellow highlighter.

Read through one chapter as a test. If you're able to scan the pages without thinking it's God's gift to readers everywhere or it's the worst writing ever done and you'd better stop now, then you are good to go.

6. Don't try to fix anything at this point.

7. If ideas come of how you might change or correct something, or questions you might want to ask yourself about that section, write notes in the margin of the first draft.

8. Continue reading and marking up your first draft until you finish your book.

The Dilemma of Creative Tension

Do you know someone who can't keep a secret? Most people do. It's often not because this person is bad, but because they just can't tolerate the inner tension of knowing something and being asked to keep it to themselves. They have to spill it, to someone, somewhere, and they feel intense relief at doing so.

Similar pressure builds as our book begins to cook. This inner tension is very much like a marvelous secret, something we know and feel excited about. (Or not excited, depending on how the writing goes that day.) If the build-up gets too intense and our ability to handle this creative tension is pretty low, we spill the book.

We share our secret with anyone we can get close to for a few minutes. The tension dissipates.

That's, actually, not such a relief in book writing. It's a big problem. Why? Because it's quite hard to build back up the tension, to fuel the writing again. We can't figure it out; it just seems like that lovely momentum is now flat. The precious secret is now not just our secret, it's the world's.

Worst case scenario: We choose poorly and the person we share our book with does not treat it well. It gets trashed; even without meaning to be, the feedback is deflating.

Most often, it's not actually the feedback that causes us to stop writing after prematurely sharing our work. It's the fact that all creative tension is gone. There's no more steam to propel the creative engine forward.

I've done this more times than I can say, embarrassingly

enough. I've shared my work with spouse and friend, stranger and coworker, and I've learned from many, many hard experiences when the writing's not really ready. From hardship, I've taught myself how long to hold the work inside, how much I can share and still keep the creative tension pumping.

When the skill of holding creative tension is developed, you can move forward quite fast on your project. An internal hum is always there, it lives inside you, and the people and places on your pages are part of you now. You know the work momentum isn't in danger of disappearing.

That's the best time to find good support, the right feedback to help your writing reflect back to you, from someone else's objective eyes, what it really is saying.

Learning to handle the creative tension with our own writing process, knowing when it's time to take the risk to bring that work out into the air for others to see, these are big steps in the process of becoming a writer. They lead to self-confidence in our own work. Self-confidence leads to willingness to risk more.

It's all a beautiful circle.

Exercise: What If?
TIME NEEDED: 15-20 MINUTES

This exercise was inspired by a wonderful writing book called *What If?* written by Pamela Painter and Anne Bernays. Using their book always opens me to limitless possibilities in my writing. It's a great exercise to give feedback to yourself on a stuck chapter.

1. Read one of your chapters that seems incomplete.

2. Highlight the section that seems most confusing.

3. Make a list of any questions you could use to open doorways for yourself. What haven't you said, explored, tried yet, with this part of your book?

List ten possible answers to the question this "What if?" exercise generated, letting yourself explore any ideas that come.

Then, implement one of the new ideas into your incomplete chapter—see what happens. Did it open a doorway for you?

CONGRATULATIONS! YOU'VE COMPLETED PART TWO OF THE BOOK-WRITING JOURNEY!

An objective read-through is the last big step in writing your book. Now you hold a printed first draft in your hands. Together with your storyboard, you're ready for your final stage of the journey: revision.

Like you did at the end of part one, take time to celebrate this accomplishment, one that many book writers never achieve. Remember the letter of congratulations you wrote months ago, after you built your first storyboard? Now's the time for another.

Write to yourself about all you've accomplished in these past weeks or months. Note how far you've come in writing your book—crafting islands, working with your storyboard and three acts, creating the draft you now hold in your hands.

Again, be sure to plan some fun time for yourself as a rest and reward. More celebration ideas from my students, especially for the end of part two:

✓ A real vacation—somewhere exotic
✓ Long drive in the country
✓ Front-row tickets to the playoffs
✓ A day alone at home—just me!
✓ A concert

- ✓ Weekend at the cabin
- ✓ Fancy dinner out with the family—who've supported me through thick and thin
- ✓ Throwing a party for my writers' group

Part Three

Develop:
Making Your Book Shine

DEVELOP:
MAKING YOUR BOOK SHINE

Developing means refining your book—taking what you wrote and shaped in the planning and writing phases, then switching even more to the reader's point of view in order to see the manuscript anew. This is true re-visioning. More than just line or substantive editing (although they are certainly important), revision work asks the questions: Is this the book I set out to write? Is it speaking the truth I wanted to share? Is it an engaging story that will keep my reader involved?

Developing your book will require that you let go of what is not serving your story—but it's also the most rewarding of the three stages because your book is almost ready!

19

Revision: Refining Content, Structure, and Language with the Questions List

Before a painter picks up his brush, he studies the landscape before him, carefully considering what to include. His eye passes over a wealth of wonderful material that lies before him: trees, bushes, a winding road, several houses, three flower gardens. He makes a frame with his two hands, looking for the arrangement that will be most pleasing on canvas. He tries various views. In the end he focuses in on what he wants, and in the process, chooses what to edit out to make the painting stronger. He makes a detailed sketch and then looks at what he chose.

In revision we do this too. We step back and consider what we've created.

Revision asks us to get an objective view of our first draft, to notice where our unconscious tendencies for wordiness or sparseness might have taken over. We see where we need to expand and contract, what's not working and what is. We gain new appreciation for our story—as it becomes more than we ever thought it could be. We are looking at what needs to stay and what needs to go to create the strongest manuscript.

I love revision—but I didn't always love it. My affection came gradually, from working as an editor at a small press for eighteen years, where I revised hundreds of manuscripts. The goal was never to makeover the manuscript. Instead, I looked for the book's original spark and tried to bring that potential to the page. To do that, I needed to study the strengths and weaknesses of content, structure, and language in each book.

As I learned to master revision, I began to notice changes in my own writing. My first drafts were becoming clearer from the get go. I was publishing more easily. At first I didn't connect this improvement with learning the art of revision.

We gain new appreciation for our story—as it becomes more than we ever thought it could be.

255

Then I published a short story and the literary journal's editor asked me if I had any editing background myself. When I said yes, she nodded. "I can always spot the writer who knows the joy of revision," she said.

You've come a long way with your manuscript. You've crafted islands and developed a storyboard with a three-act structure. You've built your first draft, filling in the missing pieces from character to container. You've done great work! Now you are on the final leg of your book journey. You'll need to cultivate a new mindset for this part of the process: detachment.

You need to step back from your book to get an overview of your work. It's the only way you can accurately analyze its content, structure, and language, and look at unconscious tendencies. You need to objectively see where you tend to expand or contract your narrative, giving too many details or not enough, skipping over important setting descriptions or transitioning too quickly from one scene to another (usually during a highly emotional moment). You need to notice those tricky sections where you overwrite—tell something when it is already well shown on the previous page or over-explain what is obvious. Or where a love for tight prose gets in the way of deepening the moment into meaning for a reader.

Revision, literally "seeing again," is the point in the journey when you consider your book as a whole and take it to a new level of universality.

You'll be doing more than catching awkward sentences, typos, and misspellings. You'll be asking thoughtful questions of yourself and your story.

The goal is to uncover emotional truths, to shape your writing so it can offer these truths to your reader. You want to let your story touch your reader's life as much as it touched yours.

The Search for Emotional Truth

Tom, one of my students, came to me with his manuscript, an inspirational business book; it was ready for revision.

Tom had an agent interested in his book. This was good news. The bad news was that Tom was stuck, his deadline fast approaching with nothing solid to submit.

Each book signals a journey that is unique to the writer, an exploration of a particular truth that fascinates him. Tom's lifelong pursuit was to grasp how two individuals talk with each other in a way that satisfies both of their needs. From his workshop notes, he'd collected over two dozen stories of negotiators in business, family, and community life.

A natural storyteller who knew how to craft engaging anecdotes to illustrate almost any topic, Tom presented important ideas in a personal way. Because of Tom's popular workshops on negotiation, his agent was confident this book would be a winner. Tom wasn't so sure.

Publishers buy manuscripts when they communicate passion for a topic, presented in a unique way that speaks to a reader. To get this passion, revision lets the emotional truths we've learned during the process of writing this particular story come forward. We revise to make this truth as unimpeded and clear as we can. It's a bit like cleaning a window to let more light in, or as Pulitzer-prize-winning author Wallace Stegner said, "All you want in the finished print is the clean statement of the lens, which is yourself, on the subject that has been absorbing your attention."

Publishers buy manuscripts when they communicate passion for a topic, presented in a unique way that speaks to a reader.

Another way of looking at this: Revision's goal is to let the manuscript become strong enough to stand on its own without the author having to make any interpretations. In my writing classes we talk about "getting out of the room" and letting your book and its readers have that wonderful conversation that all good literature fosters. Without you, the author, having to be there to make sure the reader is getting it.

This concept was frightening to Tom, a first-time book writer, who wondered, *What will happen to my theories if I'm not there to explain them?* Or worse: *If it changes entirely—will it still be mine? Will revision cause it to lose its original spark?*

This is where Tom was stuck.

For me, the refinement that comes in revision lets in the real music of a book. There's a sense of multiple sections in an orchestra finally playing together. They create a sound larger than any individual part.

But to get this richness of sound, Tom needed to look at revision in each of its three aspects, and in this order: first content, then structure, then language.

Content—The First Step

Content is the foundation of any book. It's the plot in fiction, the defining events in memoir, the information in nonfiction. There's a certain amount that must be present for the book to make sense to a reader. In a writer's head, the content is there. But when revising for content, you want to make sure it's also on the page.

So we take an inventory of the book's content.

I like to do it in two stages. I start with the whole manuscript, reviewing the table of contents or my storyboard of topics. Does each larger section have substance? If yes, I examine the book's chapters and the material within each chapter, looking for any parts that feel incomplete, where information is missing or extraneous.

It is in content revision that you'll discover if you are a naturally contracting or expanding writer. Do you prematurely edit your islands too much, so that the first draft feels more like a brief sketch, with sentences counted out like coins? If so, the richness of your book's sound may be underdeveloped and content revision will show you where you need to expand your story.

Or maybe you feel unsure about whether your reader will get the picture you're trying to paint, so you add a bit more than is really needed. You sense it doesn't contribute to the story's flow but you're worried about leaving it out. You may need to take a deep breath and choose to delete some content. Less is sometimes more in content revision.

Your Questions List

So, as you read for content, you are going to see problems. You will be tempted to make notes on your manuscript, such as, "fix this description" or "make dialogue longer."

Too much of this will turn your manuscript into a deadening list of chores that can stop you in your tracks. Instead, craft the problems you see as questions.

The first task I asked Tom to try was the questions list. A list of questions will automatically put a writer in the position of curious observer, the fascinated inquirer. They allow you to become open to new ideas that maybe you weren't ready to grasp during the planning and writing stages of your book journey. And questions *always* attract answers—in a truly synchronous way.

Some examples of content questions from Tom and my other students:

- *Does the reader need to know more in chapter 2 about listening skills?*
- *How does John get from the cabin to downtown Poughkeepsie? Do I need to add a traveling scene as transition?*
- *Which of Mary's phone calls is most important to the plot? (This writer saw the need to delete one.)*
- *How can I best explain the backstory on page 45 in fewer pages?*

> *A list of questions will automatically put a writer in the position of curious observer, the fascinated inquirer. And questions always attract answers—in a truly synchronous way.*

Exercise: Content Inventory and Questions List
TIME NEEDED: 1-2 HOURS

1. Skim through each chapter of your manuscript; then, at the top of the chapter's title page, write one sentence that describes the meat of that chapter—its purpose in the larger story. Continue until you have all chapters described.

2. Carefully read these sentences in sequence. Are there any places where you see missing steps or scenes that would be needed to make your story flow better for a reader? Are there any places where you've added unnecessary material? This may show you exactly where you need to expand or contract.

3. Now open to a new page in your writer's notebook. On the top of the page write "Content Questions." List what you discovered during your review, but write these problems as questions, as in the examples on the previous page.

The Extras File

As I review each chapter during content revision, often I find material that is missing—but equally often, material that has to go. All that work! I'd spent weeks on some of those paragraphs.

Rather than just delete them, I open a new document on my computer. I name it "Extras." It becomes the holding tank for excess sentences, phrases, and paragraphs I still love but don't serve the manuscript. (Once I even put four chapters in my Extras file!)

It always makes me feel better to know I am not throwing these gems away forever. They are safe in my computer, waiting for their right place. Not surprisingly, I find myself using them later—during other parts of the revision process, for example, when I need a bit more backstory or another line of dialogue.

Structure—Step Two: The Arrangement of Islands

If your content inventory shows your book is aligned, great! Now it's time to look at the alignment within each chapter. Structure considers the placement of each island within a chapter, as well as the order of chapters within the entire book.

It creates a logical and intuitive flow of material, organized from the reader's point of view.

This is key. It's essential to transition fully to a reader's viewpoint during structure revision.

Some writers aren't able to analyze their books' structure without feedback from another writer. Tom was one of these. He suspected his book's structure needed rethinking but he didn't know where. He needed a fresh reader. That's where I came in. I read it carefully and saw a big concern: Would Tom's reader be able to understand chapter 2's material so early in the book?

At first Tom was reluctant to change the placement of chapter 2. He thought the order made sense, but I asked him to consider his reader and try switching chapter 2 with chapter 4. He was amazed; the structure was much stronger.

Structural revision is good medicine for manuscripts. You approach it like a jigsaw puzzle, and you use questions again: Does your current placement of islands make sense for Act 1? How about Act 2? Act 3?

My first novel went through a similar experience as Tom's book, in its structure revision. I couldn't figure out why it wasn't selling to a publisher. After a year of submitting the manuscript and receiving no takers, a Midwestern small press sent me two pages of very helpful structuring feedback. Two editors advised jettisoning the first four chapters—they said the story actually began in chapter 5. Like Tom, I was stubborn about making the change. But once I tried it, I saw the wisdom immediately. The structural revision now started the story more squarely in its true emotional arc—the relationship between father and daughter.

After I reworked it and began sending it out again, the manuscript was accepted by a publisher within a month. Good medicine, indeed.

I was lucky these editors took the time to do a structure read. I would have saved time if I had had a reader check for structure before sending the manuscript out, or if I had done the exercise that follows.

Does your current placement of islands make sense for Act 1, Act 2, and Act 3?

Exercise: Structure Read
TIME NEEDED: 3-4 HOURS

1. When your manuscript feels revised for content, read through it in its entirety.

2. Now craft a short sentence that gives the purpose of each main event or turning point in the book ("John leaves the house after the fight" or "how to position the hands on the keyboard"). List these sentences in your writer's notebook, in the order the events appear in your manuscript.

3. Study the list of sentences. Does this order create an easily followed sequence? Does your opening launch the reader immediately into your topic (if nonfiction) or the tension of your story (if memoir or fiction)?

4. Without looking at the manuscript, rearrange the sentences to see if a new order might serve better.

Language—Step Three: The Passion of Your Story

Subtlest of the three areas of revision is language. (We'll explore its attributes of pacing, voice, and theme in the following chapters.) To start revising the language of your book, you must look for the passion you started with.

Passion engages a reader by saying, "This book offers you a unique and useful viewpoint on a vital subject." If enough of your passion for the story ends up on the page, your language will reflect that. Your passion will be revealed in your choice of words and the tone of your writing—for example, scholarly versus friendly, dramatic versus understated. You will make visible your own heartfelt journey with your book's subject.

At language revision, it's time to revisit your original reasons for writing the book, the three questions from chapter 1. Have your reasons changed? Or have you just lost track of your GPS during the sheer work of writing? Now's the time to connect your manuscript back with the passion that began it.

You can tell whether you've kept the passionate edge or not because passion is about risk. It requires you to explore new things. As you work on language revision, you look for too-safe passages that hide your true beliefs from the reader. Scout out any careful and controlled prose and replace it with vivid voice (see chapter 22).

Passion means connecting your heart, mind, and spirit with your writing so that it reflects what you care about, what you believe in. The reader senses authenticity in your words, the connection between your life and your writing. Your book begins to ring with emotional truth—that elusive element we talked about at the beginning of this chapter.

Passion means connecting your heart, mind, and spirit with your writing so that it reflects what you care about, what you believe in.

Exercise: Language Questions
Time needed: Ongoing

1. In your writer's notebook, dedicate a new page to "Language Questions."

2. Set a timer for twenty minutes and begin to list any questions still unanswered about your book. Focus on questions that have meaning to you personally: why you are writing this book, your involvement with the material, your concerns about it going out into the world.

3. Notice any discomfort generated by these questions. Ask yourself, *How is this discomfort connected to my life? What parallels do I see? If I focus on addressing a question in my outer life, does it help answer the question for my book?*

I found it helpful to persist with this list until I had twenty to thirty questions. A few that greatly assisted the language revision on my novel were these:

- *How does it feel to be fully known and received by another person?*
- *Does that state of being fully received change a person? How?*
- *Does it change others around the person?*
- *What if this change could result in others around the person being rescued from themselves?*

This isn't always easy. Sometimes we unconsciously repeat patterns that have worked in our writing in the past. When this happened to me with one of my books, at first I didn't even have words to form fresh questions. Only old images surfaced. I looked back at my collages and image-based representations of my current story, and eventually words finally came to define new questions, creating a dance between what I knew and what I was open to not knowing. Each creative work should leave us looking at the world anew—this is what keeps our language fresh.

Brenda Miller and Suzanne Paola say it well in their book, *Tell It Slant*: "Revision becomes not a chore, but the essence of the writing act itself. What came before cleared the way for what is to come."

As Tom worked through his language revision questions, he began to realize he was actually bored with his topic. The writing didn't quite communicate Tom's own struggles with the art of negotiation, as the stories in his workshops did so well. His passion was not evident in the words and images he'd chosen. This accounted for its too-pat approach.

He realized he'd been under such pressure from the deadline given by the interested agent, that he had sacrificed quality. As the passion for his book project faded, he unconsciously began reducing his participation in the story. This deadened the prose, producing lackluster writing.

So Tom began to write about this unease with his manuscript, revisiting the passion he originally had for his topic. I suggested a few ideas on how to get it back on the page:

1. Bring in new topics you don't know about (*What don't I know here? What do I need to find out?*).

2. Adventure into what scares but fascinates you (*What if I try this? Why am I holding back?*).

3. Connect with something you believe in (*What do I really feel or think about this?*).

As you become aware of dead language in your manuscript, you rework the wording with more vivid verbs, more interesting images. You begin to insert more of your own journey with your book's topic. You may even find that your keenest interest lies in a slightly different slant. Tom did. He discovered that his real passion lay in family negotiation rather than business deals, especially communication between teenagers and parents.

When you take risks, your writing becomes fresh.

This change of perspective produced writing so fertile, so much the opposite of his experience with being stuck, Tom said it felt like a faucet had been turned on. The agent was pleased too.

When you take risks, your writing becomes fresh. Language revision often awakens a completely different perspective on your book.

Exercise: Rekindling the Romance
Time needed: 20 minutes

1. Set a kitchen timer for ten minutes. Ask your book: *What did first I love about you?*

2. List whatever you really love about your topic. Maybe there are certain aspects of the setting or characters or the story you're telling that ring true.

3. Set the timer again. Freewrite (without editing) for ten minutes about what you intended to say in this writing. What was the original point of the piece?

Revision creates a manageable way to allow what we still don't know about our book to emerge, to reacquaint ourselves with its beautiful shadows. Most readers want to hear about the struggle as well as the goal achieved. Through polishing your writing, you shine light into dark places, make them visible.

Remember, a well-painted landscape shows shadows as well as light. This is why writing with conscious revision becomes a way of healing ourselves, as well as revealing the whole story.

20

FINDING THE RIGHT RHYTHM— THE ART OF PACING

On my first visit to the Metropolitan Opera in New York City, I saw Puccini's *Turandot*. It was a vast and elegant production, with a story that brought me to tears.

Much of the Met's success comes from top-notch performers and elaborate staging, but as a new operagoer, it was the pacing of *Turandot* that did it for me. I was so engaged in the flow of Puccini's story, I totally forgot I was sitting in a packed auditorium.

Pacing is one of the most complex and exciting tools to use at the revision stage of your book journey. To get certain emotional effects, you need the right pacing. Your pacing choices control the amount of dialogue, tell you where to intensify the action, where to pause for description. As you learn to work with pacing, you can begin to perfect the speed of your delivery, the balance of anecdotes and concepts.

Puccini's opera doesn't boast about its strong pacing—as an engaged viewer, I was only aware of the excellent story. Your book's pacing needs to be so invisible to the reader that he can move through your material without stumbling, skipping, or having to read anything twice. Good pacing means your reader never awakens from the literary dream you've been so busy crafting.

Pacing as Rhythm

Pacing has two levels that a book writer must attend to. First, you need to listen for the rhythm of your outer story, the events in your book and how they unfold for the reader. Once you have discovered this external rhythm, you move on to the more subtle level of pacing work: the rhythm of the

Good pacing means your reader never awakens from the literary dream you've been so busy crafting.

inner story, the level of emotional meaning.

This may seem odd, but many professional writers swear by it. Stuart Dybek, author of many books including the short-story collection *Coast of Chicago,* writes, "It's difficult for me to bring a story to its conclusion unless I feel that I've found not just its rhythm but also its sound." I call it external and internal pacing. Rhythm, or external pacing, provides the movement of your story. Internal pacing (sound) gives flow to its meaning and how this meaning unfolds for the reader.

So your next task in the revision process is to become aware of the step-by-step progress of words, sentences, paragraphs, and chapters on each page. Not unlike adjusting the radio dial to eliminate static, you begin to tune in to the external rhythm of your book. Once you start to do this, it becomes easier to see where the flow stops and starts. Then you can begin to adjust words, sentences, paragraphs, and chapters to let this flow move forward unimpeded.

The second level of pacing work is more subtle. You must figure out where the emotional arc of each chapter lies—where it peaks with the biggest emotional impact for the reader. I like to imagine a bridge spanning my story from beginning to end and a reader traveling across the arc of this bridge, getting more and more involved with the emotional meaning of my book until it reaches a peak emotional moment. You manipulate this by how you place the moments of container (the physical setting and emotional environment of your story—see chapter 16) and the amount of scene versus summary.

Pacing the Outer Story

How fast is your story moving? Does it gallop through each moment or does it linger? Speed is the main factor in pacing your book's outer story. And speed depends on very mechanical things: how many syllables in your words, how often you vary sentence and paragraph lengths, how you begin and end each chapter. (An easy example: Compare a page from a Stephen King thriller with one from a book by Ian McKuen, and see how the language impacts pacing.)

One way to see this is to read each chapter of your book aloud and listen to the rhythm of word, sentence, and paragraph in each chapter. As novelist André Dubus wrote, "Reading aloud allows me to get physical and use my body so I can see mistakes more clearly. Is this the wrong rhythm? Are these repetitions? I hear things that I don't see."

When I use the technique of reading aloud, I can tell by my word choice which sections are slow because my voice slows down, usually because there are too many multi-syllable words and long sentences.

Other writers study external pacing by looking for the amount of white space on each page. One novelist I know prints out his chapters, laying the pages next to each other in a line to study the visual effect of white space against paragraph blocks of black text, an easy way to notice where you have too slow or too fast passages.

Other writers study external pacing by looking for the amount of white space on each page.

From these two simple techniques, you can learn which types of prose move faster than others. For example, whenever I try the white space exercise, I can immediately see that dialogue passages contain much more than descriptive sections. So it makes sense that dialogue is a speedier part of a book.

I also look at any one-line paragraphs. These are tiny stop signs in the middle of a narrative. The reader takes notice, pauses to absorb the effect. I make sure the effect is worth pausing for, at that point in the narrative.

One of my students, Judith, was working on her nonfiction book. It contained about seventy case studies. As she revised it, she began to adjust the rhythm of how her stories worked with her book's information. Judith said this process of learning pacing "completely altered" how she presented her material in the final version. "I learned the value of varying sentence length, where material seemed repetitive, where to condense sections of dialogue," she said. "Pacing showed me how to move material around in a way that breathed life into my pages."

Pamela, a published poet, was revising her first young-adult novel and saw how proper pacing created tension in her stories. Pacing worked much better, she said, than the "contrived plot twists" she was using to get tension before. Pacing does pay off fast, in Pamela's case by creating an instant page-turner.

But you can probably guess why pacing is a revision process, not something you work on in first draft. Until you put all your islands in place, until you know what your inner story is about, you can't really "hear" how everything works together. You're not able perceive the rhythm of your book yet. So I always tell writers to put pacing to the side while writing initial islands, crafting the storyboard, working on the first draft of a new book. It's only at revision that we are able to get the overview that's essential for pacing.

As you begin working on pacing in your outer story, remember that the goal is pretty simple: keep the pace varied. Make sure you vary the pace of every level of your outer story—from words to full chapters.

This will greatly affect the pacing of the inner story, as we'll discover later in this chapter.

From Words to Paragraphs

Readers know intuitively whenever writing bogs down from too-slow flow, or when it moves too quickly and causes us to lose our breath—and our footing in the story. We usually stop reading and put those books aside. When I began writing my own books, I studied how my favorite writers kept my interest, how their word choice, sentence length, and paragraphs created a smooth pace I couldn't let go of.

Then I became a professional editor, working on the pacing of other writers' manuscripts. I saw how easy it was to adjust pace with just three steps.

1. **Make every word count.** Choose vivid verbs and image-rich nouns, and avoid unnecessary adverbs (*really, very, utterly,* etc.) whenever possible because they slow things down. Watch out for empty adverbs too: *beautifully, sadly, cleverly.*

2. **Vary the sentence lengths within each paragraph.** Whenever you have more than two or three sentences back to back that are longer than ten words, make the next few sentences shorter.

3. **Vary paragraph lengths.** When you want the reader to linger to absorb reflective writing or the meaning of something that's just happened, try longer paragraphs. Consider one-sentence paragraphs for very strong impact.

Word choice is learned by reading good writing. It educates you to what's possible—a great image, a use of a new word. You begin to notice the flavorless spots in your own prose, you replace *tree* with *oak, car* with *red Chevrolet.* You might also see how often you use ten-dollar words when a fifty-cent word will serve your reader much better.

Learning to vary sentence length is even simpler. Look for where you want emphasis, where you want to wake up your reader. Use shorter sentences there. By the way, gone is the rule that sentences must be complete. Not anymore. Much writing these days is conversational in tone.

Of all these steps, the most important—and the most underused—is varying paragraph length. Most of us are ridiculously unconscious about our paragraphs. We write in a set rhythm, a pulse that feels good. We don't really notice that we're churning out page after page of five-line (or four-line or three-line) paragraphs. We don't notice the sleepy pace this creates, no matter what excitement is happening in our plot or subject matter.

So when you do your visual check of white space and dense text on each page, notice paragraph lengths. Monotonous

Word choice is learned by reading good writing. It educates you to what's possible—a great image, a use of a new word.

visual rhythm imprints surprisingly fast on your reader's mind. It overshadows the actual meaning of your writing. As I mentioned on page 271, whenever I suspect this is happening with my own writing, I print out a chapter and lay the pages sequentially on the floor. If I squint at them, I can see patterns of white space and text—the visual rhythm of the outer story.

When I look at paragraph lengths, the fun begins. I play with them, making some longer, some shorter. Five lines here, two there, seven there. I look for natural moments to break each paragraph, moments that enhance what's being said.

Page-Turners: Your Chapter Endings

For twelve years, I wrote a syndicated weekly newspaper column. I only had six hundred words so I learned to wrap up the column neatly. The ending was always tied up with a clever image, a bright red bow on a tidy package.

Then I went back to college for my M.F.A. in fiction. One of my teachers noticed my tendency to neaten up my chapter endings. "Do you really want your reader to close your book after each chapter?" she asked me. "Or do you want a page turner?"

I definitely wanted a page turner.

She advised me to read the last paragraph of each chapter and rework it slightly, to leave readers with an unanswered question, an unfinished situation, or a foreshadowing of problems to come.

For a closure lover, this was a challenge. My teacher was asking me to leave my chapters in a state of wondering, of inquiry, not concluded. The poet John Keats touched on this with the theme of "negative capability" that appears in much of his work—the willingness to be unresolved and accept that uncertainty is a good thing. Another poet, Rainier Maria Rilke, also explored the value of unanswered questions as a way to get deeper into writing. In his 1903 book, *Letters to a Young Poet,* Rilke advised "to have patience with everything unresolved in your heart and to try to love the questions themselves as if they were locked rooms or books written in a very foreign language."

He told his student that the answers to these questions "could not be given to you now, because you would not be able to live them. And the point is to live everything. Live the questions now" in hope that we can "live [our] way into the answer."

Readers enjoy this suspension, this openness, in books as a whole and at the end of chapters in particular, but at first, this idea felt impossible for me as a writer. I had to deliberately unlearn twelve years of a certain writing style. It took months to figure out new endings for my chapters, but once I began to play with the idea of creating incomplete endings to my chapters, leaving something unresolved, the pace of the outer story increased dramatically.

When my novel was published, readers confirmed this. I still have the letters and emails saying, "I stayed up all night reading your book" and "I couldn't put it down—I finished one chapter and had to begin the next one to find out what happened."

Pacing the outer story will leave you with these kinds of results. It's definitely worth the time in revision to pay attention to how your story structure flows.

Once I began to play with the idea of creating incomplete endings to my chapters, leaving something unresolved, the pace of the outer story increased dramatically.

Exercise: Studying Outer-Story Pacing
TIME NEEDED: 1 HOUR

1. Find a published book in your genre and open it at random. Squint at several pages, studying the ratio of white space to dense text.

2. Read two pages aloud. Listen for the rhythm. Does it feel fast or slow? Where does the pace vary?

3. Locate a chapter that contains a suspenseful moment or turning point. Notice if the sentences are short or long, if the verbs are particularly vivid. Are there any adverbs? How did this writer adjust outer-story pacing to create this tension?

4. Next look at the chapter transitions. Study the paragraph that ends one chapter and the paragraph that begins the next chapter. What effect does it have on you? Are you left with a need to turn the page, read on? Or is there a feeling of things being wrapped up?

5. Copy three paragraphs from this book into your writer's notebook, changing where the author started and stopped. See what effect you get with different pacing.

OUTER-STORY PACING

1. Read aloud to hear the rhythm.
2. Print pages to check the visual balance of white space to text.
3. Vary short and long words.
4. Replace ordinary words with more vivid ones.
5. Vary length of sentences.
6. Vary length of paragraphs.
7. Create "cliffhanger" chapter endings.

Inner-Story Pacing

Jo was struggling to pace the scenes in her historical novel, the narrative sometimes moving so fast that even she felt no meaning from it. She tried to slow things down with longer sentences and paragraphs, the tools of outer-story pacing, but this just turned the writing sluggish and stale. I suggested the pacing problem wasn't external, that it had to do with the inner story. She needed to figure out the emotional arc in each chapter and begin to work with the inner-story pacing to bring the emotional meaning forward.

As Jo began to play with this, she learned something new: the emotional level in any one scene had to be strong enough to reveal her characters to us, to make something happen in the plot, or to heighten tension. She was forced to go inside the minds of her characters, think about what they were doing and feeling. Each small emotional moment in her scenes built on the others, creating the arc of the inner story in that chapter.

To slow down the internal pace of the story without replacing dialogue and action with denser text, Jo began adding small sense details—sounds and smells—at certain moments of the emotional arc. Suddenly her inner-story pace felt smooth and powerful, an undercurrent the reader could pay attention to. It resulted in stronger characters, more believable setting (key in historical fiction), and more meaning in the actions.

Using sensory images is one of the most powerful inner-story pacing tools I know. Because such details naturally slow down the pace, if well placed they can highlight important moments so the reader can linger a bit.

Using sensory images is one of the most powerful inner-story pacing tools I know.

Another student, Beth, added an emotional moment in her memoir when she wrote about the sharp antiseptic odor of a hospital hallway, and how it got stronger as she watched her mother being trundled down the corridor on the gurney. In Samuel's nonfiction book, a revised anecdote now included the sudden peal of bells which startles the crowd at a hanging in an old English village. Simple, but effective.

Exercise: Inner-Story Pacing
TIME NEEDED: 20 MINUTES

1. Print out a chapter from your manuscript. Read through it, asking yourself, *Where does the emotion peak in these pages?*

2. Look at the pages before and after this peak. Can you revise them to enhance the peak moment, to make the emotional moment stronger? See what sensory details you can add to the moment itself.

Tense action, such as a chase scene, requires more outer than inner story. So the use of inner-story pacing might be saved for a slower-paced section that follows, which lets the meaning of the action become clear.

What about metaphor? Some writers like to use metaphor to enhance the inner story, but it's tricky. "The river swung around the bend like an elderly woman on the dance floor" requires us to detach from the current moment for an instant to first picture the river, then the woman, and compare them in our minds. Every now and then, metaphor can be beautiful, but too much creates dozens of pictures that readers must visualize. It becomes very tiring to exit and re-enter the story over and over.

Expansion and Contraction: Working with Scene and Summary

Every book balances immediate writing in present time and writing that feels more reflective, that shares a passage of time or an overview of events. This is what English teachers call "scene" and "summary." In revision they need to be considered for placement and quantity in your book because each creates a different effect.

Imagine a story with nothing but scene. It feels very close-up and personal, with everything happening right in front of us, right now, a string of individual moments, all important and vivid. The pace is ridiculously fast so there is little time to absorb the meaning of what's happening. This is scene writing.

Scene's opposite is summary. Summary spans time, condensing a repeated event that takes place over a period of days, months, or years, like driving cross-country. If scene is like "showing," summary is like "telling." If scene gets our hearts racing with the tension of the story, summary feels more like a collection of digested impressions.

A strong book will alternate the two, placing them for effect. You may not use scene to give a blow-by-blow description of a cross-country trip, when the important action doesn't happen until arrival, as in Andrew Pham's memoir *Catfish and Mandala*. Pham uses summary to show the passage of months of his bicycle journey through a foreign country: "When I was hungry or thirsty, I stopped at ranches and farms and begged the owners for water from their wells and tried to buy tortillas, eggs, goat cheese, and fruit. Every place gave me nourishment; men and women plucked grapefruits and tangerines from their family gardens, bagged food from their pantries, and accepted not one peso in return."

But Pham switches to scene's immediacy when he meets someone of consequence who has great impact on the story: "His Viking face mashes up, twisting like a child's just before the first brawl. It doesn't come. Instead words cascade out, disjointed sentences, sputtering incoherence that at the initial rush sound like a drunk's ravings."

Joan Didion's *A Year of Magical Thinking*, which recounts the months after her husband's sudden death from a heart attack, contains a great deal of summary which balances Didion's sparse prose, short sentences, and simple words—as well as her traumatic story. "I recall a fight over the question of whether we should go to Paris in November," she writes. "I did not want to go. I said we had too much to do and too little money. He said he had a sense that if he did not go to Paris in November he would never again go to Paris." The reader is kept on edge because there's plenty of meaning in this contracted summary—regret and despair at what might have been and can never be now.

So you learn to evaluate where you want the impact, how to see your natural tendency to expand in scene or contract in summary. You revise now to balance this tendency. Expansion writers learn to focus the ideas from the island stage, where there is always more to add—one more flashback, one more setting detail, one more idea. Contraction writers learn to let their prose breathe more fully. Their island writing may be as sparse as Didion's, where each word costs a million dollars, and now it must expand to create good pacing.

You learn to evaluate where you want the impact, how to see your natural tendency to expand in scene or contract in summary.

If you have too many expanded scenes, contract some into summary. Too much summary? Expand key emotional moments for more meaning.

Exercise: Expansion and Contraction
TIME NEEDED: 1 HOUR

1. Set a kitchen timer for fifteen minutes. Begin to write about a childhood event that influenced you greatly. Don't overthink this exercise, just let it rip. No editing along the way!

2. When you're done, read the piece out loud to yourself. Whenever you get interested, as you read, highlight the paragraph that pulled you in. (It's essential to read out loud—you're switching from a writer's viewpoint to a reader's.)

3. Pick a paragraph that really speaks to you. Contract (condense) it into one sentence, as short as possible, without losing the essence of the larger paragraph.

4. Now expand this one sentence into five new sentences (a new paragraph).

5. Which was easier for you, expansion or contraction? Think about what this short exercise taught you about your natural tendency as a writer.

6. Return to your original freewrite about the childhood experience. Select another favorite section. Apply the aspect (expand or contract) that was the most difficult for you in steps 3 and 4. If you had trouble with expansion, expand the section to three or more paragraphs. If you had trouble with contraction, condense the section to half its length.

7. Read the new writing out loud. Can you notice the difference in flow, in music, in pacing?

21

THEME:
THE RIVER RUNNING
THROUGH YOUR BOOK

After months of revising the first draft of one of my novels, I was still stumped as to its theme. My chapters hung together pretty well but the manuscript lacked that wonderful sense of wholeness that a theme-rich book delivers.

One evening I was reading a scene to my writers' group. When I finished we talked about the characters, especially the main character, a search-and-rescue pilot. One of the writers, bless her, asked me that pivotal question that opens huge doors inside.

"They're all circling the wilderness of their lives, aren't they?" she said quietly. "Everyone in your book is on a search-and-rescue mission for themselves."

She'd just given me my theme.

You may be aware of the separate parts of your outer story, how the acts work together, where the tension builds. You may even know a bit about your inner story, what meaning you're trying for. But until the theme is identified, there is no sense that your book is greater than the sum of its parts.

Most of my characters were indeed "circling the wilderness" of their lives, trying to land, yet afraid to. Here was my theme. My writers' group friend had given me words for my book's undercurrent—and now all my islands made sense.

Theme can't be rushed. It doesn't surface until it's good and ready, until we have understood enough to see beyond the narrative, the basic story. At revision, we step back to see if we can notice the way all the parts of our book are connected. Only then do we begin to perceive theme.

Often, our theme is already intact, as in the case of my novel. I'd built in the clues to my theme without knowing it.

At revision, we step back to see if we can notice the way all the parts of our book are connected. Only then do we begin to perceive theme.

They were there. Now I just had to enhance them.

In the early stages of the book journey, it's correct not to notice theme. We are way too busy keeping the boat afloat to see the steady movement of this river. By now, in revision, we are getting the distance required to feel it.

Theme can surprise us with its scope—often much larger than we set out to present. Professional artists sometimes speak about years of making their art, watching it evolve into something greater than anticipated, and their gratitude when a viewer or reader says, "Your piece spoke to me in such-and-such a way," even when the artist had no intent toward that result.

This is the beauty of theme—its potential to transform an audience. Writers are astonished witnesses to this glory in their work; the good news is that during revision, we can also help it happen.

Finding Theme through Repeating Patterns

How do you start finding the theme in your book? Thematic hints sneak into our writing at the very beginning, even as we explore the book idea. They can emerge from the dreamy right brain and find their way into early islands, if we're lucky.

Writer Flannery O'Connor called these hints "happy accidents." We're rarely conscious of putting these into the manuscript, but later, finding them during revision, we feel very grateful that they've escaped the editing pen of the Inner Critic, who would've dissuaded us of their usefulness in the story—one reason the island method of writing is so helpful. As you let yourself wander aimlessly through your story during its early drafts, the Inner Critic is lulled into believing you're not really working.

At revision, these thematic hints show up as repeating patterns: images that recur again and again, an object a character obsesses over, something lost that's remembered frequently, houses or lakes or countries that are visited often, lines of dialogue that repeat. There can be more than one major theme, but usually there is one that's larger and sends out more hints than any other.

Think of the repeating image of yellow roses that threads through each of the three separate stories in Michael Cunningham's *The Hours*. First it's piped on a birthday cake, then gathered from Virginia Woolf's garden, then bought at the florist for Clarissa's party.

This repeating image becomes thematic as it links the three very separate stories. It speaks of the fragile beauty of life, the brief lives of Cunningham's main characters.

Or take the neighborhood setting in Vivian Gornick's memoir *Fierce Attachments*, where a daughter and mother converse on their daily walks in New York City's noise, roughness, and edginess. The setting becomes a thematic image that mirrors the two women's difficult but hard-to-abandon relationship, just as the old New York neighborhoods last through generations, despite each generation's attempt to flee.

What repeats in a book? Finding that is the first step to discovering what theme you've planted in your own story—without even knowing.

What repeats in a book? Finding that is the first step to discovering what theme you've planted in your own story—without even knowing.

Exercise: Looking for Thematic Patterns in Published Books
TIME NEEDED: 2 HOURS

1. Writer's notebook in hand, look over a favorite book in your genre that you have recently read. Record any repeating images you notice—objects, images, conversation, location.

2. Look for places where the author develops both a good sequence of outer events and demonstrates the meaning behind those events (often indicators of theme).

3. Ask yourself, *What lingered with me after I finished this book?* Theme is often present wherever we can't get a story out of our minds.

Finding a Theme Outside the Writing

While I think it's best to let your theme evolve organically from looking over your freewrites and islands, there are some writers who need to know their theme first. Often they find it by looking outside their writing.

One student in my class, a professional editor who was working on her memoir, said that after six months of writing islands she could not write anymore. "I need to know where this is going," she said. "All these islands look like so many shells on the shore scattered about." Then she discovered a book on women's myths that talked about how women are silenced, not just as young girls as my student had thought, but at key stages throughout their lives. This book, *The Heroine's Journey* by Maureen Murdock, made her realize that being silenced was a universal theme. "Reading that book made me feel less alone in the wilderness. I knew what I wanted to write about, but it wasn't until I read the book that I realized that it could actually be the overall theme to my book," she told me. "Now my islands make sense."

It's fine to go for the theme before you establish the story (you know what you want to say thematically, but you haven't yet told the tale that demonstrates it). But keep the doors open inside; stay aware that you are still looking for the thematic glue that will make sense of your writing. Otherwise the Inner Critic might derail the process.

Missy, another student in my class, experienced this. She wanted her inspirational book to be lighthearted and happy, showcasing her theme that people are good at the core. It was a belief that sculpted Missy's life and her dedicated volunteer work, made her the generous-hearted woman our class loved. But the Inner Critic latched onto this theme as Missy began to write her initial islands. She found herself so fixated on her book's upbeat theme in early drafts that she consciously discarded any memories that didn't fit her happy viewpoint: the early death of her mother, the struggles of her father as a single parent working the family farm, her eventual escape from the farm in her twenties, her subsequent divorce. These events revealed that, contrary to her theme, bad things happen and people are sometimes not good at the core.

At revision, Missy was stuck. She had a great theme but an unreliable story, unbelievable to a reader.

I advised her to write a letter to the Inner Critic, asking for a reprieve from the protection it was offering her. She needed to write the dark as well as the light, forge the inner story of struggle that could logically frame her outer story of joy. Then I suggested she go back to island writing, exploring first the untimely death of her mother.

It wasn't easy. But as Missy wrote, a repeating image came forward of the Midwestern plains surrounding the family farm. Despite all the tragedy, these vast stretches of land and sky were always constant in her life. Each spring they awakened, each winter they slept. Missy realized her story was about the steady cycle of seasons, how beauty inside can grow even stronger with life changes such as the ones she had lived through.

Her initial theme was too black and white. Yes, people could be good at the core, but life threw curve balls that made them do terrible things. As Missy let some necessary grey come into her story, her book became truly inspirational.

She needed to write the dark as well as the light, forge the inner story of struggle that could logically frame her outer story of joy.

Exercise: Searching for Thematic Patterns in Your Own Book
TIME NEEDED: 30-60 MINUTES

1. Choose any five chapters from your manuscript.
2. Yellow highlighter in hand, skim your chapters for repeating images—place, objects, images, conversation. Underline them with the highlighter.
3. Review what you underlined and list them in

your writer's notebook. Can you see any hints of theme?

4. Next, get out your storyboard and scout it for similar repeating images. Can you add to your list?

5. If your list is thin, explore your inner and outer story again. Review each chapter to be sure both inner and outer story are present. Especially focus on your inner story, looking for the natural framework of any evolution of spirit that you want to show us. Doing this may well reveal hints of your theme.

Questions to Find and Enhance Theme

Once you realize what your book's undercurrent is trying to say, enhancing it is great fun. When I got the hint of my novel's theme—about lost souls circling and never landing—I began playing with it to bring it out more clearly. I started planting deliberate thematic images of denial and escape, rescue and loss.

Earlier in my book journey, the Inner Critic would've put me through a shaming firestorm to even consider this lofty idea for my novel. But now at revision, my theme was organically present in many of my islands. My job now, at revision, was just to make it more so. I began with a main character, the small-plane pilot, Kate, who was indeed circling above her own life, as lost as the missing crash victims she searched for. I explored her take on my newly discovered theme by forming a question: *How does a woman fully land in her own life even as she's rescuing others?* Then I did a freewrite to answer this question, letting my writing go wherever it wanted. The freewrite gave me further clues; I began to weave levels of this theme through every section of the book.

Theme surfaced in my nonfiction book, *How to Master Change in Your Life,* via a similar path. From feedback in the revision stage, I became aware of a repeating image in this memoir/self-help book of roads and pathways. The opening anecdote was about something that happened during my solo trip across the U.S. when I was twenty.

I was driving through the Ozarks when the highway ended suddenly at a lake. I didn't know what to do—turn around and go back the way I came? Wait?

I waited.

After a while, cars began to line up behind me, and a ferry appeared to take us across. This image fit my book's theme perfectly. I crafted a question to develop it further: *What do you do in your life when the road you're traveling on disappears?* Good theme for a book about dealing with change.

Theme emerged in both these books precisely because I allowed myself to write in islands (see page 24). These nonsequential scenes brought out something deeper, when the linear part of my writing self, which doesn't recognize or appreciate theme, was not the only voice being heard.

In *Thunder and Lightning,* Natalie Goldberg describes a writing exercise she tried in a class after she'd read *Borrowed Time* by Paul Monette, a memoir of Monette's experience when his partner Roger was diagnosed with AIDS. One of Goldberg's students commented that AIDS gave Monette his voice as a writer, this moment in a writer's life when "something crosses our lives, brings us to our knees."

This discussion evolved into two questions that Goldberg posed to the group: *What brought you to your knees?* and *What do you love with your whole heart?* When I applied these two additional questions to my search for theme in my novel, and particularly to the primary dilemma of my character, Kate, an even more complex picture emerged. Why? Because as in real life, fictional characters follow Goldberg's example above; the thing that hurts my character the most may also lead her to a new understanding of herself.

To further test the theory that theme is revealed through opposing elements, I offered Goldberg's two questions to my class. I asked them to switch between the questions randomly, intuitively sensing that the tension this random switching

This discussion evolved into two questions that Goldberg posed to the group: What brought you to your knees? and What do you love with your whole heart?

created would help the linear mind relax, and theme might come out.

Ellen, one of my long-time students, was brought to her knees with her husband's sudden stroke. Ellen wrote about how his stroke changed their lives, shaking her faith in the safety of the world. When she switched to writing about something she loved, she didn't write about people—to her surprise—but about trees. Ellen's first piece told of her husband falling, how she had to catch him before he hit the glass window of the bedroom where they were breakfasting. Juxtaposed with the lyrical passage about trees, we saw how her strong husband was like a huge tree, and how shocking it was when he was felled by a stroke. Everyone in the class saw the intersection of these two short, raw pieces of writing, how theme emerged unexpectedly.

For many writers, the combination of deep love and aching loss often brings a book to a place of theme. It helps us deliver our story in a unique and original way. The beauty of it is that we don't even need to know how to do it. We already have these connections intuitively in place, and we just need to trust that in the areas where raw truth appears in our lives and in our writing, theme does too.

Repeating Your Theme

Rebecca McClanahan, author of *Write Your Heart Out* and *Word Painting*, teaches a theme-revealing writing technique called "plant and return." When you discover a particular image that repeats in your book and may indicate theme (my disappearing road, for example), you plant it deliberately, early in the book, then return to it often enough to emphasize it in the reader's mind.

As you play with this "plant and return" technique, you'll learn whether it holds true. Is that image the real theme your book is addressing? Is there another image that is stronger?

Note: Writers erroneously think it's the *understanding* of images, the *interpretation* of the meaning of an object or a conversation, that communicates the most thematically. Actually, it's the images themselves that reach out to interact with the reader. Theme speaks to the right brain rather than the linear left brain.

Students frequently ask: When do you plant an image? Where? How often? I usually try to place a thematic image no more than four or five times in the book, and I choose exceptional story moments to do this—when I want to alert the reader to a shift in understanding, a moment of great emotion, a big change in the plot.

More than this seems artificial to the reader.

How the Five Senses Strengthen Theme

One of my favorite nonfiction books is *The Loon: Voice of the Wilderness* by nature writer Joan Dunning. I discovered it one summer at a cabin in the Adirondack mountains.

On the lake that summer, two pairs of loons were nesting. They yodeled to each other day and night, and their calls haunted our sleep. As I read about the fragile existence of these birds, I was drawn in by Dunning's stories of living close to them, an experience that echoed my own during that vacation.

If you've ever heard a loon calling its mate, you never forget the sound. Dunning used sound liberally in her book, as well as the other senses. You probably remember from our discussion of container (see chapter 16) that using the five senses makes writing slower, and more emotional for the reader. It also enhances theme. I don't think Dunning's story of the loons' range of calls would have been as poignant to me without her detailed descriptions of sound syllables that signify danger, longing, loneliness, joy. Dunning doesn't stop with loons; her descriptions include an auditory attunement to nature that brings her book alive, in as simple phrases as "around the lake the crickets have begun to fire up that vibrating and equally indecipherable communication that makes hot afternoons have that slightly dangerous sound that is a sign of summer's end."

Theme speaks to the right brain rather than the linear left brain.

Smell and taste also enhance theme. Writer Marcel Proust once wrote that the "smell and taste of things remain poised a long time, like souls bearing resiliently, on tiny and almost impalpable drops of their essence, the immense edifice of memory." The olfactory bulb is one of the structures of the limbic system, which affects memory. Perhaps this explains why using the sense of smell in your writing will evoke a memory response from many readers.

Sound is probably next as far as its potency in our writing. Maybe because it's a big part of our survival instinct—if you observe animals in the wild, you'll notice how sound sends warning much sooner than visual cues. In her little book on loons, Joan Dunning uses the sense of sound to communicate her theme of distance and intimacy, how they co-exist between nature and humans. Dunning's book captivates the mystery of a species we adore but must stay away from, so it can survive. Her anecdotes don't talk about this mystery directly. Theme never does. But every vignette she writes illustrates the conundrum of being pulled toward something you can't be close to.

To explore this more in your own writing, you may want to spend time with two amazing books on the senses. *A Natural History of the Senses* by Diane Ackerman travels through each of the five senses, showing how they impact our daily lives and how, with increased awareness, they can enhance our enjoyment of life. Jonah Lehrer's *Proust Was a Neuroscientist* explores the senses from a different angle: through the often-unique viewpoint of visual artists, poets, writers, and musicians such as Paul Cezanne, Igor Stravinsky, and Virginia Woolf.

SENSES IN ORDER OF THEMATIC EFFECT IN WRITING

Smell

Sound

Touch (air temperature, weather, texture)

Taste

Sight

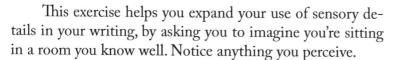

Exercise: Theme via Five Senses
TIME NEEDED: 40 MINUTES

This exercise helps you expand your use of sensory details in your writing, by asking you to imagine you're sitting in a room you know well. Notice anything you perceive.

1. Choose a room that you remember well, one that has emotion for you—the hospital room where you spent many hours watching over a critically ill parent, partner, or friend; your childhood bedroom lined with rock-star posters; the "outdoor" room of a favorite garden. Write about this room for five minutes without censoring or editing yourself.

2. Read over your writing. Circle any word or phrase that evokes a visual image. Count up these "sight" occurrences. Write the number at the top of your page. Write *sight* next to this number.

3. Do the same with words that evoke sound—verbs like "rustle" or "clang," nouns like "harmony" or "bells." The total goes at the top of your page with *sound*.

4. Continue with "smell," "taste," and "touch" words or phrases—"touch" implies texture, hot/cold, moist/dry. Note the totals.

5. Compare this with the thematic ranking of senses on page 292. Can you increase your smell or sound memory of this room? Based on the natural tendency you noticed, which sense do you rely on most in your writing? Which ones do you ignore?

6. Set the timer again for five minutes and continue writing about the same room. This time, write with attention toward the sense you were least comfortable with.

22

YOUR WRITING VOICE—
KEEPING CREATIVITY ALIVE

Many years ago, one of my students, Jay, took a poetry class to discover voice in his writing. The instructor gave them an assignment to draft a sonnet about people who loved each other. Jay decided to focus on his elderly father and mother.

He began writing a poem about his parents' enduring passion through fifty years of marriage, but then he found himself contrasting this passion with their tendency to ignore each other.

Jay's instructor helped him through early drafts where he wrote about listening to his parents talk, and about their silences. As he wrote, he remembered a time as a young college student, visiting home. Unobserved, he'd watched his father pause in the hallway, listening to Jay's mother sing off-key from the kitchen.

As Jay jotted notes about this experience and began to weave this memory into his poem, something changed in his writing. In capturing this memory-image in specific detail as an eavesdropper, the poem suddenly had a unique voice. It took the simple act of putting himself in the picture—along with the feelings he had for his parents, the way he valued their love despite the misses—to make the writing tangible and emotionally rich.

Alison Smith, author of the memoir *Name All the Animals*, spoke about this too. Early drafts of her book didn't satisfy her but she didn't understand why until she realized she'd told the story from outside of herself, focusing on her older brother's death but leaving out her own part in the story. "Leaving yourself out of your own life story is quite an oversight," she said.

It took the simple act of putting himself in the picture to make the writing tangible and emotionally rich.

297

The real tale, Smith realized, was the effect of her brother's sudden death on the family, how everyone unraveled and how impossible it was to know if they would ever put themselves back—a story that could not be told without the presence, the voice of the storyteller, Alison Smith.

This is voice. It's all about putting yourself in the picture, in your book.

All books, from self-help to documentary nonfiction to memoir to novel, contain the voice of the writer who penned them. Voice contains the conscious and unconscious choices the writer makes during the book-writing journey, the realizations we have along the way.

Yes, it's true that all writing reflects a writer's beliefs, values, and way of moving in the world. This reflection, whether it's delivered directly or indirectly, does contribute to voice. But for a fully developed literary voice, a writer must be willing to be present in his own writing. He must know himself, the place he occupies in his narrative.

As Smith discovered, life experiences, when told truly, don't allow the writer to be absent.

Constellation of Images

In the last chapter, we saw how theme emerges organically as you develop the inner story. Voice also grows organically with the experience of wondering and exploration. Voice depends on the writer learning her unique fascinations. How? By noticing which images get repeated in her writing.

A great method to hasten this discovery is to work with your "constellation of images." Writing instructor Rebecca McClanahan, in *Word Painting,* tells us that the term comes from poet Stanley Kunitz, who, as McClanahan says, "once called the sources of a writer's originality her 'constellation of images.'" These are images that recur almost unconsciously in our work: roads or pathways, a certain kind of tree, specific colors, the sound of trains, twins, whatever proves to be a strong metaphor for the writer's view about life. McClanahan proposes that we look for this constellation of images in our writing and begin to work with these images consciously, advice I've found quite valuable in strengthening my own writing voice.

Voice begins to strengthen as our values and beliefs as a writer—seen in these repeating images—are included more deliberately. We begin to weed out inauthenticity.

What the Voice Says

When I was revising my first novel, I became aware that I hadn't yet addressed a question that fascinated me. I knew I was afraid of it. Probing would take me into inadequacies from childhood. But the question wouldn't leave me alone.

In the novel, my main character, Molly, grows up lacking a sense of where she stops and where her sensitive artistic father begins. She spends the first chapters asking him to help her find this boundary, to help her see herself more clearly as someone apart from him, but he's never able to answer her questions.

There's one scene in the book where Molly holds up a mirror, studying first her own face then her sleeping mother's face. She comparing physical details, trying to see the differences between them—eyes, hair, beauty. Many other characters help show her various sides of her identity, just not the one she feels is the "true" Molly—the one she finds midway through the story with her lover.

But even a lover's reflection is not the true you. I tried to go further, crafting a question from Molly's dilemma: *When a character holds up a mirror but can't see herself, what's the inevitable outcome?* But I was unable to really answer it. It felt too personal to my own life.

The plot did indeed create a fall for this character, as well as the breaking of all the mirrors she holds up. In the end, this character has nothing but herself to look at. But it wasn't until I was revising the last draft that I saw how much I was diluting certain scenes.

I was deliberately making this girl less desperate—

Voice begins to strengthen as our values and beliefs as a writer—seen in these repeating images—are included more deliberately.

when in reality, for the good of my story, she needed to be pushed closer to the fire. I realized that I didn't want to go there. I even caught myself sharpening pencils and doing the laundry—clearly avoidance tactics. What was keeping me from bringing the writing to the place where the story so very much wanted to go?

I thought of myself at sixteen, the same age as my character. Using the Dialogue exercise below, I asked this sixteen-year-old self an important question: *Why are you silencing Molly's voice?* I learned that the Inner Critic as Gatekeeper was trying to protect me by keeping the writing from revealing the vulnerable memories of those teen years.

Once I became aware of this, I began to work each writing session with the Dialogue exercise. Slowly the scenes came alive with new intensity, letting my voice fully emerge.

Exercise: Dialogue with Your Creative Voice
TIME NEEDED: 1 HOUR OR AS NEEDED

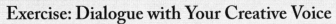

1. Locate an uncomfortable or deadened area of your writing that seems blocked. It might be an unsatisfying character, an undeveloped anecdote or a tepid theory. Write for ten minutes on this question: *What about this gives me pause?* You can also begin this freewrite with "I am challenged by this in my writing because . . ."

2. Then write for ten minutes without censoring or judging what comes, in response to this question: *What am I most afraid of saying or revealing?*

3. Next, approach this challenging area as if it is a silenced part of yourself. Ask it: *How can I help you have a voice?* Write for ten minutes.

Conscious and Unconscious Controls

From this exercise, I learned a lot about how we put controls on our own expression, our creative voice. We silence ourselves without meaning to, and our writing falls short of true.

The Inner Critic wants to keep us safe. It doesn't want us to stand out from the crowd and possibly get our heads cut off. So, as we get close to deepening our writing voice, the Inner Critic sometimes uses somatic resistance—headaches, irritation, even an upset stomach.

A professional writer in one of my classes began to have migraines every time she began writing early childhood scenes from her memoir, especially incidents that took place when she was in elementary school. She'd excuse herself, take an aspirin for the pain, and sometimes leave class early. It looked like she was going to have to abandon her book project because her body wasn't going to take it anymore.

One day I suggested an alternate plan. Would she consider a few minutes spent writing to the migraine itself, as if it were a person? She could ask it why it showed up during these passages, maybe find out what it was trying to protect her from.

She did. Under the migraine was a fierce Inner Critic, honed by years of training, hiding a childhood memory of hurting her head in a traumatic accident. It happened the same day as a big event in her family that caused everyone great pain. Both levels of pain had been ignored for years; the writing brought it all back.

After many tears and much journaling, the writer went back to the elementary-school scene. She was very surprised when the migraine disappeared, and the more she wrote, the more her voice began to come out in her writing. Processing this memory was exactly what she needed to do for her book, but the migraine sent by the Inner Critic had effectively blocked it.

Specific Ways to Develop Your Voice

Theme often invokes images for the reader, but voice is specifically revealed in the words you choose, the rhythm you

Theme often invokes images for the reader, but voice is specifically revealed in the words you choose, the rhythm you use. It varies for each person, unique as the writer.

use. It varies for each person, unique as the writer. Theme can be the same in two writers' books; for example, a theme of loss. But voice is how it's uniquely expressed.

We aren't trained to develop our voice in school, except perhaps in creative writing classes. Educator Steve Peha, from Teaching That Makes Sense (*www.ttms.org*), says that in many subjects, students all learn the same rules and same collective theories about math, history, science. Creative writing, on the other hand, is supposed to showcase the individual, how unique we can be and still communicate well.

Voice makes one person's writing different from everyone else's, writes Peha. "The set of all the different choices a writer makes, and the collective effect they have on the reader, is what is often called 'voice' in a piece of writing."

But because uniqueness makes us stand out, the Inner Critic gets understandably anxious. It doesn't want us to be so visible, so open to possible rejection, so it begins altering the tone of our writing, diluting its individuality.

We start copying others' voices, longing to sound more like John Grisham or Eudora Welty. We imitate instead of finding our own way; we then revise toward blandness. We become timid about letting our voice develop and the uniqueness show.

Voice is about not conforming, not sounding like others.

But it's hard to break the training of conformity, to risk making the personal choices that develop voice. "The trick is in letting that voice come through," says Peha, by getting in touch with the most unique part of ourselves, the part that is not like anyone else.

This is the voice that's formed from our personal experiences. If we're able to find these experiences and mine them, our writing becomes more genuine, authentic, and rich—which in turn makes our books stand out.

Exercise: Recurring Images and Voice
TIME NEEDED: APPROXIMATELY 2 HOURS OVER 1 WEEK

1. Over the coming week, read through at least ten short islands of your own writing. Underline any words or images that repeat, even subtly. Make a list of these recurring images. Note any additional images from the theme list you created in the last chapter.

2. Pick three of the most potent images you discovered. Freewrite in three separate ten-minute sessions about each image, letting yourself remember times these emerged in your life.

3. Now write down three values or beliefs that are important in your life. Perhaps you believe in honesty, or that everything has more than one side to it, or that life must continue no matter what.

4. Write each value on a separate index card. On the reverse side of each card, brainstorm concrete images that describe or give feeling to this value. A road? A broken vase? A Band-Aid?

5. Compare these concrete images with the ones you've brainstormed in step 1. Where are the connections?

When You Really Get Blocked

Jim's novel was almost finished. He was spending a last weekend on it at a cabin in the mountains. He thought he was ready to complete the revision and get it ready to submit to publishers.

"I love this method of writing in 'islands,'" Jim told me repeatedly in class. "I have zero writer's block and even in revision, I know exactly what to revise, where to make changes."

Our class wished him well and waited to hear how the retreat went. I got the first SOS email from Jim. "Help!" it read. "Now at the eleventh hour, I am experiencing a weird

When a book writer can see the end of the journey and the vehicle stalls, it's more than frustrating. It's frightening.

kind of writer's block where I have no idea how to finish this manuscript and get it off my desk."

When a book writer can see the end of the journey and the vehicle stalls, it's more than frustrating. It's frightening. "I keep waiting for one of my characters to open his mouth," Jim added, "say something new to give me direction. But nothing happens. I'm losing energy waiting here. I'm beginning to doubt I'll ever complete this."

I asked some questions. Jim's terror had emerged because his book had taken on a voice of its own. Now that he was away from his normal life, he could see it. He no longer recognized himself in the story. Where was *his* voice?

What Jim was experiencing was actually the best news possible. The book had just become its own person because it now had its own voice.

It's an empty-nest syndrome of sorts, and having published so many books, I'm familiar with this phenomenon. As with parenting, the writer has a few choices on how to respond. If the writer becomes so fearful of what's emerging on the page, so clueless about where he's going, that he silences the dialogue, words will trickle to a stop. If he's willing to let the book's voice be the stronger one, let the book become its own self without any need for the writer's presence, the story can leave home with new strength and purpose.

But often this last stage of developing your manuscript is the hardest to deal with. Too easily, the writer will abandon the project or begin to believe he has nothing to say. His book is worthless after all. Better to find out now, before the embarrassment and rejection.

These are only passages, dark nights before dawn. They actually signal the writer that a search for the truest, most sustainable voice in his work has begun. Both changes in voices and silent passages are expected as the writing matures. Often the experience is making us probe our writing for any unasked questions that remain.

"The role of the writer is not to say what we all can say,

but what we are unable to say," wrote Anais Nin. Sometimes your book can say it best of all.

Using Container to Bring Out Voice

Certain writers have unmistakable voices that pull a reader in; the voice engages us so powerfully, we can't stop reading. It's perhaps easy to find this voice in fiction and memoir, but non-fiction also brings it out. Two writers who come to mind are Malcolm Gladwell and Mary Roach, both journalists who have earned fame for their ability to enliven potentially dry topics.

In the preface to his book of collected essays, *What the Dog Saw and Other Adventures,* Gladwell says, "Good writing does not succeed or fail on the strength of its ability to persuade. It succeeds or fails on the strength of its ability to engage you, to make you think, to give you a glimpse into someone else's head—even if in the end you conclude that someone else's head is not a place you'd really like to be."

In class we discussed a section from Gladwell's *The Tipping Point,* marveling at how we so quickly engage in his unique way of presenting facts: the healing of a crime-ridden neighborhood, the comeback of Hush Puppy shoes. "I don't care about Hush Puppies. Really," said one student. "But I did when he talked about them."

Mary Roach's books *Stiff* (about corpses) and *Packing for Mars* (about astronauts' life in space) also convince me that voice isn't dependent on topic, even a writer's passion for something they must write about. Engaging writing comes from the writer's ability to sustain inquiry into that topic, to adequately describe the environment of the topic so well, we can't help but follow her into its exploration.

One weekend I taught a workshop on how writers produce the engaging writing that Gladwell is talking about. We read an essay by Susan J. Miller, excerpted from her book *Never Let Me Down.* Miller's father was a well-respected jazz musician who hung out with the likes of George Handy and Stan Getz. But he was also a heroin addict, and her life was

> Engaging writing comes from the writer's ability to sustain inquiry into that topic, to adequately describe the environment of the topic so well, we can't help but follow her into its exploration.

terribly affected by this. Her memoir is heart-breaking in its detailed description of the horrors of addiction, and some of the writers in the class were repulsed by it.

Some couldn't finish it. Others loved it. No one was neutral.

We had a lively debate, trying to understand why the essay affected each of us so deeply, why Miller's voice was so compelling. We concluded it was because of her extraordinary ability to describe in full the living environment of her story. That living environment is the container for her story, and it delivered more strength of voice than plot, characters, topic, or structure.

Heroin addiction is not on my list of fun things to read about. But I was totally engrossed by Miller's tale, and I selected examples of her strength of voice, particularly one paragraph that was especially vivid—where her father takes her on a train ride then gleefully whispers that he just dropped acid. It conveys her sheer terror. She is aware that her father might at any moment decide the train car is a tomb and try to jump off. What can she do? She's just a kid. She has to ride out the ride. "The train rocked furiously back and forth," Miller writes, "its lights flickering, racing at sixty miles an hour through the pitch-black tunnel on the longest nonstop run in the city, from 125th to 59th street." We get messages of impossible urgency via:

1. **details of physical setting** (watching the night flash by outside the grimy windows, the crowded train car, the newspapers on the seat)

2. **five senses, especially sound** (the overwhelming screech of the train's wheels on metal, the whisper of her father's voice against her ear as he tells her his secret)

3. **physical body sensations** (the rocking of the train causing nausea)

4. **word choice that echoes the sounds of jazz being played** ("screech" and "whisper")

5. **jerky paragraph length and flow** (Miller uses a series

of short clauses, separated by commas, rather than complete sentences—this mimics the jerky movement of the subway train, the pulse of jazz, even the drug state)

How do you know what kind of voice most naturally occurs in your writing? How do you find where this voice is clearly present and how you can enhance it?

> **A few ways to describe voice—**
> **Do any of these describe yours?**
> lyrical
> conversational
> warm
> cool and distant
> crisp, staccato
> minimalist
> intellectual

Start with a chapter of your manuscript you really like, one where you suspect authentic voice is present. This should be a chapter that engages you so much, you might wonder if you really wrote it. Like Jim discovered, this may be where your book has taken on a voice of its own. Like in Miller's work, there may be plenty of sensory detail present.

Remember: your writer's voice is often unlike your voice in real life. How you describe events or people in your writing is not necessarily how you would describe them verbally.

How do you know what kind of voice most naturally occurs in your writing? How do you find where this voice is clearly present and how you can enhance it?

Exercise: Discovering Your Voice
TIME NEEDED: 1 HOUR

1. Pretend you're a movie camera. Scan one of your chapters, marking in the margin when the camera zooms in or out. Does your writing often zoom in for close-ups? Or pull back a lot for distant views?

2. Pick one section. Ask yourself about its tone. Is it distant, crisp, cool? Are you giving an overview, reporting, clinically examining a situation? Or is the tone friendly, warm, full of heart? Does it make your gut wrench when you reread it?

3. Practice rewriting the section using the opposite tone—if your writing was zoomed out, come closer; if it was intense, back away. Turn a friendly, conversational tone into an intellectual one. Heat up a cool passage with warmer verbs and more sensory detail.

4. Notice if authenticity grows as you play with these extremes. Does voice emerge?

23

FEEDBACK FOLLIES AND FORTUNES—CRITIQUE AND SUPPORT

Noah was ecstatic. He emailed me to say that his manuscript was finally finished. He had taken it through all the stages described in this book, with the support of many writing workshops along the way. He'd spent three months revising it and was confident that the book was good and ready for the world.

"Who has read it?" I asked, sure that he'd also taken the necessary steps to get feedback, to let him know if his vision had truly translated to the page.

"I don't want anyone but the agent to read it," Noah said firmly. "Comments from other writers will just mess with my head."

So I wished him well and I waited.

Sure enough, the following year I heard from Noah again. This time he wasn't so gleeful. He'd queried eighteen agents, and of those who asked to read the first twenty pages of his work, not one got past the opening chapter. "They don't even know what they're missing," he moaned. Then he was quiet. "What do I do now?"

I told him he'd been very brave to send his manuscript out into the world without first getting feedback. But feedback was what I recommended now. "You need readers to report back what they find on the page," I told him. "Kind, constructive feedback is one of the last stages of the book-writing journey, one that can't be skipped."

No writer is an island, although in the final stages of book writing you may feel like one. It's essential to swim back to readers, not only to break the isolation but to hear how your work sounds to people outside your own head. Feedback at this stage of the book journey gives you the final

It's essential to swim back to readers, not only to break the isolation but to hear how your work sounds to people outside your own head.

polish you need, because readers will tell you where things went right or wrong.

Yes, it's a risk.

Like Noah, some writers are afraid to muddy the waters. Others circumvent the feedback process by begging relatives, spouse, children, or best friends to read a few pages and tell if they like the writing—or not. Close friends and family aren't usually the best evaluators of your art.

Noah gave in reluctantly. He went to his local community college and found a writers' group, got to know a few members, and exchanged manuscripts. It took him a few months but when he called me to say how valuable the experience had been—how it opened his eyes to certain things he'd overlooked—I wasn't surprised. I congratulated him on taking the extra time to get his book right.

Now that you're almost at the finish line, feedback is required. Learn how to get the help you really need, whether it's a writers' group, writing partner, online support, or professional editor.

Even for Professional Writers, Feedback Can Be a Touchy Experience

As Noah thought about his reluctance to get comments on his manuscript, he realized he was really afraid someone would tell him it was worthless. This is actually quite common, even among professional writers. We don't necessarily get better at receiving feedback as we publish more books—because each book is a brand-new adventure into our most tender selves. But the good news is that we do get better at asking for the right kind of feedback, and we get smarter at managing the process, for example, knowing how to sift through the responses, then letting them sit for a while, and finally taking just the ones that really make sense.

Most important, we know how to keep writing, in spite of feedback—good, bad, or indifferent.

Many years ago, I attended a once-a-month writers'

group that met at Dunn Bros. coffee shop in downtown Minneapolis. The writers were professionals; nearly all of them wrote for a living. Their reading of my work was always thoughtful and caring.

I love writers' groups. I appreciate the honesty that each group develops over months of meetings, as members get to know each other's work. We learn to speak our viewpoints with kindness, trusting that our fellow writers have enough experience and professionalism to hear what we have to say about their work objectively. When the collective is clicking, everyone respectful yet frank, we all grow tremendously in our art.

This takes time because a writer's journey toward belief in her work takes time. My voice must be louder than the voices of feedback. My love for my work must be strong enough to listen to all the comments—the good and the bad.

So in this Dunn Bros. group, I learned to take risks and let the group have at my book. I always survived (actually, thrived from) the feedback. But one week, I took a bigger risk than usual.

I was writing a section of a new novel and wanted to see how a character came across to others. That Saturday at my Dunn Bros. group meeting, there were plenty of compliments: my character came across well, my imagery was good, the setting believable, the conflict engaging.

But one writer—I could always count on her to find the missing piece in my puzzle—challenged me about what I was up to. "Tell us," she said, "where is the juice for you in this chapter? Where is the real emotion?"

Suddenly everything felt flat. The pages on the table in front of me seemed worthless, and I was more than discouraged—I couldn't even answer her question. I knew what she was saying: there was no passion in my writing at all.

I gave a passable response and we moved on to another writer's work. But I was noticeably silent the rest of the

When the collective is clicking, everyone respectful yet frank, we all grow tremendously in our art.

meeting, with only enough composure to thank this writer and say I'd think about her question.

By the time I left, I was fully in my role as outraged artist. Why did I subject myself to such questioning? Who *were* these people to ask me something so personal? They knew nothing about my work, my life, my art.

I blasted myself home, picked up the phone, and called a writing friend to complain about the group. I wasn't sure I'd even go back.

My friend knew me well. "Is it really the group?" she asked.

"Do you think it's my writing?"

"Do you?"

Not you too, I thought bitterly.

But in my heart, I knew she was right. My close-to-finished novel was in need of a strong dose of something, and the writers' group member had nailed it.

It was almost impossible for my lips to form the words. "It wasn't the group," I mumbled. "The chapter died weeks ago. I knew it before she opened her mouth at the meeting. I guess I went there to confirm it to myself."

This took a lot to admit. My friend, a clear thinker and someone who doesn't beat around the bush, asked me how I felt about saying this.

"Rotten," I said. But I felt more rotten about my passionless writing.

"So revive the chapter," she said. "You know the drill. Put it away, get some distance, do freewrites."

"It's *so* not revivable," I said. "Besides, I don't want to work on it anymore. I don't even want to speak to the characters. We're in separate corners."

My friend laughed. "It sounds like the feedback showed you that you need marriage counseling with your book."

I imagined a couple in marriage counseling, in opposite corners, hurt and defensive. Sounded a lot like where I was with my novel. I needed a therapist to reawaken my passion via good questions: "Remember the time . . ." "What did you first love about her . . ."

Levels of Feedback

Like a long-term marriage, your relationship with your book can become ho-hum. Instead of getting more exciting as you near completion, the book journey just gets old. Revising is tiresome. You make only half-hearted attempts to enliven chapters, maybe pass off what's not quite working and tell youself it's good enough. You begin to take for granted the images and ideas that once excited you and excuse yourself for "not fixing everything."

As much as I stung from the truth of it, feedback was just the prescription to snap me out of my complacent state. I needed just this level of tough love to do it.

Early in the book process, as with any creative project, feedback must be entirely supportive. You want to hear only what's working, because that's all you need at the planning and writing stages—encouraging words to keep you going forward. Positive comments at early stages lead to more writing, and often more confidence in trying new ideas. Nurturing is perfect for exploring the book's possibilities.

"Nonsense," some writers say when I espouse this in my classes. "Everyone needs critique." But in my experience as a writer and teacher, it's only in the later stages of the book journey that criticism becomes beneficial. Remember my reaction—and this from a much-published writer after two years spent on her book? It took me making a whining phone call and taking off several days to recover my balance from that one simple question.

Criticism can devastate new book writers. They will abandon their projects faster than you can say, "Rejection letter."

In the later stages, when you are getting ready to submit your manuscript to readers and then to the world of publishers, editors, and agents, you are committed to your book

> *Early in the book process, as with any creative project, feedback must be entirely supportive.*

and you are ready for a different kind of feedback, one that keeps your edge alive—like being in love. You need to sustain the energy and excitement for your book that brought you this far. As novelist Ursula LeGuin said, "The unread story is not a story; it is little black marks on wood pulp. The reader, reading it, makes it live: a live thing, a story."

Finding the Right Feedback

It's important to match the type of feedback with both your personality and your writing needs. A very gregarious person might prefer gathering with others in a lively writers' group that loves plenty of conversation. A more reclusive writer may do better with the one-to-one feedback of a writing partner or a writers' group that meets online. Pick the feedback that's right for you.

Writing Partners

Writing partners are equal-exchange opportunities. You give her your chapter, she gives you hers. You each read, you each comment. It's a fairly intimate creative relationship, where trust is built over time.

You can usually find writing partners through writers' groups and classes. Look for someone whose writing you admire, who gives useful feedback in class, who opens doors with her insights. It's worth waiting for the right partnership, because if good, it can last for years. Writing partners have been instrumental in many of my books. Without them, I don't know if I would've finished and published as many.

Writers' Groups

Groups are different from one-to-one feedback. I've belonged to many different kinds of writers' groups, most hugely helpful.

In my current writers' group, I email everyone two book chapters each month, and each group member sends me their work. We are writing in different genres, everything from essays to short stories to poetry. It doesn't seem to affect the feedback. When I email my chapters, I usually add a note that points the group in a certain direction, such as "These are early drafts, so be kind; I'd like feedback on whether Molly's argument with Zoe is believable." Some group members pay attention to this feedback structure and are most helpful. Others give me whatever they notice, and I have to sift through their responses to find what is most meaningful to me.

Groups also diverge in their opinions. This isn't necessarily bad for the listening writer, but you have to know what to do with it.

Some clues:

1. If someone is passionately against a topic in your book, don't take that kind of feedback to heart. We can't all agree on everything. Only pay close attention if the *way* you've written the topic is critiqued.

2. If two people love the scene and two people don't, consider it a wash—they cancel each other out.

3. If five out of seven are confused by a certain passage, pay close attention. There's usually something that needs refining.

After a group meeting, try to give yourself a small reward—a lunch out with friends, a walk, a good book to read. Don't immediately go back to your desk and fix the chapter. You need time away from the feedback to let it settle, to figure out what you agree with and what doesn't feel right to you.

But if your writing feels very tender, don't show your work yet. Instead, look for a writing group that meets to do writing exercises from prompts. A great resource is the International Women's Writers Guild (*www.iwwg.org*), based in New York with branches all around the world. IWWG members gather for "Kitchen Table" meetings, where women gather and share their work. Membership is low cost; with it comes a list of Kitchen Table meetings in your area. Try one out. They might give you just the feedback you are needing.

If your writing feels very tender, don't show your work yet. Instead, look for a writing group that meets to do writing exercises from prompts.

Or visit a local writing school, a university English department, and scout postings for writers' groups. Many have bulletin boards that list these. For instance, the Loft Literary Center in Minneapolis has an extensive website (*www.loft. org*) that connects writers in the five-state area around the Twin Cities. Often the groups aren't based on geography—you are meeting through the Internet.

Email the coordinator of a group that sounds interesting, and ask questions. Find out how people work together, whether they exchange writing or just write from prompts. If it's local, ask if you can sit in on a few meetings to see if it's a good fit for you. This should be welcome, as long as you are willing to not comment heartily on others' work until your own is up for comment as well.

Attend writing classes. Look for classmates with similar interests, whose way of giving feedback is both honest and helpful. Do their ideas open doors for you? Do they seem willing to respect your work? Then ask them to join you in starting up your own group.

Structuring Feedback to Best Suit Your Writing

We're not born with an inherent ability to give good feedback. Most people, even professional writers, are lousy at it. They don't necessarily offer comments that the writer can actually use. And they give feedback for all sorts of wrong reasons—to show off how much they know, to make everyone aware they'd never be caught dead making a mistake like that, to boost literary egos.

Obviously, this does nothing good for the receiving author-to-be.

That's why I've come to believe that questions are the most untapped form of good feedback. In teaching writing for over twenty years, I've found that questions open doorways for the writer. They let us see (1) there's something unaddressed or unanswered here, and (2) there are ways to find out what it might be. When we are asked a question, it allows new information to come up organically from our interior worlds. A lot of my first-time students don't believe in the power of questions. But after one exposure, they get it.

You really had to be there, to get the full impact of the question, to see the writer light up with new awareness and love for his manuscript, but perhaps some of these questions will trigger ideas on this form of feedback.

1. *What would happen if Jonah didn't say yes to Ann at that moment?* (In response to a chapter where two characters fall into a pseudo-agreeability, where they really need to get more separate, this question caused the writer to catapult into an new realization of Ann's angrier side. We'd seen Ann simmering for weeks, but this writer hadn't yet, and it was deadening the chapter.)

2. *What's the most outrageous thing this woman could do?* (In response to a stuck character, this question caused the writer to have her go into a bar and bargain sex for a ride to L.A., a totally unexpected action that was entirely believable and got the writer excited once again about this person.)

3. *What was always in your mother's refrigerator?* (A memoirist suddenly remembered her mother's quart bottles of diet Pepsi, which brought the realization that she hadn't yet written about junk food and constriction, an essential theme in understanding her family.)

4. *How does lightning play out in your life?* (In response to a skilled writer's struggle with finding theme in his nonfiction book. He went from writing sequential and slightly repetitive scenes to interspersing musings on the nature of lightning, personally and topically, which helped his book rise from the ashes.)

Any feedback in class needs to be monitored by an instructor, who has the welfare of the students in mind. If there

Any feedback in class needs to be monitored by an instructor, who has the welfare of the students in mind.

are writing classes in your area, try them out. Online classes are easy to find and are good forums for learning feedback skills.

Professional, Paid Feedback: Writing Coaches and Editors

Writing coaches can be professional writers, a teacher you took a writing class with, or an editor someone recommends. They have publishing experience as editors; usually they are published themselves. They work with you one-to-one, in person or by email or postal mail.

Writing coaches can be hired for any kind of feedback you want. I've had some coaches keep me moving forward on a project with weekly or bimonthly check-ins. I've worked with others to evaluate my manuscript and help me see what to work on next. It's valuable if you need persistent support from someone well trained to give it.

With most manuscripts, I reach a point in the later stages of development where I need to hire an editor to read through and evaluate my work. I'm one of those—I work as an editor-for-hire for publishing houses, reading and evaluating manuscripts—but when I have worked on a book for over a year, it's hard to see the final corrections myself.

What does it cost? Manuscript evaluation, which should include (1) a detailed report of strengths and weaknesses and (2) some margin notes, runs anywhere from $400 to $1000 at this writing. Many evaluators will give you an estimate based on word count. They should also be willing to refer you to other writing clients who have worked with them so you can get a sense of how the feedback comes across. Be sure to interview your future reviewer as you would any service person. Some only work by email or postal mail; others will read your manuscript and meet with you in person to discuss it. The last option is often more expensive, so if you can just get the printed notes and work from them, it's the most economical way to go.

The best place to find good paid feedback is not necessarily in the ads in the back of writers' magazines, although there are some excellent reviewers listed there. I would suggest that you go to the local college, university, or writing school. Why? Because teachers who teach writing are often good at manuscript evaluation. They can show the writer exactly where and how to correct or improve the work, rather than just blue pencil "awk" (for "awkward") in the margins. So you get more for your money.

Assessing Your Feedback Needs

Noah found a writers' group in his Detroit neighborhood, one he's been with now for two years. He sees the group members for coffee and chapter exchange one Saturday morning each month, and each writer has grown tremendously from the feedback.

At first, Noah said, the group was large and not very committed. Over time, the original ten members shrank to five steady writers who showed up at each meeting. Those who didn't submit work eventually dropped away. Noah's writing was gently critiqued, chapter by chapter, until he collected good feedback on his entire book. He now knew more clearly why agents never got past chapter 1—and he's hard at work on a more informed revision.

To assess your feedback needs, spend some time with your writer's notebook or journal today. As you think about where you are in your manuscript revision, make some honest notes about your concerns and eagerness for feedback. Then, when you feel you're ready, take one small step toward reaching out.

Go online, visit community bulletin boards in your local bookstores, or make a call to the English department of a nearby university or college. Research some possibilities for a manuscript exchange with a writers' group, writing coaches, or writing partner.

Discover how constructive feedback can help you take your manuscript to the finish line—and the publication that awaits there.

As you think about where you are in your manuscript revision, make some honest notes about your concerns and eagerness for feedback.

24

ACCEPTANCE AND REJECTION: PREPARING TO LAUNCH YOUR BOOK INTO THE WORLD

One spring, I was wallowing in the discontent of rejection letters. I'd sent my first novel to agent after agent, publisher after publisher. No one wanted it. This new novel crossed genres—it was written from the point of view of a young woman but it was meant for adult readers.

I believed in the book and wanted to see it in the hands of potential readers. But my disappointment was so great that I had no energy left to keep trying.

A friend talked me into attending a presentation at Wisdom House, a spiritual and teaching center near where I lived in Connecticut. The director of the University of Connecticut's writers' project had gathered six artists—an actress, a sculptor, a painter, a poet, a composer/musician who worked with Broadway shows, and a writer—to discuss acceptance and rejection.

Perfect, I thought. Misery loves company.

But the panel wasn't about misery at all. Although most of the artists talked about the pain of receiving rejections for their work, many went on to discuss the meaning of rejection in the life of an artist. And then they went even deeper—into self-rejection and self-acceptance. How that comes first, and how belief in your work is paramount to success.

Two comments stayed with me. One point was made by a composer: It isn't the composing that scares him. It is thinking about it. "When I'm actually doing it," he told us, "I'm completely happy." The act of making art gives pleasure. The thinking about writing was what was hard.

As creative artists, we want our work to be viewed and appreciated, but this by itself won't keep us going. We need to do it for the love of it.

The act of making art gives pleasure. The thinking about writing was what was hard.

What if you wrote something and it got accepted right away? asked a panelist. Would you be as happy as if you struggled to earn it? The others said no, not in their experience. Most agreed—and these were quite well-known, well-respected professional artists.

Easy or unearned success can destroy your future successes, even prevent you from producing any work at all. Publishing is rife with stories of writers who couldn't write a second book after their first was a runaway bestseller.

The other important point the panel made: Always try to retain an amateur spirit with your work. Write for the freshness and the vivacity that it gives you.

One panelist told us that the word *amateur* comes from the French word, *amour*. *Amateur* means "out of love." If you can keep putting love into the process, you'll be fed from it. So love becomes the most logical reason to keep going despite rejection. As Robert Henri, artist and author of *The Art Spirit*, said, "Do not let the fact that things are not made for you, that conditions are not as they should be, stop you. Go on anyway. Everything depends on those who go on anyway."

Acceptance and Rejection—The Balance Inside

I went back to my writing office refreshed by these insights from the panel. There was more to explore with my writing and the stalled novel.

I reviewed what I had done: Nine years had gone into this novel. I'd received positive feedback from mentors, editors, other writers. I'd researched agents and small publishers, sent the manuscript off, answered questions, made countless revisions.

There had been hope along the way: One publisher said it was very good but not quite their kind of book. Two agents gave me extensive feedback before deciding, also, it would be too hard to sell a cross-genre book.

I kept faith, was persistent in trying to manifest my dreams. I've published widely, so I know to keep going and I did for a long time, even when fellow writers advised me to give up this one, go on to the next. After reviewing all I'd done for the book, I realized it could very well be time to put it aside, as a book for the filing cabinet, not the bookstore shelves. I loved my novel, but after so many rejections, I was tired of trying to sell it to a publisher.

Not long after the panel, I heard about an upcoming meeting of Connecticut women writers. The location was two hours from my home, not convenient on a weekend when I had Monday classes to prepare to teach, but the nudge was strong. I decided to go.

We sat in a circle. Each writer introduced herself. The talk here was also on acceptance and rejection. One writer spoke of a colleague who had finished a new novel but the search for publishers had been hard. The novel was cross-genre and broke from the norm for most publishers. But she'd eventually been accepted. After the meeting, I asked this writer about her colleague, got the name of the publish-er, and drove home, wondering whether to pursue this lead.

I emailed the publisher my well-worn query letter and, over the next few weeks, got some interest. They first looked at sample chapters, then they asked for the entire manuscript. So I shipped it off to their chief editor in California.

I'd done this step many times already. I didn't hold much hope. I tried to let it go completely.

Months went by. No word from the editor.

But I wasn't ready to let my book die. When a student mentioned a new web site for self-publishing that produced excellent work quite cheaply, I considered publishing the novel myself. Of course, I had doubts. Several colleagues of mine in publishing looked down on self-published books; they were not good enough to find a "real" publisher. But musician friends always asked me why writers didn't release their own books, as musicians did their own CDs? Artists set up their own shows, sold paintings off web sites, and although gallery entrance was a cachet in the art world, it wasn't the only vehicle for getting work out to viewers.

If you can keep putting love into the process, you'll be fed from it. So love becomes the most logical reason to keep going despite rejection.

I knew more and more writers were having success with self-publishing, selling their books in major bookstores and online. It had changed a lot since the last time I'd checked it out. What did I have to lose? I knew with self-published books, it is up to the writer to sell and distribute. Did I care about high sales anymore? No, I just wanted my novel to be read, even if only by a few people.

So while I waited I explored self-publishing sites (see pages 346–49), spent two weeks setting up the book into a version that looked typeset, designed a cover, and sent it off to get printed. In two weeks, I received my self-published novel in the mail.

I spent the day on the couch, reading my book, crying and laughing, falling in love with it again. Even if it never saw the light of a bookstore, it had been a heartfelt literary cycle that felt complete.

I slipped the novel onto the bookshelf with my other published books, turned to my next project. I could now move forward.

Getting Past Discouragement

The word *discouragement* comes from the root word *cœur,* or *heart.* It's the process of losing heart, losing perspective. It happens to all writers, over and over again, no matter how often we've been published.

It's a terrible moment when your work gets rejected. It's hard to imagine how you're going to move forward, especially when you read reviews of other (wonderful) writers and sigh with the impossibility of ever getting published.

When I was working on *Your Book Starts Here,* I was lucky. I had a wonderful editor. At revision, I sent chapters for her polishing comments. Each time I got my edited chapters back from the editor, I marveled at how much better they read.

But one week, when my life was so much spaghetti thrown against the kitchen wall—you know the kind, where family and work challenges, money troubles, and illness all converge at once—my editor sent back a few newly revised chapters that I had thought were almost ready. She didn't. She had much to suggest.

This was our third call-and-response session (I call out, she responds with edits). But I felt intense discouragement. I thought the book was nearly finished and now I needed to rethink a whole section.

I closed myself in my office and took some deep breaths, then set about finding what felt true for me in her suggestions. What might she be seeing that was invisible to me? As I thought about the global changes she suggested and the smaller changes she was recommending, I felt myself move into a different viewpoint—that of the reader.

It didn't take long. I saw how 90 percent of her suggestions actually made the chapter flow much more smoothly for a reader.

That week I thought long and hard about my writing and the book I'd worked on for so many months. The blues swept over me and I knew I needed to somehow regain my courage for the final leg of the race. Had I really improved as a writer in the process of this manuscript? Or were my blind spots always going to be with me?

I reminded myself that writers never really get completely clear of blind spots. We all will always have them, and they are unseen until we get perspective, often through the process of rejection or acceptance. Seeing anew is a sign of growth.

I went back to my desk and began making the manuscript changes that made sense to me. Some of them were so big they caused tremors throughout the chapters but I reminded myself this rearrangement was growth, and I wanted my book to be the very best it could be.

I felt grateful now, not discouraged. And curious —would this learning translate into a changed skill? Would my attempt at the next chapter come out better because of what I'd just learned?

This is the goal—to learn new skills from the rejection.

Seeing anew is a sign of growth. This is the goal—to learn new skills from the rejection.

Yes, there's discouragement, losing heart, but there's also the joy of developing skills—if you keep on keepin' on.

When Your Book Is Accepted by a Publisher: That Phone Call We Wait For

I opened this chapter with the story of submitting my novel manuscript and receiving rejections for over a year. I persisted, I believed in the book, I revised it as agents and editors gave me sensible feedback. I tried to keep my courage. I'd given it my best effort then given up.

I was getting ready for bed one evening when the phone rang. It was late, my caller ID didn't recognize the number, so I decided not to answer, to let voice mail pick it up.

But something said, "Answer the phone, now!" so I answered on the last ring. I wanted to say, "Why are you calling this late? Don't you know what time it is?" But all I said was hello.

"I'm calling from California." It was the editor at the publising company where I had mailed my manuscript many months before. "We love your novel and want to publish it."

I don't remember much of the conversation—in fact, I had to email her the next day to be sure we'd had it. But I did recall the three times the editor said, "What a very fine novel this is!" because that was the best news I'd received in a long time.

We met some months later when I was on vacation in the Bay Area. As we sat at a small coffee shop in downtown San Francisco, the editor told me again how lucky they were that I'd contacted them. The publisher had wanted to expand their line of young-adult titles for a while, but with books that were also for adult readers.

My cross-genre novel fit perfectly.

Do You Love Your Book Enough?

If you talk with published writers, you'll find these kinds of stories. They are our war stories, our badges of courage, that show us we've navigated the publishing world and survived both acceptance and rejection. It seems to make us stronger.

It certainly educates us about why we are writing our books. Do you have enough belief in what you are doing? Have you put your heart into your book? Do you love your project enough?

Author Barbara Kingsolver wrote, "This manuscript of yours that has just come back from another editor is a precious package. Don't consider it rejected. Consider that you've addressed it 'to the editor who can appreciate my work' and it has simply come back stamped 'Not at this address.' Just keep looking for the right address."

Along the way, courage comes from unlikely sources. During my bouts with rejection, I often searched for hopeful facts. The ones below are from the Internet, from articles I've read, so take them as urban legends, if you wish. I consider them facts to give us all the lift of heart we need.

Do you have enough belief in what you are doing? Have you put your heart into your book? Do you love your project enough?

Urban Legends about Famous-Author Rejections

Madeleine L'Engle's *A Wrinkle in Time* was rejected 97 times and went on to win the coveted Newbery Award in 1963. It's now in its sixty-ninth printing.

Kate DiCamillo's *Because of Winn-Dixie* got 397 rejections before it was published. It's now a movie.

Ray Bradbury has had about 1000 rejections over his career, according to a Barnes & Noble interview, and he's still getting rejected.

A Time to Kill **by John Grisham** got 28 rejections.

Jonathan Livingston Seagull **by Richard Bach** got 140 rejections.

Gone with the Wind **by Margaret Mitchell** got 38 rejections.

The first *Harry Potter* **book by J.K. Rowling** was rejected by 9 publishers before an editor said yes.

View rejection as a chance to look differently at your book. Maybe it does need more work. Maybe, as Kingsolver reminds us, you just haven't found the right home for it. You can struggle through rejection, learn from it, and watch how the process gets easier the next time. Or you can put the project aside and never have a breakthrough to a deeper place.

Susan, a writer in my book-writing class, told this story. "I'd been studying Tai Chi for years, and one day I learned something about my tendencies. Someone was sparring with me and I kept pulling away from her. When I spoke to my teacher about it, I told him it was my instinct to pull away. My teacher said, 'Your *instinct* is self-preservation; your *habit* is to pull away. Unless you let go of your habit and let her pull you, you will never face the decision of what you will do.'"

Rejection lets you rise above the habit of discouragement and face new decisions about your faith in your creative expression.

Rejection is often overwhelming, difficult, disheartening. But there's no choice, say most successful artists. You have to try. You'll stagnate if you stay where you are.

Self-Care to Keep You Going

Creativity coach and author Rosanne Bane (*www.rosannebane.com*) introduced me to the concept of self-care and how it's essential to keep going forward when you're working on a creative project. In her "Writing Habit" class at the Loft Literary Center in Minneapolis, Rosanne encourages students to commit to self-care as one of the recommended practices that empower writers to maintain steady forward movement.

When I first took Roseanne's class, the concept of creative self-care was completely foreign. But the way she explained it made so much sense.

Think of a runner preparing for a marathon. Self-care is so essential—the body will be asked to perform beyond its norm, so the athlete must care for it attentively. A woman about to give birth to a child is told to rest a lot, keep her feet up, eat nourishing foods. A businessperson on a long trip across several time zones will schedule an extra nap to make up for the body's sleep deficit.

So must a writer think of how to put her self-care in the picture during the final stages of completing a book. To acknowledge the effort and strain on her systems.

Our exercise in this chapter asks you to consider the months ahead, when you will be starting your journey into publishing, and plan one self-care item for each week. If things are tense on the rejection front, make it twice a week. This simple decision helps bolster your stamina, your belief in yourself, and your ability to move forward.

Rosanne encourages students to commit to self-care as one of the recommended practices that empower writers to maintain steady forward movement.

Exercise: Planning Self-Care
TIME NEEDED: 15 MINUTES INITIALLY, THEN 1 HOUR A WEEK FOR 4 WEEKS

1. Brainstorm a list of things you love to do for fun and/or things that nurture you. They may include:

   getting a massage

   meal out with a friend

   trip to an art museum

   curling up for an hour with a great book

   taking a hot bath

   nap on the couch

   movie or concert

   phone date with a close friend who lives far
   away

   sports event

   manicure or pedicure

   long walk in the woods with the dogs

   gardening

   playing basketball

   Saturday fishing trip with buddies

2. In your calendar or datebook, choose an hour a week and assign yourself one of these self-care activities. Make it a serious date—block out the time.

3. Do this for one month. At the end of each week, write for ten minutes about the effects of this self-care date. What obstacles did you encounter? What benefits did you notice?

25

WELCOME TO THE WORLD OF BOOK PUBLISHING

Congratulations! You've planned, written, and developed a book, and it is ready to be launched into the world. You've honed it, you've gotten feedback from a writing partner or hired editor, and you're ready for the next steps.

This chapter takes you through the process of publishing—whether you choose to self-publish, work with a small press or regional publisher, or contract with an agent and/or large publishing house.

Just like the planning, the writing, and the developing, selling your book takes hard work.

But millions of writers have managed the process, and you can too, provided you approach the industry with knowledge, detachment, and persistence.

Just like the planning, the writing, and the developing, selling your book takes hard work.

Getting Real about Publishing

Some writers live in la-la land as far as publishing is concerned. They don't really want to sell their book; they just want someone to walk up to them and turn their creative genius into instant fame and fortune.

A good example was a very intelligent woman in my class who finally finished writing a good mystery. It had interesting characters and a watertight plot. She loved her book and was sure everyone else would too. New to publishing, she decided to go for broke.

She made ten photocopies of her book, packaged them up, and shipped them off to ten agents whom she had read about in *Writer's Digest* magazine. These agents were supposed to be top in their field and open to new writers. She heard back from only two.

In very brief emails, they said: "We don't handle mysteries.

Next time, read our website."

This writer came to me, mad. How dare these people not even look at page 1 of her book? What was wrong with them? I tried to tell her that it wasn't that the publishing industry was so unapproachable, it was because she hadn't placed her beloved book in hands that would welcome it.

She needed to make some decisions about what she really wanted for her book. Then she had to do some research to manifest her dream and reach the success she desired.

What's Best for Your Book?

Let's look at the three main avenues for publishing: agented manuscripts submitted to large houses, unagented manuscripts submitted to small presses, and self-publishing. Then we'll consider electronic and multimedia, and print-on-demand.

Are you a first-time author, with few writing credentials? Then think small, think local. First-time authors have the easiest time with small presses or self-publishing, especially in today's industry.

Small presses and self-publishing options are growing, because large houses have such a huge overhead they can only afford to publish known blockbuster authors. They are very careful of what they accept from new unknown writers. Some agents advise that, once a writer has published one book and it's selling well, it's easier to find larger publishers who will be interested in your next book.

Are you an experienced author who is switching genres (your first novel after many nonfiction books)? Try agents first. But also consider small presses, or, if your mailing list of clients or potential readers is large and you have ways to promote and sell your book, you might want to opt for self-publishing. Once you have sold over 5000 copies, you can approach a larger house.

Do you have a book that is hooked to a timely political or social event? This is often an excellent catch for an agent.

Find yourself a good agent who can recognize the time-sensitive window of your material.

We'll look at agented manuscripts first, then check out the other options.

How Do You Find an Agent?

First, don't make the same mistake as our mystery writer and assume that any agent will want to read your work. Do your research, educate yourself. A lot of agents specialize. Save yourself an unnecessary out-of-hand rejection.

A great way to find an agent is to look at recently published books in the same genre as your manuscript. Turn to the acknowledgements page of each book—this is where writers often thank their agents.

Then visit Jeff Hermann's *Writer's Guide to Book Editors, Publishers, and Literary Agents,* a wonderful industry resource. It has the names of agents and what books they represent, especially recent titles sold. Get a sense of the type of literature your potential agent likes to represent: medical thrillers? Cutting-edge gay/lesbian fiction? Coffee-table gardening books? Inspirational books for holidays? If the bulk of an agent's "list" is close to your book's premise statement, you may have a good match. Google the agent's name. See if he or she has a website.

Collect a starting list of at least twenty agents who pass this test. This will take research. Do your work now. It'll save you much time and anguish later. You're looking for that perfect someone who can treat your book well.

Query Letters

Once you compile your list of agents who seem right for your book, begin crafting your *query* letter. A query is a one-page, single-spaced document that sells the concept of your book in exciting language. Its sole purpose is to get an agent interested in the next thing—your proposal packet.

Query letters are not easy to write. Plan to take some time with yours. One agent I know receives four hundred

A great way to find an agent is to look at recently published books in the same genre as your manuscript.

query letters each week. Often an agent or her assistant has only a few minutes to spare to read yours. It needs to grab attention immediately.

A query letter has three parts: (1) a sales pitch for your book, (2) a short bio, and (3) the reasons you are approaching this agent.

For the sales pitch, go back to chapter 9. Find your premise statement, that sentence you honed and perfected. Open your query letter with the premise statement as your first sentence. Expand it to two or three paragraphs, using the same exciting prose. This makes up the body of your query letter.

Next, write a few sentences about any writing or business credentials that demonstrate you're the right person to write this book. Include publishing credits.

Finally, add one sentence from your research of the agent's work: tell her why you want to work with her, specifically. Mention a book she represented that you liked.

Some writers wonder: Why not work into it gradually, maybe beginning with a sentence like "I love your agency and would love it if you represented my book"?

If you're the agent who gets four hundred query letters a week, imagine reading the "I love" sentence four hundred times. The letter would go straight into the round file. Agents are in a business to sell books so it's essential to make that first sentence engaging, even electrifying—and about your book. You worked long and hard on that premise statement; now use it.

The goal is obvious. You want the agent (or agent's assistant who screens query letters) to read on.

In *Making the Perfect Pitch*, a collection of interviews and articles by agents, you can read some dynamite query letter openers, such as:

> "I am a Vietnamese American man, a witness to the fall of Saigon, a prisoner of war, an escapee, a first-generation immigrant, and an eternal refugee."
>
> —from *Catfish and Mandala*
> by Andrew X. Pham (memoir)

"When all the kids around him were coming of age,
Robin MacKenzie was coming undone."
—from *The World of Normal Boys*
by K.M. Soehnlein (novel)

The Proposal Packet

Out of the twenty agents to whom you mailed or emailed your query letter, you may get a few who will ask to see your proposal packet. This is great news! Now you're ready for the next step: creating a proposal packet. This packet contains a synopsis of your book, a chapter outline, platform (marketing niche) information if your book is nonfiction, and two to three sample chapters, or the "partial" manuscript.

Proposal packets must contain your very best work. One publisher I spoke with said their editors read the first two manuscript pages only—and if they aren't grabbed, the proposal is rejected. So polish carefully.

Proposal packets must contain your very best work.

Again, read these two bibles to proposal crafting: *How to Write a Book Proposal,* by Michael Larson, and *Write the Perfect Book Proposal,* by Jeff Hermann. Although geared toward nonfiction writers, there's great information in these. Larson's book is a classic, reprinted often. Also for nonfiction, *Think Like Your Editor* by Alfred Fortunato and Susan Rabiner.

Hermann's book is unique because it gives ten proposals that actually sold. You can read the packets and see what's in them—and how fine-tuned the language must be to capture an agent's attention.

Fiction and Memoir Proposal Packets contain:

1. cover letter (your query letter can be reshaped)
2. bio (one page)
3. chapter outline (one to two pages, with two brief sentences about each chapter)
4. synopsis (one-page overview of the plot and meaning of your story)

5. sample chapters (usually two, amounting to anything from twenty to one hundred pages)

Nonfiction Proposal Packets contain:

All the above, plus:

6. platform plan and marketing analysis (how you'll help sell your book)

7. competitive titles (six to eight books in your field, published recently, and why yours is unique)

Agented Manuscripts

If the agent decides to work with you and you agree, you continue the process. First you sign a contract which allows your agent to represent (show and hopefully sell) your book to publishers. For this service, the agent gets a commission which is a percentage (usually 15 to 30 percent) of whatever you earn in royalties on your book, including advance royalties. That commission is good for the lifetime of that book. (If the book goes through twelve printings, the agent will continue to get a percentage of royalties.)

Remember that an agent is a broker for your work. Agents develop working relationships with certain editors they know. These editors are employees of different publishing houses and each editor handles a genre, such as mystery, cookbooks, or literary fiction. Because of this, agents often specialize in specific genres.

Good agents do not charge reading fees, although some ask to be reimbursed for photocopying and mailing expenses. Good agents will also suggest revisions when necessary. An agent helps you find the best house for your book and helps you negotiate the contract, including all the various subsidiary, electronic media, and foreign rights. Good agents also make sure that any legal issues will be the responsibility of the publisher. Reputable agents are members of AAR (Association of Authors' Representatives).

Some professionals say the law of averages applies to getting an agent's attention. One told me it takes seventy-five queries before there's a click of interest. This may discourage some writers, but if you approach querying knowing you need to put in your time to work these averages you won't fall apart at the first or fifth rejection.

A wise writing mentor once told me it's like looking for real estate. You count on research, on many visits to many potential houses. Your book is also looking for a home. It pays to be careful and take your time.

Your book is also looking for a home. It pays to be careful and take your time.

Changing Role of Agents in Modern Publishing

Since 1987 when my first book was published, I've seen many changes in the role of literary agents. My first agent brokered my proposal packet to editors at publishing houses he knew well. He helped negotiate the contracts, which included what I would make for sales of hardback and paperback editions, how the publisher would sell foreign rights (if my book was sold overseas) and reprint rights (future uses of my book's material in other books or in short excerpts), and handled the royalty checks (the percentage of sales that I received after my advance was paid off) when they arrived. He was literarily an agent for my books.

Thanks to all the cutbacks in publishing, editors these days, especially in large houses, don't have time to read all the over-the-transom query letters and proposals. Agents have now taken over that function. Manuscripts must also be sparkling clean before submission. Your agent will work with you, sometimes for months, to get your manuscript in shape. Some agents even act as line editors—which means they work closely with an author to refine and shape a manuscript line by line, something that used to be the province of in-house editorial staff at a publishing house.

But here's the catch: agents are over-the-top busy too. They are very careful about taking on a writer whose manuscript is not well edited or focused. They ask new nonfiction writers to have a good "platform," a developed reputation in their field or a unique niche to sell from that is attractive to modern readers. I've spoken with agents who regularly require new fiction or memoir writers to have well-established platforms too, before they will even present their book idea to publishers. It's harder for agents to sell books, so they need the writer's help.

It's good if your book topic is newsworthy, is historically interesting, touches an industry trend or a current social or political idea. If you've done the work of researching what's in the bookstores and your book is really ready, your agent's experience should be able to find the best home for your book. But if you haven't done your upfront work, the agent can't open the door.

This change of roles—the new position agents are in—is both helpful and confusing to writers. A novelist in my class sent her very strong manuscript to five agents; all were interested in it, all gave different suggestions for rewriting. Who was she to believe?

Another writer rewrote per an agent's suggestion for over a year of back-and-forth emails and letters and phone calls; in the end, the agent said, "Sorry—the editor I had in mind for this project has left the publishing house and I don't know who else to sell it to." So the writer had no agent, and her manuscript was now unrecognizable to her.

Others have had wonderful experiences, but rest assured these writers did their research well.

Research also lets you know about the few unscrupulous agents who promise the moon and never get close. Visit Victoria Strauss's excellent website, *www.writerbeware.com*, for an updated list of agents and small presses to avoid.

If you're smart, if you've done your work on your manuscript, working with an agent can be your best next step. Most agents love good books and are sincerely interested in these books finding their way to publishers.

Agented manuscripts are still the best way—often the

only way—to get noticed by a major house. Agents are also invaluable in negotiating rights—film, foreign, reprint.

Learn how to work with agents. Respect what agents can do for writers by studying two classic guides to working with agents.

How to Get a Literary Agent, by Michael Larson, goes through a step-by-step process of finding and working with an agent.

Making the Perfect Pitch, mentioned earlier, is edited by Katherine Sands. It interviews fiction and nonfiction agents and shares great information on the best way to submit work to an agency.

I also recommend subscribing to Chuck Sambochino's free e-newsletter, "A Guide to Literary Agents." At the time of this writing, Chuck was the editor for *Writer's Digest* magazine. His newsletter features interviews with agents and with writers who've sold books to them (*www.guideto-literaryagents.com/blog/*).

Unagented Manuscripts

Many small presses and some regional publishers accept manuscripts that come directly from the author rather than through an agent. These are called "unagented."

To work directly with a small press, again you use a query letter, followed by a proposal packet and sample of your manuscript. Sometimes writers send the entire manuscript. Each press has its preferences. Research small presses in *The Writer's Market*, an annual listing of all publishers, agents, and periodicals.

The upside to small presses is that they are often open to new authors and new genres. The downside is that many small presses do not sell to the big chain stores because their distribution channels are small or limited to a certain geographic area. Because small presses may have smaller distribution, the writer must get involved in publicizing her book, getting reviews, and possibly arranging her own book signings.

Many small presses and some regional publishers accept manuscripts that come directly from the author rather than through an agent.

Working with a small press is often a great way to get your first book published. If your book has a specific audience, and you can find a publisher who focuses on that audience, you can submit your manuscript directly to the press. But be sure to study the press's list—what they currently publish—and their submission guidelines. Most will have a website or you can call and ask them to send you their submission guidelines.

Small presses can take a long time to respond—up to a year—so consider multiple submissions (sending out your packet to more than one publisher at the same time). You need to let each know immediately if your work is accepted elsewhere.

Self-Publishing

Self-publishing has made it easier, quicker, and cheaper for authors to see their book in hand—and avoid the challenges of trying to sell to traditional publishing houses.

If you self-publish, you'll be in notable company. Lewis Carroll self-published *Alice's Adventures in Wonderland* and most of his other books. Mark Twain, Zane Grey, Upton Sinclair, Carl Sandburg, Anais Nin, George Bernard Shaw, Edgar Allan Poe, and Edgar Rice Burroughs were all self-published for one or more of their books.

Up until the advent of the Internet, self-publishing used to be denigrated (originally it was called "vanity publishing"). Now thanks to improved and affordable printing techniques, it's become a very acceptable option. Here you prepare the manuscript yourself for printing. Since you are the publisher, you shoulder all the costs of preparation, design, printing, and distribution.

Self-published authors sometimes find their way to fame and fortune, as did James Redfield who originally self-published *The Celestine Prophecy* and was later picked up by a commercial press. A January 2009 article in *The New York Times* talked about the self-published author Lisa Genova, whose novel, *Still Alice,* was originally released through iUniverse but ended up with Pocket Books. Genova got a mid-six-figure advance and a place on the *Times* bestseller list.

Most self-publishing businesses use digital printing. You choose either POD (print on demand), which means you order only the number of copies you want at one time, or a standard offset-printing run which supplies you with a set number of copies of your book, usually at lower cost per copy. Some writers opt to only publish electronically, releasing their novel or memoir as an e-book. E-books are usually printable by the buyer from a PDF. Most books can be formatted, for an additional fee, for electronic readers, such as the Kindle or the iPad.

Self-publishing companies typically do not charge very much, they don't pressure you to add extras, and there aren't hidden fees.

Self-publishing is a good option—especially if you want to get your book in the hands of readers for seminars, self-promotion, or a personal mailing list. Sometimes self-published books will be picked up by the large wholesale book distributors, such as Ingram or Baker & Taylor, which means they can be made available for sale to large bookstores and libraries, but this is less frequent.

The Self-Publishing Experience

Mary Cummings, author of several books published by traditional publishers, went to self-publishing for her book *And the Baker's Boy Went to Sea* (Sparkling Press, 2006). "Self-publishing has many drawbacks—it also has some benefits," Cummings said. "For some people, it's the right decision for getting their book into the hands of readers who will love, enjoy, and learn from the book, and maybe even be transformed by what they read. For me, it was right (though not to say 'easy'). I had editorial assistance from a freelance editor, and copyeditor. I also had sixteen WWII submarine veterans provide me with factual information, and four of the subjects also read the manuscript to check for accuracy. I hired a book designer, which, while pricey, gave the book the look I wanted."

J. Michael Orange, author of the self-published memoir *Fire in the Hole: A Mortarman in Vietnam* (2001), told me, "A friend who was a graphic artist at my work place created the cover using a public-domain photo I provided her and chose the type font. I indicated the blurbs I wanted on the back cover and also wrote the book jacket copy (synopsis)."

Michael went with *www.iUniverse.com* as his publisher and says they produced the cover almost exactly as he planned.

He adds, "When I bought my first hundred books, I was very worried that I would not be able to sell them. I felt the same way when I bought my last supply of hundred books. I have moved 1,400 books so far."

Bev Bachel, author of *What Do You Really Want? How to Set a Goal and Go For It*, said about a book she coauthored with a colleague: "We explored several different concepts, hired a designer to design cover and page layouts, reworked and rearranged copy, sent the final copy to designer, then proofed and proofed. We sent it to Bookmobile (*www.bookmobile.com*) for printing. They came highly recommended, so we didn't get prices from anyone else."

My own experience in self-publishing has been with CreateSpace (*www.createspace.com*) and Lulu Press (*www.lulu.com*). Since I have desktop-publishing experience, I set up initial page layouts on my own computer, played with different ideas until the pages looked the way I wanted, then hired a typesetter and cover designer for the final production.

I learned things: get your ISBN number and bar code from *www.bowker.com*, be sure to get at least two pre-publication reviews (blurbs), and don't forget important things like the copyright statement.

A brief answer to the question almost all new writers ask: How do I keep other writers, agents, and publishers from stealing my book idea? First, this rarely happens. Publishing is a *very* small world and word about stolen book ideas gets around. Call me naïve, but in my experience people in publishing are generally honest; most want to help good writers succeed—because then they will succeed too. If you're really worried, add this copyright statement to your material: "© [current year] [your name]. All rights reserved." Register your book with the Library of Congress in Washington, D.C., by sending them a copy of your book and a completed registration form and fee (visit *www.loc.gov* to find out more).

If you begin to feel like a second-class citizen publishing your own book, remember the list of authors above. When I am looking over publishing options, I try to remember that Walt Whitman self-published *Leaves of Grass*. Or that Virginia Woolf was married to her publisher. And Marcel Proust was rejected three times and decided to self-publish.

What would the world have done without these writers? Whichever avenue you choose, realize—if you can—that the outcome may have less to do with your book's quality and more to do with the industry. Find a way to get your book out to the readers who will love it.

That's the main goal, isn't it?

And while you're at it, don't forget to plan your publication party!

Exercise: Your Publication Party
TIME NEEDED: 1 HOUR

I believe in the power of visualization, and for those of you who like to read the end of a book first, here's a great exercise. You can use it to launch your entire book-writing process, or you can end with it as a celebration.

1. At the top of a clean sheet of paper, write a date when you can imagine yourself at the publication party for your book.

2. Close your eyes and daydream into this—then open your eyes and take some notes:

    where does it take place?

who attends?

what kind of music?

what kind of food?

who hosts the party?

what do you say in your speech?

what are you wearing?

what's your favorite moment?

3. Now daydream a bit about your book. Copies are stacked on a table, waiting for your signing. Guests are eager to get their own copy. In your imagination, study your published book. Write the answers to these questions, or whatever comes to mind as you visualize the book.

    what does it look like?

    how does the cover feel? the pages?

    is it a nice, solid weight when you hold it?

4. Finally, write a couple of paragraphs as if your party has just happened and you're looking back with real satisfaction on the months of work. How well it's paid off. Brag a little on paper.

Launching Your Book

Once you reach the very lucky position of not only finishing the writing of your book, but having sold your manuscript to a publisher or published it yourself, you're now ready for an exciting question: *How do I want to launch my book?*

You're about to be onstage —and that's a good thing.

Long ago, publishers did this work. Writers stayed behind the scenes back then, but now we know that publishers no longer launch our books for us, unless we've written proven bestsellers. We must do our own singing.

Often there's very little publicity budget once your book is published, and most publishers depend on writers to do the legwork: for example, find the reviewers and set up their own book events to help readers find out about their books.

You can't be shy now—you have to believe in your book enough to design, dream, and deliver a successful launch. Dilbert's creator, Scott Adams, was said to have written a positive statement about his cartooning career each day, which kept his belief in himself strong (he talks about learning this process in his book, *God's Debris)*. Adams penned the same statement fifteen times every day. The theory is that his focus stayed on the potential instead of his fears. I don't know what he wrote, but it was something like, "I will be a famous cartoonist." And so he was.

I use this exercise every time I am wanting to manifest something really good—like an excellent book launch. It helps me remember the potential rather than the fears in this crazy life of writing books. Hint: The exercise works best if you keep the statement beneficial to more people than yourself (another universal principle).

Some examples from my writing students: "I'm delighted with my published book." "My published book is everything I've dreamed it could be." "Readers are loving my book and it's changing lives for the better." "My book is practically writing itself—and I am thrilled at how it's coming together." "My writing feeds my soul."

Make sure to write the statement fifteen times at one sitting—because something shifts around the tenth or eleventh time you pen that statement. It starts to sink in and you can feel a change in your attitude.

This little but powerful practice never fails to focus me on the highest dream possible for my creative efforts, which is what this book-writing journey is all about.

Exercise: Penning Your Future Success
TIME NEEDED: 20 MINUTES

1. Come up with a positive statement about your book journey. Put into words what you've achieved and what you hope your book will do in the world.

> You can't be shy now—you have to believe in your book enough to design, dream, and deliver a successful launch.

2. Write this statement fifteen times.

3. Notice your feelings changing as you write—is the truth of this settling into your body and mind? Let it in; it's time to celebrate!

Ending Notes

Ending a book isn't easy. I feel a little sad, very hopeful and excited, afraid I've forgotten something important. You'll find this, perhaps, when you finish your book. There's a lot more to say, but you need to say goodbye for now.

I hope the stories, examples, information, and exercises I've shared from twenty years of teaching and book publishing have helped you. To wrap up, I'll share the exercise I end my book-writing classes with:

1. Take ten minutes and write down the three most important things you learned from reading this book.

2. Make a list of questions that spoke to you in regards to your book.

3. Carry your questions close to your heart—in your writing notebook, on the desktop of your computer.

4. Live with the questions, as Rainer Maria Rilke says, so the answers can find their way to you.

Thanks for reading my book. I look forward to reading yours. Please email me and let me know when it comes out—I'd love to hear about your success.

I wish you happy writing!

Mary Carroll Moore teaches online and in-person classes based on this book. For more information, see her website: *www.marycarrollmoore.com.*

Email her at *mary@marycarrollmoore.com.*

Visit her book-writing blog for free weekly writing exercises at *http://HowtoPlanWriteandDevelopaBook. blogspot.com.*

APPENDIX

A List of Writing Exercises in This Book

Favorite Books on Writing and Creativity

On the creative process:

Andrews, Elizabeth, *Writing the Sacred Journey*

Aronie, Nancy Slonim, *Writing from the Heart*

Atchity, Kenneth, *A Writer's Time*

Bane, Rosanne, *Dancing in the Dragon's Den*

Berg, Elizabeth, *Escaping into the Open*

Brande, Dorothea, *Becoming a Writer*

Burnham, Sophie, *For Writers Only*

Cameron, Julia, *The Artist's Way*

Dillard, Annie, *The Writing Life*

Friedman, Bonnie, *Writing Past Dark*

Goldberg, Natalie, *Thunder and Lightning*

Hendin, Judith, *The Self behind the Symptom*

King, Stephen, *On Writing*

Lamott, Anne, *Bird by Bird*

Lauber, Lynn, *Listen to Me*

Levasseur, Jennifer, and Kevin Rabalais, *Novel Voices*

Maisell, Eric, *Fearless Creating*

McClanahan, Rebecca, *Word Painting*

McClanahan, Rebecca, *Write Your Heart Out*

Messer, Mari, *Pencil Dancing*

New York Times, John Darton, *Writers [on Writing]*

O'Connor, Flannery, *Mystery and Manners*

Phillips, Jan, *Marrying Your Muse*

Rico, Gabrielle Lusser, *Writing the Natural Way*

See, Carolyn, *Making a Literary Life*

Sher, Gail, *One Continuous Mistake*

Taylor, Jill Bolte, *My Stroke of Insight*

Thomas, Abigail, *Thinking About Memoir*

Ueland, Brenda, *If You Want to Write*
Vogler, Christopher, *The Writer's Journey*
Welty, Eudora, *One Writer's Beginnings*

On writing skills:

Burroway, Janet, *Writing Fiction*
Butler, Robert Olen, *From Where You Dream*
Clark, Roy Peter, *Writing Tools*
Elbow, Peter, *Writing Without Teachers*
Forster, E.M., *Aspects of the Novel*
Gardner, John, *The Craft of Fiction*
Gardner, John, *On Becoming a Novelist*
Gornick, Vivian, *The Situation and the Story*
Hills, Rust, *Writing in General and the Short Story in Particular*
Love-Denman, Margaret and Barbara Shoup, *Story Matters*
Miller, Brenda, and Suzanna Paola, *Tell It Slant*
Prose, Francine, *Reading Like a Writer*
Truby, John, *Great Screenwriting* (audiocassette/CD)
Zinsser, William, *On Writing Well*

On getting ideas:

Bernays, Anne, and Pamela Painter, *What If?*
Epel, Naomi, *Writers Dreaming*
Epel, Naomi, *The Observation Deck*
Goldberg, Natalie, *Writing Down the Bones*
Hemley, Robin, *Turning Life into Fiction*
Snow, Kimberly, *Word Play, Word Power*

On the politics of writing and creativity:

Bly, Carol, *The Passionate, Accurate Story*
Woolf, Virginia, *A Room of One's Own*

On healing via writing:

DeSalvo, Louise, *Writing as a Way of Healing*
Pennebaker, James, *Writing to Heal*

On editing and revision:

Browne, Renni and Dave King, *Self-Editing for Fiction Writers*
Kaplan, David Michael, *Revision*
Strunk, William, Jr., and E.B. White, *Elements of Style*

On publishing:

Herman, Jeff, *Write the Perfect Book Proposal*

Herman, Jeff, *Writer's Guide to Book Editors, Publishers, & Literary Agents*

Larsen, Michael, *How to Write a Book Proposal*

Larsen, Michael, *How to Get a Literary Agent*

Lerner, Betsy, *The Forest for the Trees*

Sands, Katherine, *Making the Perfect Pitch*

BIBLIOGRAPHY

With gratitude for the opportunity to use excerpts from the following works:

Adams, Scott, *God's Debris* (Andrews McMeel Publishing, 2004)

Atchity, Kenneth, *A Writer's Time* (New York: W.W. Norton & Co., 1995)

Butler, Robert Olen, *From Where You Dream* (New York: Grove Press, 2006)

Cameron, Julia, *The Artist's Way* (New York: J.P. Tarcher/Putnam, 1992)

Campbell, Joseph, *The Hero's Journey* (Novato: New World Library, 2003)

Carson, Rick, *Taming Your Gremlin* (New York: HarperCollins, 2003)

DeSalvo, Louise, *Writing as a Way of Healing* (Boston: Beacon Press, 2000)

Diaz, Adriana, *Freeing the Creative Spirit: Drawing on the Power of Art to Tap the Magic and Wisdom Within* (San Francisco: HarperSanFrancisco, 1992)

Didion, Joan, *A Year of Magical Thinking* (New York: Vintage, 2007)

Dunning, Joan, *The Loon: Voice of the Wilderness* (Dublin: Yankee Publishing Inc., 1985)

Epel, Naomi, *Writers Dreaming* (New York: Crown Publishing, 1993)

Estes, Clarissa Pinkola, *Women Who Run with the Wolves* (New York: Ballantine, 1996)

Franck, Frederick, *The Awakened Eye* (New York: Vintage Books, Inc., 1979)

Gardner, John, *The Art of Fiction: Notes on Craft for Young Writers* (New York: Vintage Books, Inc., 1991)

Gilmore, Mikal, "Bruce Springsteen," *Rolling Stone,* November 5–December 10, 1987

Gladwell, Malcolm, *What the Dog Saw and Other Adventures* (Boston, Back Bay Books, 2010)

Goldberg, Natalie, *Thunder and Lightning: Cracking Open the Writer's Craft* (New York: Bantam Books, 2001)

Hendin, Judith, *The Self behind the Symptom* (Easton: Conscious Body Institute, 2010)

Henri, Robert, *The Art Spirit* (New York: J. B. Lippincott Company, 1923)

King, Stephen, *On Writing* (New York: Scribner, 2000)

Lamott, Anne, *Bird by Bird: Some Instructions on Writing and Life* (New York: Doubleday, 1994)

Lauber, Lynn, *Listen to Me* (New York: W.W. Norton & Co., Inc., 2004)

Le Guin, Ursula, "Staying Awake: Notes on the Alleged Decline of Reading," *Harper's Magazine, February* 2008

Levasseur, Jennifer, and Kevin Rabalais, *Novel Voices* (Cincinnati: Writer's Digest Books, 2003)

Louden, Jennifer, *The Life Organizer* (Novato: New World Library, 2007)

Love-Denman, Margaret, and Barbara Shoup, *Story Matters* (Boston: Houghton Mifflin Company, 2006)

McClanahan, Rebecca, *Word Painting* (Cincinnati: Writer's Digest Books, 2000)

_____, *Write Your Heart Out: Exploring & Expressing What Matters to You* (Cincinnati: Walking Stick Press, 2001)

Miller, Brenda, and Suzanne Paola, *Tell It Slant* (New York: McGraw-Hill, 2004)

Miller, Susan, *Never Let Me Down: A Memoir* (New York: Holt, 1999)

National Public Radio, *The Best of NPR: Writers on Writing* (National Public Radio and Time Warner AudioBooks, 1999)

Nin, Anais, *The Diary of Anais Nin,* Volume 5 (New York: Harcourt, Brace, Jovanovich, 1974)

Ogilvy, David, and Sir Alan Parker, *Confessions of an Advertising Man* (Manchester: Southbank Publishing, 2004)

Pace, Eric, "Terry Southern, Screenwriter, Is Dead at 71," *The New York Times,* October 31, 1995

Pachter, Marc, *Telling Lives: The Biographer's Art* (Philadelphia: University of Penn Press, 1981)

Pham, Andrew, *Catfish and Mandala* (New York: Picador, 2002)

Plimpton, George, Ed., *Writers at Work: The Paris Review Interviews,* Eighth Series (New York: Penguin Books, 1988)

Proust, Marcel, *Remembrance of Things Past* (New York: Random House, 1934)

Rilke, Rainier Maria, *Letters to a Young Poet* (BN Publishing, 2009)

Sands, Katherine, ed., *Making the Perfect Pitch* (Waukesha: Klambach Trade Press, 2004)

Schrader, Paul, and Kevin Jackson, *Schrader on Schrader and Other Writings,* (Bloomsbury: Faber and Faber, 2004)

Smith, Alison, *Name All the Animals* (New York: Scribner, 2005)

Stone, Hal and Sidra, *Embracing Your Inner Critic* (New York: Harper-One, 1993)

Taylor, Jill Bolte, *My Stroke of Insight* (New York: Plume, 2009)

Thomas, Abigail, *Thinking About Memoir* (New York: Sterling Publishing Co., Inc., 2008)

Ueland, Brenda, *If You Want to Write: A Book about Art, Independence, and Spirit* (www.bnpublishing.com, 2008)

Vonnegut, Kurt, *Bagombo Snuff Box* (New York: G.P. Putnam, 1999)

Welty, Eudora, *One Writer's Beginnings* (New York: Warner Books, 1985)

INDEX